The RUCKSACK

Published under licence by Brown Dog Books and
The Self-Publishing Partnership Ltd, 10b Greenway Farm, Bath Rd,
Wick, nr. Bath BS30 5RL, UK

www.selfpublishingpartnership.co.uk

ISBN printed book: 978-1-83952-929-0
ISBN e-book: 978-1-83952-930-6

Cover design by Andrew Prescott
Internal design by Andrew Easton

Printed and bound in the UK

This book is printed on FSC® certified paper

FSC
www.fsc.org

MIX
Paper | Supporting
responsible forestry
FSC® C013604

The
RUCKSACK

Debra
Castle

BROWN
DOG
BOOKS

To Fraser … You gave me something precious,
the best lessons in life I have ever had. God bless.

It's said our experiences from a very young age influence and shape who we become and, on the whole, I believe this. But what happens if we are unhappy with our lives, if we start to question ourselves, if we are uncomfortable with who we have become? Is it possible to change ourselves, our mind, our life's path, our future?

This book explores this and is my personal journey to self-love and happiness. It was not an easy choice to write and publish but I felt it was time to share my story in the hope that people who can relate can feel inspired to choose the life they want. I would add, I am not qualified in any way to give advice or guidance, this is simply my story which I hope shows that, with sheer hard work, support, discipline and determination, you can find your own self-love and happiness. I would also add, I'm in no way an experienced writer, in fact I'm not a writer at all, this is my first attempt and something I've been working on for the past four to five years and I can honestly say I have found it enjoyable and very cathartic. So, here it is, it's unpolished, it's raw, it's honest, it's sometimes unbelievable, even for me but ultimately, it's my story and one I am no longer ashamed of.

CHAPTER 1

The Foundation

Do you have a first memory and do you remember where, when and what it was? Whatever and wherever it was, could it have been the start of your foundation? I'm not qualified to answer that but I personally think it starts before this. I believe it starts when we are born and even though we might not remember, our influences, in my opinion, have already begun.

My first memory was at three years old, maybe that's the average age for first memories, I don't know but for me it was. I can visualise myself sitting on a bed in Tilbury hospital. I don't remember going in or the build-up to this, I just remember being there. I remember the bed, it had a wrought iron frame and it was painted in a beige colour, I relate it to those seen in old TV movies, when hospitals still had matrons. And sitting there on that bed is my only memory whilst I was there. However, the story goes, I constantly fretted and I cried the whole time. I was having my tonsils out which wasn't uncommon but I have no recollection of my behaviour whilst there. By all accounts I cried so much my mother and father were questioned about my welfare, my treatment at home, their parenting. I found this quite bizarre when this story was shared with me much later in life but it seems their response was spot on. When questioned, my parents simply said, 'she just wants to come home.' The hospital must have been happy with this as I was released after about a week and my next memory was me skipping along the road heading home. We didn't have a car, which wasn't that uncommon for most families we knew back then so we walked everywhere. But that walk, or should I say skip, was a very happy one. And considering I wouldn't eat in the hospital, as soon as I arrived home and was asked if I wanted something to eat, I immediately answered yes and promptly ate egg and beans. The crying also stopped. I think it was the bed. It's the thing I remember the most. I can still visualise that little girl sitting on that bed feeling very vulnerable and very frightened. I hated that bed.

So where was home? We lived in a very small council house in Christchurch Road, Tilbury. It was my first home. I shared it with my two siblings, one almost two years younger, her name was Aline, and one just over two years older and her name was Jet. Jet was the quiet one of the three of us, she wasn't disruptive in any way and she was what you might call a good child. Whereas Aline, well, she was the drama queen and I laugh at some of her antics. She was about the age of three, maybe four when, on a regular basis, she would threaten to leave home if she had been told off, which was followed by her packing one of her little child baskets with a couple of jumpers and trotting off down the garden path. And if she had been smacked for some reason, she would rub the whole area of the incident in Germolene, making sure it could be seen which sometimes meant holding her dress up, and then she would sit on the stairs saying, 'I hate Mummy' whilst rocking back and forth. Aline liked rocking, she did it regularly, particularly on the sofa, just rocking back and forth, sometimes singing which I don't think I ever understood. She once told our dear old neighbour that Mummy had a man in the cupboard, no idea where that came from but Aline did like to fantasise or stretch the truth but I guess it showed she had a vivid imagination and a sense of humour, something she still has today. But, that aside, she was definitely the naughty child although I do look back on it with humour. So, Aline and Jet were very different, as was I, but we'll explore that a little later.

Our house only had two-bedrooms and as we were a family of five including my mother and father, it made it rather small and cramped. The gardens however, were large, both front and back, so we had plenty of room to play and as our house was in a cul-de-sac, we also had a large area outside the garden to play. It was a very safe environment with very few cars so there was never much fear if we ventured beyond the garden gate. Aline, Jet and I spent many summers playing outside in the garden and beyond. We were all very young, pre-school age, so spent a lot of time together. We also made a couple of friends who lived in neighbouring houses who sometimes joined us with our main source of amusement being playing with a ball or skipping rope, or playing chase or hide and seek, it was all pretty simple and innocent. Winters were a bit different. We went outside if it snowed but mostly, we had to play inside and with it being such a small house this brought its challenges, mostly for my mother and father I guess, but we managed to amuse ourselves despite this, playing the odd board game or building a tent in our bedroom.

We had the obligatory pets, like guinea pigs or rabbits and we also had a bird which I think was a budgie. And, of course, we had the odd goldfish or two who were always kept in one of those little bowls but never seemed to survive for long. But the main pets of our household were my father's racing pigeons. I call them pets because I guess to my father they were. They needed a lot of attention, they needed training, they needed feeding and watering and of course the loft where they were kept needed to be regularly cleaned. The pigeon loft was situated at the end of the back garden, I remember it vividly and I remember sitting on the step of the back door watching my father taking care of his pigeons, his pets. I think this hobby was something he really enjoyed, he seemed quite dedicated which really showed during the time when the pigeons were racing. Now, during these times the pigeons would be put in baskets, taken to the pigeon club along with all the other entries, placed on a large van and driven to their starting point. Each entry would then wait for news of the time they were released and the time expected home and this information was mainly passed through word of mouth from one pigeon fancier to another. During these information exchanges you would often see pigeon fanciers strutting up and down the street sharing what knowledge they had to others who lived nearby. This was good old-fashioned information sharing, no landline telephones as this was something most people couldn't afford, just simple, honest face-to-face communication. Anyway, the race was on. Whose pigeon was going to win the race? Who was going to the pigeon club that evening feeling more like a peacock than a pigeon fancier because they managed to achieve first place? It was full of anticipation. Now, this whole affair affected Aline, Jet and I for one reason and one reason only, the garden became a no-go area during race times. You see, these little creatures, on their return, needed a quick and smooth entry into the loft in order to quickly remove the ring on their little leg and punch it into a special pigeon clock which established its time home. This would then be shared at the club that evening and the peacock would be established. So, noise in the garden when they were due home was definitely not allowed and if Aline, Jet or I forgot and appeared in the garden laughing or screaming, or just appeared, period, we were quickly shouted at and ordered indoors. I remember us three moaning but mostly I remember us giggling and the more we tried to be quiet, the more the giggling intensified, much to the dismay of my father. But amongst it all, you could not deny my father's dedication to his little feathered friends and in all honesty, he rarely shouted at us, perhaps that's why we took notice when he did, even though we found it necessary to giggle when his back was turned. One thing I was too young to appreciate at the time however, was how clever those racing pigeons were. They are incredible little creatures. Who else goes all the way to Scotland and finds their way home without a map or satnav!

So apart from having to run indoors for the return of the pigeons, we spent most of our time outside, weather permitting. I loved being outside and I seem to remember very long summers. Maybe it comes from the mind of a child but I am certain the summers were longer than they are now. However, I also have vivid memories of winter snow. It snowed most winters but it didn't deter us from having fun in the garden. We would run around enjoying the fresh fall having fun with snowballs but more importantly we loved making a snowman, I think we enjoyed this the most. I remember having proper lumps of coal for the eyes and a row of coal lumps placed nicely to create a smile. We had an open fire in Christchurch Road so coal was readily available and if we were really lucky, we had a proper carrot for the nose. When I look back, we made some very ugly snowmen, there they were, standing proud with piano teeth and a long orange nose. But we were happy with our builds and never noticed how the ugliness increased as it slowly melted away. It could end up with one eye, two teeth and all the buttons lost from its coat. And as for the carrot, that always disappeared, believed to be eaten by some kind of animal during the night which was probably true. But those snowy winters were fun, just like the sunny summers, we always found things to do.

It's strange looking back comparing our lives to current times. We were not a wealthy family, in fact, we were quite poor, yet we seemed to have everything. I think this is no more than a state of mind, what you get used to, not knowing any different and I think warmly about the innocence surrounding those times. However, there are two things that for me no amount of innocence could defuse. The first was a tin bath that hung on a hook outside of the house on the side wall. I can still envisage it hanging there in all its glory from a rusty nail just waiting for its next appearance indoors. And that indoor appearance was every Sunday. In those days, and this may not be the case for everyone, but it was for a lot of people, there was no double glazing, no central heating and no running hot water which made winters quite challenging. I remember washing in a little sink in our small bathroom. The sink would be filled with hot water that had been boiled in the kettle on the gas stove and my mother would wash us down. But then Sunday came and in came the tin bath, appearing like a higher being, a gift from God. And I guess it was, especially as it would be put in front of the open fire and filled with not one, but several kettles of hot water, it was a game-changer, a luxury but still I hated it. And there was some sort of pecking order, I don't think it was intentional but mostly Jet would go first, maybe because she was the eldest, then me, then Aline so Aline and I never got first dibs. On the odd occasion Aline would go first, being the youngest, then me then Jet but for some reason I always seemed to be second. It's a funny memory to have, a strange thing to remember and I have to question whether my foundation was unknowingly being created.

The second distinct memory, and the worse by far, was the outside toilet which was located on the side of the house where the tin bath hung. The route to the toilet was out of the back door, turn left and turn left again through a small gate. The door was on the left, it was wooden with gaps at the top and bottom and I think it was painted green and it had one of those metal latch locks. It was a very cold place, even in the summer months. The walls and floor were all concrete, it had no personality and was the coldest place I had ever been, particularly when the winter hit. It had one of those traditional style toilets with the cistern at the top and a long chain hanging from the side, and it was black which totally matched the feeling in that room. However, it was our only toilet so could not be avoided. It also housed many spiders which I hated. I used to watch them for any movement, praying they would stay put. I grew up petrified of spiders which I put down to this room but I think it was fuelled by the fact that an elder male cousin once chased me with a spider. I thought I'd never get away and I remember feeling like I was running so fast but getting nowhere, like one of those frustrating dreams. I remember which cousin it was to this day but I doubt he would remember. Maybe this added to my fear. Thanks for that dear cousin. However, that aside, I don't think I ever got used to that particular room or the whole experiences that came with it.

I would not describe us as a well-educated family and I don't mean this in a derogatory way, we were simply more streetwise than academic. Tilbury was a very working-class dock town back then with a couple of schools, a few shops, some playing fields, some pubs and two or three working men's clubs. We rarely ventured outside of the town, so subsequently, all our experiences were centred around one place. Tilbury Docks provided a lot of the employment and this is where my father worked. This was in the days prior to containerisation so the work was hard. I always remember the hook that used to hang from my father's trouser belt, something that was required to do his job but I was never sure what its purpose was. My mother stayed at home with us three girls looking after the home, cooking, cleaning, taking us to school etc. It was quite normal in those days for wives/mothers to stay home with the children. Mothers working was quite uncommon and unlike today, the work opportunities for women were less and of course, if they did work who looked after the children? It just wasn't the accepted thing to put children into nurseries, I'm not even sure there were any around. Life was very different compared to current times. I guess it would have been ideal if my mother could have worked as we would have benefited from some extra money. My father's money didn't stretch far and with a wife and three children all under five to look after, times were tough. We often wore hand-me-down clothes but we weren't alone, it was normal for a lot of families. Money was simply not in abundance and I remember funny details like, if our shoes got holes in the bottom, we would put cardboard inside and hope it didn't rain. We really didn't find this unusual, we just did what was required, it was normal, a little innocent and necessary to survive.

Looking back, I feel like I simply floated through life as a child, drifted along, dealt with whatever came my way. I don't think as a family we were unusual, no different from the neighbours, we were all in this way of life together. However, I often felt like I was what I can only describe as, on the outside looking in, somewhat detached. It was like I had no sense of purpose, a feeling of not belonging, like I didn't fit in. Sometimes my mind would go to places I didn't understand, imagining situations, which was all very strange at such a young age. I didn't understand these feelings and had no idea what to do with them or how to express myself so I drifted along, deep within my own thoughts, until I found a way of dealing with these feelings, which we'll explore later in the book.

As I grew, it was interesting to learn about some of my childhood behaviours as told to me by Jet, Aline and my mother and although we laughed, I thought they were a little, shall we say, strange. It turns out I wasn't the most attractive baby and looking at the odd photo, I would probably agree! My sisters, particularly Jet, had lovely hair and black/brown eyes whereas me, I sported a little ginger quiff and light brown eyes. It was a standing joke in the family that I was not an attractive baby, in fact I was known as the ugly child and that maybe I was the milkman's who was short and ginger at the time. I was also referred to as 'donkey' because for some reason I used to kick my big sister, Jet. I also used to pinch my younger sister Aline's bottle, when it was full of milk and hide behind the sofa drinking it. Whilst I don't remember all of this, to my older self I would say these were all attention-seeking traits and although we all laughed about them, including me, because at the time it was funny, somewhere deep in my subconscious mind I must have locked them all in as, strangely enough, I found myself discussing them in counselling many years later. I'm not suggesting any of my family intentionally tried to hurt me, they didn't, and I myself found these stories hilarious but I think it showed the level of attention I was seeking. Now, why was I seeking this attention? Did I feel 'different' from my siblings? I certainly looked different and looking back, I can now see I was competing with them, not intentionally, but I clearly had this need to be like them and I didn't see this as a bad thing. They say there is a thing called 'middle child syndrome' and I actually believe this. In fact, I think whatever order you are born can make a difference to your views and personality and I don't think the treatment of each child by their parents is intentionally different, it just happens.

By the time I started school, I had my own personal issues as I was incredibly shy and hated the thought of getting anything wrong for fear of being ridiculed. I would never raise my hand to answer any questions the teacher may have put to us for fear of being wrong. I have no idea why I was like this but I remember it being an awful feeling. I hated the thought of the embarrassment of answering a question incorrectly and if it ever happened, I would feel my face flush and my eyes fill with tears. I do feel that I was too young to be feeling like this but I did, and I hated it. Playtime was my favourite time where I could run free and I loved it. My foundation was definitely taking place.

And talking of behaviours, one thing I remember when living in Christchurch Road was my relationship with my father. For some unknown reason whenever he tried to cuddle or kiss me, I would push him away. My memory of this is quite vague but what is in the forefront of my mind is my mother telling me that I was upsetting my father by doing this. I had no idea what to do with this information, after all, I was five years old at the time and didn't understand myself let alone understand such an adult comment. To this day I have no memory of how this was dealt with going forward and I still don't understand why I did this but there must have been something lurking in the back of my mind. Why didn't I want affection from my father? He wasn't a bad man, it just didn't make sense. He was not ordinarily a man of great affection, it's just the way he's wired but this behaviour has always puzzled me.

Summing all this up, and looking at it through older eyes, something was definitely occurring in my mind. I had things going on I didn't understand, my thoughts and behaviour just sat with me shaping the child I was. I had no idea how to explore this or express myself nor did I realise the impact it would have on my older self. The insecurities and the lack of confidence would cost me dearly.

So, the day came when we had to move from Christchurch Road, we had simply outgrown our home and the council offered us a three-bed home in Kelvin Road, Tilbury which was a few streets away. I was five years old when we moved and I have some very distinct memories of this time both funny and scary. Firstly, the move. I look back now with such laughter, there was no money for removal vans etc. so everybody around chipped in to help. I remember this wooden box style wheelbarrow that was loaded up with what little we had and wheeled up the road. It did several trips, balancing chairs, a table, mattresses and anything else it could take. The image I have in my head of this makes me smile, in fact it makes me laugh, you couldn't make it up but again, to us it was normal. The new house was not in the best shape, most houses in Tilbury in those days were pre-war and it showed. The only thing I remember in the kitchen was a butler sink and a tap, I have no memory of anything else in that room. The lounge had an open fire and the bathroom had a bath and sink and was on the ground floor. Upstairs housed the toilet, which was a small room off the landing, as were all three bedrooms. And now to the gardens. The back garden was something else, it was so overgrown that the grass was taller than us three children so we were not allowed to go out the back door. It was about 100 ft long and we had no idea what was at the other end and the task of finding this out would be left to my father. However, one thing for certain, there were definitely mice running around out there and occasionally they would make an appearance inside the house. In fact, I remember years later having visiting mice which I believe was due to the fields at the back of the house, it seemed to attract them. I hated the mice, they moved so quickly and you could see them at the most unexpected times. They really frightened me. They were too fast to catch so you were never sure where they ran to or from. Mousetraps were the contraption used to catch them so it wouldn't be unusual to see a dead mouse trapped just waiting for my father to dispose of it. And of course, we had spiders. Already a fear of mine, I thought we had left them behind in Christchurch Road, but no. In fact, I think they followed us and brought their families with them. They must have jumped in that wooden wheelbarrow and hitched a ride knowing it would be a bigger house with more space to run, urgh! It was great that we had a bigger house but overall, I was quite scared at the prospect of living there as it really wasn't in the best of shape. And not only had we moved but so had our spiders and we now had our little furry friends making appearances. But it was home and there was only one way for it to go … up!

It took some time but our house in Kelvin Road became liveable, my mother and father set about making it our home with what little we had with, I believe, a little help from the Council. My father worked on the garden, he may have had help from family and/or friends but it became a great place to play, grass on the left and an area dug over on the right where I remember potatoes were grown. And, of course, the pigeon lofts stood pride of place at the bottom end. We had a shed which housed a few garden tools and some other odd items and of course the occasional mice and spider who would make their homes in there. We still had our pets so our rabbit hutch was also in the shed so the rabbits were safe from the foxes who wandered around at night. So, this was it, our new home and a routine was quickly established. We would go to school Monday to Friday, spend summers mostly playing in the garden and winters building snowmen or creating games indoors, pretty much the same as Christchurch Road. At one point Aline, Jet and I were all at junior school together which I'm sure must have been quite a relief for my mother. However, in order to help finances I do remember her getting a job at Bata shoe factory in East Tilbury. It was evening work which must have been quite difficult given that she also had us three girls to attend to but I guess it helped make ends meet. But then, when I was about six years old, tragedy struck. I remember my mother trying to get downstairs but having great difficulty, so much so that she had to seat herself and slide down. She couldn't lift her arms, in fact, in my eyes, she was finding any movement difficult and was in desperate pain. Aline, Jet and I were all ready for school and were sent on our way, I believe a neighbour or my father took us but just before we left my mother put her head down and cried. She cried in pain and at that point I thought she was going to die. When I arrived at school, I tried to concentrate but found it quite difficult and then, around mid-morning I burst into tears. I was quickly taken to one side by the teacher who asked me why I was so upset and my reply was, my mother will have to go to hospital. I was sobbing, I could hardly speak but eventually I calmed down and continued with my day. The school notified my parents about my outburst and I remember my mother asking me why I was so upset. I have no idea how I answered that question but I would like to believe I was reassured as my outburst was not repeated. However, it turned out my mother had severe rheumatoid arthritis, something we would all become accustomed to living with but something I doubt my mother ever became accustomed to; it was something she would have to live with until her dying day. Terribly painful and terribly sad but I have no idea why I reacted like I did. I was so scared and I was sure she was going to die. I felt out of control, I was frightened, so many emotions for one so young but I was quite an emotional child, something I think I can safely say remains with me today.

My father continued to work in Tilbury docks, earning what he could to provide for us all. It wasn't easy, especially with my mother's illness. Our home was not ideal for any of us, particularly for someone with rheumatoid arthritis. I remember those awful wrought iron windows that were so cold that ice used to form on the insides and scraping our fingernails down them or creating smiley faces was something we found amusing. The other vivid memory was the side wall of the house where the stairs were. We were an end terrace which nowadays is a bonus but back then with no double glazing and no central heating it brought its own problems. That wall used to be soaking wet every winter and several methods were tried in order to deter it but to no avail. It was a very cold house and apart from an open fire in the lounge which was later changed to an electric fire, there was no other heating so a paraffin heater used to house itself on the landing trying to serve all the bedrooms. Hot water bottles and electric blankets were also the order of the day. This all took the edge off the cold which we all knew was better than nothing even though it didn't really do much. But it's the smell of paraffin that remains vivid, I hated it and still do, to this day. How different those days were, it's hard to imagine how we lived like this but we all did, we weren't alone, no competing, no jealousy, we all helped each other and I think it taught us a thing or two about kindness, respect and appreciation, not that we realised this at the time.

During the early years of my life, from Christchurch Road to Kelvin Road, I continued to feel insecure and remained very quiet at school. I was a bit of a loner looking back, often feeling different, shy, frightened, a whole myriad of emotions for one so young. I never really knew how to express myself with anyone including my parents, I always felt awkward and uncomfortable.

This is a brief outline of my foundation. Nowadays, through a lot of self-exploration, I can answer some of the reasons I was like I was and I would say that, if you're exploring your behaviour, understanding your foundation is very important. It's your backbone, it's where it all starts and it's vital to your journey of self-exploration. It's so easy for me to see this now and it took a lot of work to get to this understanding however, in this next stage I didn't carry this knowledge, so let's see what happened.

CHAPTER 2

Fitting In

Our lives continued in Kelvin Road, seasons came and went, winters were still tough and never seemed to improve but the strange thing about not knowing any different is, you just get on with it, you have no choice and you have nothing to compare it with. I guess that's the same about a lot of things in life, unless you find yourself being curious or hungry for different or better things. But if you don't, life just rolls along. I remained the same at school, shy, not knowing how to behave, frightened, uncomfortable, insecure. I don't know how Aline and Jet felt, I guess we were too young to talk about such things or even have an understanding of it so I just kept quiet, fumbling along, hating how I felt and not knowing what to do about it. I think my siblings were OK, seeming to fit in with their surroundings and making friends, I can only assume and hope they were. There was so much running around in my head, I just wanted to be normal, to not feel this way but I didn't know how to do that because I didn't know why I was like it. I actually don't relate to the word normal anymore, I believe it confines us to societies boundaries and is a word that's overly used. But, at this time, that was what I wanted because, for me, it meant fitting in, impressing, being liked and loved, that was my normal. I'm not saying I wasn't loved at home but somewhere in my psyche something was going on but what was causing it? Maybe I'm back to the 'middle child syndrome', my foundation, maybe I was simply born like it but these can be explored later. In the meantime, fighting for my normality was hard work, fear of rejection overwhelmed me, I couldn't make mistakes, everything had to be right, perfect, no room for error which was an awful lot of pressure to put on oneself. But it was a pattern that had emerged and so, it continued.

And then I found something I excelled at, something that attracted attention, something that made me feel like I belonged. And that something was sport.

I had always been an active child and at the age of eight or nine I discovered I was a great athlete, particularly as a sprinter, but I was generally a good all-rounder. This caught the attention of the teachers and I was swiftly tried out in all different sports but primarily it was athletics that I was pushed towards. The 100 m sprint was my best event which led to hurdles, relay and then the 200 m sprint. The strange thing is, athletics petrified me, it was so nerve-racking, you're alone, it's completely up to you what the results will be and I felt the pressure. I think the pressure was exaggerated by the fact that I feared failure, here I was being recognised, the one thing I wanted and yet, I hated it. I was sick before every event, I couldn't eat, I cried and although I now understand that even professional athletes have nerves, I'm sure they don't hate what they do. I absolutely hated waiting for that gun to go off telling you to run for your life as I knew at that point there was no going back. Run, run, run, don't slow down, get over that finish line first, do what's expected of you, don't let everyone down, you simply have to win. My father took a great interest in my sport which for some reason felt like more pressure, he used to tell others how fast I could run and I should have felt proud but instead, the pressure increased. By this time, I was representing the school at different local meetings in which we competed against other schools and I always ended up with a bunch of medals and if I remember rightly, I held a couple of records for Thurrock. Both Aline and Jet were also good at sport but I don't know how they felt about it, I often wonder but, once again, it wasn't something at that age we talked about, we just got on with it.

So here I am gaining lots of attention, everything I wanted, but feeling under more pressure than ever, and it was about to get worse. You see, when you're good at something the outcome can be that you get popular but there are people who will never share in your success and who, in fact, are jealous of it. And there were definitely kids at school who were like this. I was popular with the boys, I was fast and strong, like a lot of them. Playground games became a place where my skills would shine, much to the discussion of the boys but much to the detriment of my friendship with the girls. There would be the odd remarks, jealous jibes and I think this was my first experience of dealing with bullying and I didn't like it. Why did they hate me? And in my fragile state of being utterly needy, I suffered. I felt broken by the behaviour of some of them and then I was faced with a situation that just made matters worse. I was sitting in class feeling slightly anxious as I had been asked the previous day if I had ever had a fight. I felt the rumblings of a problem and for sure, I was right. Being very aware of what was going on I half prepared myself and then, the school bully approached me and said, 'do you wanna fight? Lunchtime?'. I froze and I'm sure I went bright red and the only thought running around my head was, what a fool I would look if I said no, so I said yes. Everybody in class seemed to be excited at the prospect of us fighting, I felt like I was being tested and I'm sure that was the case so backing down wasn't an option, what on earth would everyone think of me if I'd said no? So, lunchtime came ever closer and then the bell went and everyone piled outside and once the teacher was out of sight the bully lunged at me, grabbing my hair. I fought back, I was not going to look like a fool. My stomach was turning, my heart was pounding and my pride was hanging in the balance. A crowd had descended upon us, lots of cheering and shouting but the only entertainment they were blessed with was a lot of hair pulling. She pulled, I pulled, she swung me around, I swung her around, it was real kids playground stuff. But, to my relief, the crowd had attracted the attention of one of the teachers on playground duty who happened to be our sports teacher who I was very familiar with. He came over and broke us up, my heart was palpitating at this stage, and he told us to follow him. We were marched across the playground and all I could think was, oh my god, we're going to have to face the headmaster. But halfway there he stopped and asked us what this was all about. I immediately spoke up, explaining how this had happened, how it wasn't my fault, how I was approached in class, and the bully said very little. The teacher then said a few words, reprimanding us and some words were exchanged between the bully and I which was quickly silenced by the teacher. We were soon on our way back towards our classroom, the crowd had dispersed, we had escaped anything too serious for which I was grateful. The teacher who dealt with this was the coolest teacher in the school and I think he dealt with it fairly. Had it been anyone else, I'm sure the outcome would have been very different. As for the bully, she continued her day as if nothing had happened and spoke to me as she always had. Her mission had been accomplished whilst I was devastated. I never felt the same about her and this highlighted to me the type of person she was which didn't rank high with me. I found myself keeping one eye on her for the rest of junior school. I never forgave her. She never knew this and I would never have mentioned it to her, I just locked it away in my head, I wasn't brave enough to share such things. There were other small incidents of bullying, mostly from the girls, ranging from comments on something I was wearing to jibes just before a race about losing. But the boys still cheered me on and seemed to delight in my abilities, something I warmed to. It was my approval, but probably from the wrong source. I must add, I did have a few good girl friends at school who always stood by me and I feel warmer about them today than I did then, I remember them well.

At nine years old I discovered a sport that I both excelled at and enjoyed, it was netball. I really started to love it. In fact, I preferred it to athletics but there was one big reason why. It was a team sport which alleviated some of the pressure, we were all in it together and I liked it. I still carried on with all other sports but netball was where I gravitated to. The teacher who managed the netball teams was also our classroom teacher. She was quite strict but encouraged me with my sport. In fact, she was very supportive and at the age of ten started taking me to netball training outside of school. I think it was a local adult team but I don't remember who they were or where it was but she would taxi me too and from with the agreement of my parents. Her name was Mrs Woodgar and she frightened me slightly, I think due to her strictness. So, given her nature, I was a little surprised when Mrs Woodgar organised a trip to her house one Sunday afternoon for nibbles, fizzy drinks and games for most of the netball girls. It was a beautiful day and we were having fun with various activities but then we played a particular game that required a controller of the music, something like musical chairs except we had a large sheet on the floor that we walked around and found ourselves eliminated if we landed on the black cross when the music stopped playing. One of the girls who was eliminated, a girl a year or so older than me and not someone I was particularly fond of, decided to make it her mission to get me eliminated. As we were walking around, I watched her telling the music controller when to stop in order to coincide with me being on a black cross. As I was watched her, she missed me twice which added fuel to her mission and on the third attempt she got me. She proceeded to delight in her accomplishment which seemed to go unnoticed by many, but not me. I was mortified, it really played on my mind, why was she against me? Why didn't she like me? Why did she cheat just so she could get me eliminated? Why was she so horrible? I felt really sad and, mixed with this sad feeling was the big question, why couldn't I say anything? I never felt brave enough to stand up to people, I lacked the confidence. Maybe this, along with the jealousy, made me a great target but whatever it was, it gave me very mixed emotions, most of which weren't good. After leaving junior school, the paths of the culprit of that incident and I crossed often as we both continued playing netball at senior school, but as she was a year above me, I could often avoid her, which I really had no objection to. I avoided her at all costs and the same applied to the bully who picked a fight with me, I made it my mission to see very little of either of them.

In the meantime, my love for netball was growing, I was doing very well whilst still maintaining all other sports but I think even at that young age I knew netball was for me. I would play as often as I could and enjoyed representing the school. Then one day in class Mrs Woodgar had set us our maths task and I was struggling to complete it. I wasn't a very academic child and I often struggled but I knew straight after this I would be out on the netball court and that's all I wanted to do. The bell went for playtime but Mrs Woodgar said that those who hadn't completed the task had to remain seated. My heart sank, I felt so small, so stupid and when I was the last one remaining, I broke down in tears. Mrs Woodgar came over to speak to me but by this time I was sobbing uncontrollably and could barely speak. She consoled me and told me to go join the other girls on the netball court so off I ran feeling utterly relieved. Mrs Woodgar spoke to my mother about this incident, she clearly thought it to be unusual behaviour and I would be inclined to agree. My mother one day asked me why I was crying at school and I could only respond with a shoulder shrug. I didn't know what to say, I didn't even know why it happened. The strange thing is, I even felt uncomfortable talking to my mother about it so I quickly dismissed it. The feeling was one of shame and embarrassment, my mother never pursued it and the matter was seemingly closed. I do believe my parents were quite proud of my sporting achievements so maybe being kept from the thing I needed most was why I got so upset. I had to prove myself, not with a maths test but out there playing netball. My parents having talked to family and friends about how fast I could run, how I represented the school, were now talking about how I was also a member of the netball team which was great, but not for me. I felt pressured, on a pedestal and although this was not my parents' intention, I couldn't help but feel this way. My father particularly enjoyed my achievements and I often wonder if I was like the son he never had, he enjoyed sport and got involved which was great for him. I remember him taking me to watch Tilbury play football at the local ground, I remember the railings dividing the pitch from the spectators where he used to lean and I would be standing in front of his legs with his big coat draping around me. I was too young to understand the bond that was developing between us and it's quite sad that I felt the pressure I did as I now believe it got in the way of our early relationship. If only I could have enjoyed these times better. My father was not a bad man, he had quite a simple outlook on life and I think he genuinely enjoyed our times together for which today, I am truly grateful.

Our cousins lived in the next street which led to us all playing games together either after school in the summer or during school holidays. Apart from me and my three cousins, there were a bunch of other kids that we connected with so all in all the crowd was pretty big. These were the days when you spent most of your spare time outside. We played hideouts, jack-jack-shine-the-light, knock up ginger. We went over local fields to play on the swings, the slides, the roundabouts. But most of our time was spent in the 'alley' which was located at the back of my cousins' house. And it literally was an alley. It ran between two sets of houses and was like a meeting place for all the kids living in these two streets. I look back with great warmth about these times, playing until darkness descended, running free, having fun then going home and pulling the front door key through the letterbox which hung inside on a piece of string attached to the door knocker. Imagine that now, wouldn't even think about it! But we had a lot of trust which I think came from the fact that we didn't have much and mostly, we all helped each other. Hard to imagine that you would come to miss those days. Maybe it's not the days I miss, it's more the attitude of people, the help we gave each other, the respect we had, it's what we were taught and quite a contrast to today's society. There was also a lot of taking responsibility for yourself. If you fell off your bike or tumbled over on your skates, you were told it was your own fault for going too fast. There were many times the phrase 'I told you so' or 'I told you not to' were communicated to us from our parents but what did it teach us? Responsibility. If you messed up, it was your fault so you did your best not to do it again. And I for one do not think this to be a bad lesson in life.

My sisters also played with us in the alley, Jet being the eldest had already established some friends including a bunch of local boys and Aline joined us a little later but had also established her own group of friends. Nonetheless, our paths always crossed. Tilbury was small so we all seemed to know what everyone was doing. I think this created a sense of community, we all belonged together but it also meant, for the most part, everyone knew everyone's business which wasn't always a good thing. These times out playing were probably my happiest. I felt free, even though I often felt uncomfortable and sometimes awkward or embarrassed. I don't know why I felt like this but during these times I would bury myself in any games we were playing and would sometimes go quiet, the same pattern I had developed at school. As long as I fitted in, that's all that mattered, that was my focus, even if it wasn't a conscious one.

So, the time came to progress to senior school. I don't remember feeling upset leaving my junior school behind and I don't remember the feeling of anticipation for my new adventure, I just rolled along with what was inevitable. I had sport and surely that would be my ticket to fitting in, it had become my crutch, something that made people talk about me, something that made me feel good about myself, despite feeling the pressure, and it was something that filled my insecurities, at least that's how I saw it. Then, just as I was leaving junior school, one of the sports teachers approached me, asking if I wanted to join the local Thurrock Harriers which was an organisation that helped local athletic talent. I said I would think about it, knowing that it wasn't something I wanted to do, but how was I going to say no? I put it off until one day, the teacher asked me again. All I could think was, if I say no what would they think, nobody would like me, this was expected of me, how would the teacher feel? I was full of confusion but somehow amongst all the confusion the word 'no' escaped from my mouth. I felt terrible and despite what felt like pressure from the teacher, I stuck to my decision. I really don't know how I did this, 'no' was not a word I used for fear of upsetting people and it wasn't a word I used for many years following this, something that would prove to be very detrimental to my growth. Anyway, in senior school, I didn't say no to any sport, I threw myself into everything, I developed to the point where not a day went by without me participating in some activity. But my love was netball, I still loved being part of a team which made hockey also enjoyable. I still did athletics and anything else where I felt like I was being talked about, it was an unhealthy way of managing my insecurities but it was the only way I knew and it became a very bad habit. And then I became the interest of one of the PE teachers who was involved in netball. She also played and umpired outside of school in local leagues and she immediately took me under her wing. And so, my true netball path started.

The PE teacher in question was called Mrs Bella, I can picture her quite vividly. She was tall with short black hair which showed a hint of grey and she carried a little bit of weight around her middle. She always wore bright coloured lipstick and naturally her attire was always sportswear, favouring Adidas. Mrs Bella kept me under her watchful eye and showed an immense amount of support towards me. It was Mrs Bella who introduced me to a netball team who played in the evenings in the local league. I do believe I was actually too young to play in this league but she took me anyway and aside from the nerves, I felt pretty good. Somebody was showing a great deal of belief in me and it made me feel special. I felt I had a lot of attention which had become my fix, a dangerous drug but one I had become accustomed to. Anyway, I must have made some sort of impression as I was asked to go back. I fail to remember the name of the team but I eventually trained and played for them. Mrs Bella would be my taxi to and from venues and on occasions my father would take me. I do believe he loved coming to watch me play which sparked his interest in the game. I felt a little bit special but often felt more nervous when my father watched me play. I often wonder if deep down it was my father I wanted to impress the most, I'm not sure, I find it hard to decipher my feelings about this.

Mrs Bella continued to take a healthy interest in me, and my netball took off, I was playing regularly in the evening league and hopefully making an impression. Mrs Bella and my father continued to be my taxi and at some point, Mrs Bella also met my mother and both parents seemed to approve of her. Mrs Bella would always let my parents know where I was and what time to expect me back so all in all, it seemed fine. Then one day after a game Mrs Bella took me home and presented me with a new pair of trainers, I really didn't know what to say, for some reason saying thank you embarrassed me but my mother would always prompt me with 'what do you say?' At that point I would lower my head and say thank you very quietly but it was the most uncomfortable feeling. Now, I'm not sure what prompted the gift of the trainers but, the gifts kept coming. Maybe she had worked out that we didn't have much money which wouldn't have been difficult, maybe she wanted to help, maybe she needed someone to care for. Mrs Bella was a middle-aged single lady who had never been married and had no children. From what I understand she had no family at all and was quite a loner, not really having a social life. Her life seemed to revolve around her job and netball. And then, one Christmas I was presented with a whole heap of gifts all related to sport, socks, tops, a netball skirt and I was quite embarrassed because it wasn't difficult for others to know that my parents could not afford this, so where did all this come from? It was certainly obvious that I had many more presents than my sisters. I somehow ignored comments from friends and family, opting to say nothing and feeling very uncomfortable. I muddled through, just me and my awkwardness with zero knowledge about how to deal with this. I felt that all it was doing was separating me from everyone, going against my needs and although it was nice to have new things, it did not feed my insecurities. How could I fit in when this was happening?

Mrs Bella became more and more friendly with my parents and continued to help in every way with my netball. I was playing quite a lot now but was also still partaking daily in all other sports. I was now around age thirteen. And then one day at school, Mrs Bella took me to one side and asked me if I would like to go on holiday with her. She said it would all be with the approval of my parents and that I could ask my cousin to come along whose name was Jolene. She had obviously noticed that Jolene and I spent time together, I would call at her house in the morning, we would walk to school together and sometimes catch up during break times. So, once both sets of parents approved, the planning began. The destination was going to be Perranporth, Cornwall and we were to stay in a caravan and Mrs Bella would be driving. At the time Mrs Bella had an old-style bright orange Mini but the type of car was not something we thought about, all we knew was we were going on holiday and somebody was driving us. It was quite exciting, we didn't go away much and even though, for reasons unknown to myself, I felt a little apprehensive, I was looking forward to it. We would be away for one week but I cannot remember how we explained this to our friends given that a teacher was taking us away. Maybe it was acceptable, but was it? I had no knowledge of this happening to anyone else so I don't know why this was allowed to happen to us. It certainly wouldn't be acceptable today. That aside, the time came to head off on our holidays. Mrs Bella came and collected us both and we said our goodbyes to our families and went on our way with myself seated in the front of the car with Mrs Bella, and Jolene in the back. I remember it being a little uncomfortable, after all, it was a tiny Mini making a very long journey but we settled back making the odd conversation which I only got involved in if Mrs Bella asked me something and then my responses were short as I really didn't know how to communicate well. And then about an hour into our journey Mrs Bella took a silver canister, which I now understand to be a hip flask, from the driver's door compartment and took a drink from it. She then turned to me and said, 'if anyone asks you never saw that, it keeps me awake.' Now I wasn't very wise but her words told me this was wrong and to add to it I could smell alcohol but I assumed she did this for a good reason and said nothing. What could I say? Mrs Bella was our guardian for the week, we had no choice but to trust her. But what was really strange is I recognised this smell as I occasionally smelt it on her at school and I started to wonder what was going on. Anyway, after a very, very long journey incorporating a few stops and several sips by Mrs Bella from the silver canister, we finally arrived at the site and found our caravan. It was OK, a nice standard caravan with a little area housing bunk beds where Jolene and I were to sleep and another area with a single bed where Mrs Bella would sleep. And of course, it had the standard kitchen, shower and toilet. We settled in and Mrs Bella organised the purchasing of immediate groceries such as cereal, milk, sugar, bread etc. The weather wasn't great but nonetheless we all headed off to find our way around the site and check out the facilities. That done, it was time for a good night's sleep but a good night's sleep it wasn't. I noticed before we went to bed that Mrs Bella was drinking and I had a very uncomfortable feeling. Why was she drinking again? In fact looking back, I would say she was a little drunk. Anyway, this played on my mind and I had a terrible night's sleep which led to Jolene having a bad night's sleep, I just felt so uncomfortable. It was also very dark in the caravan, pitch black with the lights out and neither of us liked it.

The next morning, we were all up and ready to explore the site further so we first went for a walk to the coastline. Following this, Jolene and I amused ourselves at some of the activity areas and arcades but if I'm honest, neither of us were really feeling it, we just didn't like it. In fact, I think Jolene disliked it more than I did but we tried to settle. The following day we did more or less the same but we both started to express our dislike for the place. We phoned home both days we were there, which involved queueing at the only red telephone box on the site, telling our parents we were OK but not really liking it. I think at this point they simply thought we would settle down in the next day or so but we didn't. By day three we wanted to come home. Mrs Bella had been for a long walk along the coast coming back looking very windswept and Jolene and I had decided to go to a youngsters disco early that evening. But on our way, we once again queued at the telephone box, called our respective parents saying we didn't feel any better, we didn't like it and needed to come home. Now, during this particular conversation Mrs Bella appeared, came into the phone box and heard everything and I was mortified. Her face was very serious, she kind of frightened me slightly and then she took the phone and spoke to my mother who explained that we needed to come home and that we were homesick. There was an exchange of polite words between them discussing what our options were then the conversation ended and we all went back to the caravan. We listened to Mrs Bella who was quite upset at the idea of us wanting to go home but I personally think she had some idea and had hijacked our phone conversations for a reason. She knew we weren't happy and she knew we were calling home so she did her own detective work to catch us out, and she succeeded. I felt so bad because of all she had done, I felt like I was letting her down and once again my thoughts were more with her than they were with myself. I wasn't happy but I didn't want to upset her, but I had, and the feeling was of pure dread, what on earth would she think of me? But Mrs Bella was the adult and surely she would understand. Little did I know how fragile Mrs Bella was.

It was agreed that Jolene and I would go home by train, a decision I find rather disturbing. Two young girls travelling from Perranporth to Tilbury alone. Today I shake my head at the thought, seems rather bizarre but that was the decision so we packed our things and were put on a train to London the following day. I think there were two changes, one at Exeter and one at Fenchurch Street, we had our instructions and followed them closely. Once at Fenchurch Street we boarded the train to Tilbury and I think at this point, we heaved a sigh of relief as we knew we were on the home straight after a very long train journey. Our parents had been told which train we were on and I believe it was Jolene's father who came to collect us at Tilbury station. What a relief, we had made it home. We were driven to Jolene's house on the edge of the alley and greeted by our families and neighbours like royalty, after all, two very young girls travelling from Cornwall to Tilbury alone was unheard of, and I don't think I'll ever understand how this was agreed. But we were home and we were safe and at that moment, that was all that mattered. That conversation in the red telephone box in Perranporth that Mrs Bella hijacked would remain with me. Apart from the dreadful feeling of being caught and the remorse I felt towards Mrs Bella for wanting to come home, it was once again the familiar smell of alcohol that Mrs Bella carried with her, which was hard to avoid in the confines of a telephone box. Mrs Bella stayed for the rest of the week in Cornwall and when she returned, life carried on as normal. I don't remember her talking about our holiday, it was like it was a sacred subject and maybe it was, maybe it was best left alone. Needless to say, a holiday with Mrs Bella was never on any future agendas.

The school holidays were over, we were back at school and ready for the next year. Of course, my only incentive for returning was sport, I couldn't shine academically as I wasn't that intelligent so I still made sport my priority. I did have a few friends at school but not many, there was still the odd jealousy as I was popular because of my sporting achievements but that aside, my circle was quite small. I was now fourteen years old and I guess it's the age when boys start to become of interest. On this level I was still painfully shy and didn't honestly believe that anyone would be that interested so if they were, I always felt it was because I was a good sportsperson. I had already had the odd crush but one of those had been seen kissing a girl on the anchor field in Tilbury and the other wasn't really that interested so that was that. I found the whole puberty stage so difficult, never really knowing how to behave or act, not really believing in myself, shying away from compliments, it was so, so difficult. So, I focused on my chosen sport, netball, fitting in all the other sports around it, all as a means of escape. Netball continued both in and out of school with Mrs Bella remaining very close to me and my family, all other sports remained within the confines of the school for which I would partake daily. Then, one day my mother told me that Mrs Bella had called her at home late the previous evening asking for her uncle. Now, as far as we were all aware, Mrs Bella had no family so this was rather odd and then my mother proceeded to tell me that she was most definitely drunk. I didn't know how to respond to this information so I just shrugged my shoulders and said nothing. It's strange but Mrs Bella always made me feel a little uncomfortable, I felt it at school, at home and on our holiday, but I didn't know why. Maybe I didn't like the way she 'cared' about me, the way she 'favoured' me, the gifts, the support, it all felt a little odd. Plus, there was the alcohol smell. And then there was the badminton incident. I remember her pulling me aside once during a badminton game. Jet was also playing, in fact, I think we were playing doubles alongside each other. I can't remember who the badminton teacher was at the time but I don't think that mattered to Mrs Bella as her only aim was to stop me playing and the reason, to give my sister Jet a chance. Yes, she said I should stop badminton for fear of overshadowing Jet and I should let her shine. Who the hell says that to a pupil? I felt extremely upset and I didn't really understand, I felt like Mrs Bella was controlling me but I also felt I couldn't say no for fear of upsetting her. She had done so much for me and I didn't have the confidence to question it. I buried my feelings and stopped badminton immediately. I was crushed, taking away sport was like taking away my soul but I think her aim had been achieved, to ensure I didn't stray from under her wing. It's strange when I look back, there were certain things that continued to make me feel awkward and uncomfortable. Mrs Bella's interest in me I'm sure had good intentions but I think there was a dark side. Shower times at school were quite odd, she would stand at the shower entrance watching us all. As a teacher she said it was her duty to make sure we all showered, I remember her saying this, like she was justifying herself, so why did I feel uncomfortable? Also, I still wondered if it was normal for a teacher to have such a strong interest in a pupil, I had no idea and didn't feel I could address this with anyone, after all, if I upset Mrs Bella, I would lose my netball status and subsequently my connection to a world I was getting used to. It was a world where I could lose myself, just get out there and play, feel like I belonged, feel important, a place where ironically, I could hide. Nonetheless, life continued into our final year at school, I was now fifteen years old. Around this time my cousins, friends and I were allowed to go out to the local working men's club in Tilbury. We felt quite grown up going to the club, listening to live music and experimenting with a little alcohol. Our teenage years had truly begun. However, sport was still priority and Mrs Bella remained ever present, keeping a close eye on me whilst encouraging my netball career.

That final year at school seemed to drag, probably because I knew it was coming to an end, something I was happy about and it couldn't come quick enough. I would still have my netball whether I was at school or not, my release, my place to belong and that was my only focus. My final academic results were pretty average, and I may be being a little generous there, but it didn't seem relevant, I was leaving and that was all that interested me.

I look back now and can see that the foundation of my life was very unhealthy. My terrible insecurities, my need to be liked and to fit in had led to a life of never speaking up for myself for fear of upsetting anyone and all at the expense of myself, whoever that was. I can now see that due to this I made some unhealthy decisions, not knowingly, I just fell into place not knowing what was best for me. The unfortunate thing is, when you're insecure it is unlikely you will ever do what's best for you, you simply don't have enough self-love and pleasing others is one of the outcomes even if it feels wrong. The truth is, pleasing others at your own expense is like constantly taking away pieces of yourself until there's nothing left to take. A vicious circle forms and the sad thing is, that circle becomes normal and my normal was to do whatever it took to fit in.

I discussed Mrs Bella many years later in my early counselling sessions and my counsellor asked me a simple question. Was Mrs Bella a lesbian? Now there are times in counselling that I call the light bulb moments, it's when something makes total sense, it fits, you understand it and this was one of those moments. Ding, ding, ding, of course she was. We didn't know much about the gay community back then, there was no LGBT+ community as this was the seventies and such people were frowned upon. The fact that she was alone, had never married and had no children was reason enough during these times to maybe conclude that Mrs Bella was a lesbian. However, it was something that was never discussed, it was taboo, an awkward subject, but I did eventually find out that this was true, Mrs Bella was a lesbian. But whatever Mrs Bella was, she was most definitely a troubled person. Maybe it was the non-acceptance of the LGBT+ community that caused her troubles, I don't know, I knew very little about her personal life so it's difficult to conclude. I did however find out that she was indeed an alcoholic which maybe was her way of trying to deal with her life and whatever personal issues she was living with. I truly believe that Mrs Bella was a very lonely person and maybe looking after me was a way of having someone in her life, I do hope that's all it was. So many things, so many memories that today would be classed as inappropriate and maybe even come under the heading of 'grooming' but this was another unrecognised term. Respecting our elders or people in authority was something we were taught and there is nothing wrong with respect but it can get muddled in the wrong hands.

I read in our local paper some years later that Mrs Bella was found dead in her flat in South Ockendon. She was alone, had been drinking and had committed suicide. There were no known family to advise so maybe that night she called my house following a drinking session asking for her uncle was simply a cry for help. Maybe she wanted people to think she wasn't alone but it seems she was. I don't remember how I felt when I read the news of her death but I was in a whole new situation by then. I feel sadder now than I probably did then as my understanding of Mrs Bella is far greater. Mrs Bella had a lasting memory for me but the reasons for this are very mixed.

During the editing stage of my book, I felt a lot of confusion came through in my story so far, the story itself is confusing so I edited a few bits but decided the confusion was part of my story and should remain. I took myself back, writing how I felt at that time which is quite a contrast to how I think and feel today but I didn't want that to come through. I intend to continue this through my book, taking myself back to ensure the feeling and the story are right even if it feels difficult, uncomfortable or confusing. So let's move on.

CHAPTER 3

The Meeting

During our last year at school, our little group became regulars at the Tilbury youth club and Tilbury working men's club. It was mostly Jolene and her sisters and our friend Astra. Astra lived in the alley a couple of doors along from my cousins and was part of our young group who used to play in the 'alley'. Our visits to the working men's club were at weekends and the youth club was mid-week. These were fun times. The youth club had a weekly disco and the working men's club had live bands. We were still experimenting a little with alcohol and of course noticing boys. We would discuss who we fancied and got very excited if any of our selected beaux appeared for the evening. This was a time when boys escorted you home, gave you a quick kiss and would be on their way, something we discussed if such an event happened, it was just good old fashioned, innocent dating fun and, I guess, all part of growing up. My eldest sister Jet had already met a boy, they were part of the group who used to hang around the alley. He was a tall red-headed boy called Jobe who nobody seemed to approve of but since their meeting at a very young age, they became inseparable and over time Jobe became likeable. Jet frequented the youth club and the working men's club but as she got older this became less and less. Aline at this point was too young to join us but her turn would come in the not-too-distant future.

It was Christmas 1975, I was just fifteen years old and still in my last year at school and Jolene, her sisters, Astra and myself decided to spend Christmas Eve at the working men's club. It was pretty exciting, a live band playing, dancing, lots of people enjoying themselves and a great atmosphere, it was a fun time. During the evening Astra told me about a boy she fancied and pointed him out. I knew him by sight and I knew his name was Kane as he was at my school but in Jet's year, so a couple of years older than me and one year older than Astra. Astra attended a different school, she was at the local Convent so wasn't so familiar, she just spotted him at the club. Kane was very handsome, had dark hair, was fairly tall and was very smart and well presented. We discussed him and giggled about her crush whilst taking moments to glance over at him. He was very easy on the eye and had a cocky edge to him which when you're young can be quite attractive. However, towards the end of the evening, I found myself in a very difficult position. Kane had started talking to me and asked to walk me home, yes me. I was flattered to say the least, how could a boy like him even notice me let alone ask to walk me home? My insecurities were bubbling, the needy me took over, the desperate to be liked, the desperate for attention, I had only had attention because of sport but here was someone who liked me, yes me, all of which was too attractive to turn down, so I accepted his offer. Now I had to tell Astra which wasn't easy but we'd all had a little bit of alcohol which makes the lips a little looser so I went for it. She was very upset and there were plenty of tears between my friend and I but I simply couldn't get past the fact that I was chosen. Astra eventually went home after our emotional exchange as did Jolene and her sisters leaving Kane to walk me home. I was very shy but inside I was on top of the world. Kane walked me home promising to call. I stepped through my front door and into the lounge where my mum and Jet were sitting. They questioned how my evening went, had I had a good time, who was there etc. and eventually I told them I had been walked home by a boy called Kane, feeling somewhat uncomfortable, whilst perched on the arm of the sofa. However, Jet broke the ice by acknowledging the fact that she knew him, well, she knew of him as he was in her year at school. There were cries of 'oh him', 'I know who that is' and we all enjoyed a laugh together and I went to bed anticipating his call.

Christmas 1975. I met a boy his name was Kane. He had asked to walk me home, I agreed. However, I didn't realise that walking me home meant going via his house to which I agreed. I had no idea how to question this or say no. He was a handsome boy and I felt happy that I had been chosen so I went along with his suggestion. We arrived at his house and went straight to his bedroom. He was a musician he played a guitar. He put some vinyls on, we listened to the music whilst he strummed along on his guitar and I was very impressed. I was sitting on the edge of his bed. He put on Bohemian Rhapsody by Queen and came across and sat next to me. He pulled me gently so I was lying down. We started kissing and then he started touching me. I had no idea what to do or what I was doing but he seemed to know and started undressing me. It didn't feel right. Should I stop? What should I say? What was I doing? I had no idea so I let him lead. Bohemian Rhapsody was still playing. I lost my virginity with a slight pain followed by him thrusting inside me. What had I just done? I didn't really know. And I didn't know if I wanted to do this or not but it had happened. I had no idea nor did I understand my own boundaries. I was afraid of the word 'no'. I had no idea how to express my feelings. I was just fifteen years old, a child and a virgin, he was seventeen. He walked me home. Nobody knew about my Bohemian Rhapsody moment. I felt slightly ashamed. It was my secret. Little did I know how my life was about to change. It would change forever and secrets would be a big part of it. That was the meeting.

It seems obvious to me now but this should never have happened, I was far too young, still a child and in all honesty it wasn't what I wanted, I just had no idea how to handle the situation. My inability not to take control most definitely came from my early insecurities, a trait I have worked very hard to correct as I now understand the huge impact insecurities can have on your life. That said, had I known any different I would have also known that Kane should never have put me in this situation, nor should any man, it shows utter lack of respect and, given my age, utter lack of responsibility. I know this now and I also know that life would have been very different if I'd have had this knowledge, felt secure, but I didn't and that created the basis for my future. So let's see where this takes us.

CHAPTER 4

Dark Side Of The Moon

Kane did call me once all the festivities were over. We both had plans for Christmas and Boxing Day so I had to wait a couple of days, but he called and to me that was all that mattered. We chatted, he was softly spoken and seemed keen to see me so plans were made. We started seeing each other on a regular basis, walking, talking, listening to music, all the standard stuff. In fact, Kane wanted to spend a lot of time with me and I loved it. I had a boyfriend which made me feel 'normal'. It became apparent to our families that we were dating, not much was said about it, I guess to them we were just a couple of youngsters having fun. Kane wanted me to stay with him on occasions and for some reason my parents agreed, I don't remember how that happened, it's a bit of a blur but I was still only fifteen years old so I struggle to understand. When I say my parents agreed, it was actually my mother who made the decisions, my father was very much in the background, going to work and handing my mother all his wages at the end of the week for her to manage. Perhaps my mother thought I'd found happiness, a boyfriend I wanted to spend time with or maybe, just maybe, she had no idea how to say no, how to teach me boundaries, how to show real protection, right from wrong. I believe she wanted to do all of these but didn't have the tools to deliver, I also believe she felt a lot of pressure in her life and sometimes it was easier to just go along with things. I guess being a parent is difficult but whatever was going on, her intentions were good, it just felt it was lacking good guidance. I never knew my mother's parents, my grandparents, they passed before I was born so have no idea about her upbringing. She spoke very little about her life, sharing only little titbits which were never about happy times so I think there were some issues, sadness and some difficulties. And, of course, her mother and father passed when she was very young, just a teenager which can't have been easy. Anyway, all this aside, I started staying at Kane's house more and more, it was what he wanted so that's what I did. Did it make me happy? Honestly, I'm not sure but I do know that at times I felt uncomfortable, especially when I went to school from Kane's house and not my own, missing the walk to school with my cousin Jolene. Clearly everyone knew I wasn't staying at home and I felt a little embarrassed but didn't know how to change how I felt, I just buried it. On many occasions I would nip home after school and go back to Kane's again, it was his request and I ended up virtually living there. Of course, I was still playing lots of netball and was still really enjoying it and Mrs Bella was still there encouraging me. But one day Mrs Bella questioned me about a boyfriend she'd heard about. I told her I did have a boyfriend and she smiled. She asked about Kane and if the relationship was serious and if it would affect anything to which I replied, 'of course not' which seemed to make her happy. I was already juggling many balls but I was keeping everyone happy which at that time was important to me.

I was approximately three months into my relationship with Kane when I started to notice some changes. Little things started to happen, things I didn't like, things that made me uneasy. He showed signs of anger, he would rant about what I thought were small things and he showed questionable signs of jealousy. I didn't understand why going to Kane's house after school and being five minutes later than the night before was a problem. But it was to him, and I would be questioned about my whereabouts. I didn't believe that chatting with someone was cause for jealousy. But it was to him, and

I would be questioned about the conversation I might have had and in the case of males, if I fancied them. I also noticed how disrespectful he was to his parents which I didn't understand and didn't think it was acceptable but in Kane's case it seemed OK and he frequently shouted at his parents, putting them down, arguing with them, voicing his disapproval of their lifestyle, which was very quiet and unassuming. I also noticed how extremely cocky he could be, very self-assured with a grandiose idea of himself and a very inflated ego. These qualities on reflection, were the very worst for me to be around, I had no idea how to deal with them so I stayed quiet and if I'm honest, I became very afraid very early in the relationship. But I didn't want this to go wrong, we were an item, he was handsome, very well presented and we were a couple. Everyone knew we were together and I wanted it to stay that way, I didn't want anyone to know what he was really like so I smiled and said nothing. I was making this work at the detriment of my own well-being but at the time I didn't realise it, it just couldn't go wrong, what would people think? I couldn't fail at this. Kane's toxic behaviour started to extend further, I noticed his need to control everything and to prove his authority and sometimes when I stayed at his house, he started pushing me to the edge of the bed so he had more room, I was literally hanging off the side but if I objected or moved, he became angry and aggressive. It was a strange thing to do but on reflection, it was a means of showing control and authority by bullying me. The same applied when he wanted me to be somewhere or stay at his house, it was more a demand than a question and I had no idea how to say no. But he knew just how to keep me interested by doing something that I now understand as love-bombing, a technique used by narcissists and it always happened following an incident. He would be sorry, buy me flowers or chocolates, buy huge cards filled with love quotes, drawings of hearts etc. and he would be very gently spoken with soft eyes and at that point you utterly believe that everything will be OK. That is, until the next time, it was like a roundabout you're too afraid to jump from.

Kane's need for control and authority worsened and one day he truly tested me. Kane knew all about my netball, who I played for, where I played and he knew I loved it. In fact, he knew I loved sport. Then one day we were in his bedroom and he started to question me about why I played netball. I explained that I loved it, of all the sports I played this had been the one I enjoyed the most. Then suddenly he threw me on the bed, pinning down my arms, telling me to say I would give up netball for him. My mind was racing, this was the first time he had got this physical and he frightened me. What was happening, what should I do, what should I say? He was staring at me, smirking, with my arms still pinned down, so I said the only thing that made me feel safe, I said OK. He laughed and released me and all I could think was, how am I going to explain this to Mrs Bella? She had already questioned me about my boyfriend, expressing her concern over him coming between me and my sport and here I was agreeing to exactly that. She would be mortified, but how do I say no to Kane? My heart was racing. I was stuck in the middle, not wanting to displease either. I acted calm whilst my head was doing somersaults, something I had started to master. Stay calm, stay calm, keep him happy, smile, don't disagree, don't make him angry. I was crushed, frightened and sad and had no idea how I was going to explain this to Mrs Bella. And just at that moment, he pinned me down again, smirked, looked me in the eye and said, 'no, not really, you carry on playing, I was just testing you.' He had the look of victory in his eyes, like he had won my loyalty, it was pure evil. Eventually he let me go, got up and carried on like nothing had happened. I managed a confused smile thinking this couldn't be right but then I suddenly realised everything was good, I could carry on playing and didn't have to face Mrs Bella. I didn't understand the significance of this act at the time, but looking back, I can see this was the start of both the mental and physical abuse from Kane. I didn't really know what either of those were at the time nor did I understand bullying, gaslighting, love-bombing or the whole narcissism package. But I was to find out that Kane had them all in bucket loads and for him, I was the perfect target.

I was skipping through life, I had netball and I had my boyfriend and I wanted everyone to know that everything was good because failing was out of the question, that's just how my mind was wired. My ability to cover anything bad was progressing to the point of excellence, I was very capable of wearing a mask, which I found myself doing on a permanent basis as Kane's controlling worsened, as did the emotional and physical abuse. And immediately after one of his episodes came the love-bombing, always saying sorry or I love you or presenting some small gift. So confusing, but smiling on the outside whilst utterly frightened and confused on the inside became my normal. My mind was like a merry-go-round but that was normal, my stomach often had the butterfly feeling, but not in a nice way, but that was normal, my heart used to race with fear at certain times, but that was normal, but my face always smiled and that was normal. It's hard to remember how the controlling and abuse crept up on me but it did and being so young and so emotionally immature meant it was only going one way. And it did.

I was at school, out on the sports field during a PE session playing rounders. Our team were fielding and I was on first post. It was summer, July 1976, and it was a lovely day, the sun was shining and I was doing what I enjoyed most. But all of a sudden something happened, I felt a little dizzy and I could see what I can only describe as stars, was I going to pass out? But it stopped almost as quick as it started. I carried on playing rounders and had no idea what had caused this little episode and I can't remember if it ever happened again. But, in the coming week I realised something, I hadn't had my period, I was late but I was sure everything would be OK so I simply carried on. Then one morning I got up to get ready for school feeling quite unwell. I was at my own house which was unusual but probably the best place to be as I took myself to the toilet where I promptly threw up.

What was going on? I went downstairs and sat on the sofa in our lounge. I remember I was leaning forward, elbows on my knees and hands cradling my face. It was at that point my mother came in and I think there was a brief conversation about me feeling unwell and that I may not be able to go to school. Then she bent down in front of me, looked at me and said, 'have you been sick?' 'Yes,' I replied. She continued, 'have you had your period?' I didn't even speak, I just shook my head and burst into tears. All I remember after that is panic all around me and I didn't know how to react or what to do. I was told to stay off school, my mother rang the school to say I was sick, that was school taken care of. And then I waited. My mother understandably, seemed to be running around everywhere with a worried look on her face. I didn't really understand what was happening, I was too young to grasp the enormity of the situation so I withdrew, I almost pretended it wasn't happening, an art I had perfected. I stayed off school the following day and was told by my mother that I needed to have a pregnancy test. An appointment was made at the doctor's as over the counter tests were not available. I remember sitting in front of the doctor, my mother beside me, her explaining everything and me feeling nothing but shame, sadness and fear. I felt so, so sad and so, so frightened. However, I did what I was told, submitted a urine sample and waited. And waited. And waited. I think it was a couple of days later that my mother phoned the doctor as instructed and he gave her the news. I remember overhearing my mother's side of the conversation but the only sentence I actually heard was 'could there be a mistake?' Now, I may have been young but it wasn't difficult to understand what that meant, I was numb in every way, no sense, no feeling. And then my mother confirmed that yes, I was pregnant. More panic followed and my mother started to put plans in place as it was decided that a termination would be necessary. My mother had been briefed by the doctor of the process which my mother relayed to me but then realisation set in. If we did this through the doctor, the NHS, I would have to go to the local hospital where local people worked and God forbid anyone should find out. More panic. We'd have to go private, but that cost money, money we didn't have.

At this point Kane was unaware of the situation but soon the time came to tell him. I was allowed to go to his house which looking back was a little odd. However, I braced myself to tell him. I stood in front of him in his bedroom, nerves shot to pieces, petrified, head down and said the words, 'I'm pregnant'. My full memory of what happened next is a little vague but I remember the following. Here was a man (I use that term loosely) standing in front of me after hearing I was pregnant showing no empathy whatsoever. He stood tall, his cocky demeanour present and he said something along the lines of. 'so, what are you going to do about it?' Suddenly it was my problem. I felt so much fear and so much sadness but through it all I explained the situation about going private. And then I had to ask for money. Kane, at the age of seventeen and two years my senior worked so I figured there would be some cash, in fact, I hoped there would be as I almost begged for help. Kane agreed to come up with the money but not without a smirk on his face, in fact, at one point he appeared to smile but I didn't understand why. Then I understood, to him he was the hero, to him he had saved the day. I told my mother Kane would come up with the money. I think I said this with a hint of excitement, like I was helping, I felt like I had done good by my mother. She seemed relieved through what was clearly a look of distress. I suddenly felt responsible and hoped I was making a bad situation good which on reflection was way too much for me to be worrying about. I can now see I was trying to please both Kane and my mother, I was trying to keep the peace and make everything OK. The responsibility I felt weighed heavy on my fifteen-year-old shoulders so I did the only thing I knew. I buried those feelings whilst unknowingly locking them in the 'learned behaviour' category of my mind which would pave my future in an unimaginable way.

My mother decided that she would seek my auntie's help with organising the termination. My auntie was my mother's sister and her name was Auntie Cila and she lived in East London. I always liked my Auntie Cila, she had never married, had no children, had run homes for the elderly all her life and had a great sense of humour. There was something about her that I related to and I used to love the trips we sometimes made to go and see her. My mother had called Auntie Cila and explained the situation. I wasn't privy to all the conversations but Auntie Cila agreed to help. My mother then went hunting for somewhere for me to go and found a place in Brixton which to us seemed like the other side of the world but this is where Auntie Cila came in. She already lived in London so that gave us a head start, if we got to her house, we could take it from there. And so, Auntie Cila became our alibi. Our first visit to Auntie Cila was so we could go for my consultation, we made our way to her first then we all travelled to Brixton. The consultation is a blur. I can't remember exactly what happened, I think I was examined and had blood taken and was told I was accepted for the termination and a date was set which I believe was for the following week. The consultation over, we travelled back to Auntie Cila's and spent some time there, my mother staying with her sister whilst I went off window shopping. I was gone for so long that they came out looking for me and when they eventually found me wandering back there was much anger from my mother which I think incorporated the fact that she was worried. I remember overhearing a conversation between my mother and Auntie Cila where my mother indicated that I didn't understand, I was oblivious, and in that moment, I felt like I had done something wrong. Unfortunately, my mother's concern over the situation surfaced in different ways, from sadness to anger to worry, which I guess was understandable under the circumstances. But then Auntie Cila, in response to my mother, made a statement. She simply said, she doesn't understand, she's too young. And for me, that made everything OK, I felt relieved that somebody was able to say this, to free me of any responsibility, and if it had been possible, I would have run into Auntie Cila's arms and thanked her. But that would never happen and at that moment I buried the child in me. I had to deal with this, and amongst all the chaos, there I was, keeping the peace, numb, scared and many other emotions that nobody would ever know about. Eventually, my mother and I made our way home and I have no recollection of any conversations during that journey.

Of course, this unusual activity at home can't have gone unnoticed. My mother told me she had told both Aline and Jet that we had to go to Auntie Cila's but she couldn't say why. Jet, being seventeen, was probably more suspicious than Aline who was still only thirteen. I don't believe either of them questioned these unusual activities, but if they did, I had no knowledge of this. And then there was my father. My mother ensured she had everything in place before she told him. Apparently, she sat him down and explained what had happened and by all accounts he went crazy but was calmer once he knew everything was arranged. This is how my mother relayed that conversation to me. My relationship with my father wasn't bad even though our whole interaction centred around sport. I have no idea how my father felt about the situation I was in as he wasn't a great communicator, certainly not on an emotional level. And to this day I still have no idea how he felt as we have never talked about it, never discussed it and I am in no doubt that, as long as he's alive, we never will.

So, the time was approaching for the deed to take place and we were waiting on Kane to provide the money. The day Kane came to our house to hand the money over he walked in the door and with a serious look on his face said, 'I haven't got the money.' My mother went white and what seemed like a lifetime passed before Kane smiled, laughed and said, 'only joking, of course I have it', and proceeded to hand it over. It felt very inappropriate to make a joke of the situation but that was Kane, it was all part of him being in control no matter what. He enjoyed the fact that he held the solution right there in his hands but would play a little control game before handing it over. And I guess that's why my mother's face showed so many emotions. However, she just took the money, turned around and walked away without saying anything further. I can't imagine what she must have been feeling at that time, I just wished she had given Kane a big fucking slap.

The day came for the termination to take place. My mother and I had to be up early and all I know is she went into Jet's room explaining that we had to make another trip to Auntie Cila's, I'm not sure if she said anything more to Aline. Obviously, my father knew so no explaining needed there. We left very early, travelling first to Auntie Cila's with the three of us then continuing our journey to Brixton. I was petrified, I couldn't speak, I showed no emotion, I just stared out of the train window, my eyes stinging as I held back tears. Although I was only about eight weeks pregnant, I had to have an overnight stay, which was quite common in the seventies so I had a little overnight bag with me. We arrived. My mother, as my guardian, signed the necessary paperwork and we said our farewells. I held back more tears. My mother and Auntie Cila left. I was taken to my bed to settle in. The operation was that afternoon and at that moment I had never felt so alone and lonely. I stayed very quiet, not able to express any emotions. I buried them. There were several young girls and ladies all waiting for the same operation, some very clearly anything up to five, maybe six months pregnant which at that time was legal in England. I felt sorry for them, wouldn't that mean giving birth? I didn't really know. I didn't really know what they were going to do to me let alone someone so far advanced in their pregnancy. I have no recollection of speaking to any of them. I think I almost put myself and my mind somewhere else waiting for it all to end. My mother stayed at Auntie Cila's that night and was to collect me the following morning.

So, there I am, waiting. The doctor paid a visit and asked various questions, most of which I can't remember except the one about my age. I looked at him and with a very nervous voice I said, 'fifteen'. The raised eyebrow from the doctor made me feel more embarrassed than I already did, the look from him was one of disgust. I would have rather have had pity. I looked down, blocking out everything around me hoping the questioning would stop soon. Please hurry doctor, was all I could think at that time. He finally moved on to the next patient, God help those poor souls I thought, especially those in the advanced stages of pregnancy, perhaps he would raise two eyebrows at them. A short while after his visit a nurse came long and wheeled me to a room. I guess it was my turn, I was simply part of a conveyor belt it seemed. So emotionally cold. I lay there, tears burning but not being released. I was administered anaesthetic and the last thing I remember was my legs being pulled and put into stirrups and I knew no more until I woke up and everything had been put right. What a strange way to think about it, there was nothing right about it, but if I had any feelings bubbling, they were buried, shut away and stored in my subconscious mind where they remained for many years. I remained in hospital until the following morning. I was examined by the doctor. All seemed to be OK so permission was given for me to be discharged. I was subsequently collected by my mother and Auntie Cila and after their initial questions regarding my welfare we travelled back to Auntie Cila's. From there, my mother and I continued our journey to Tilbury, a journey I cannot write anything about as, once again, I have no recollection of it, it's a complete blank.

Once home, I rested for a couple of days and things simply carried on. I smiled, the smile that covered the reality of my life. I had fallen into this dark place in my head, a place full of deceit, lies, dishonesty, shame and fear. I was too young to understand this and too young to know what to do so I kept up the facade, convincing everyone that all was OK. This dark place was put aside. I didn't know what to do with it. Should I talk about it? Who would I talk to? Did I even want to talk about it? Talking didn't seem an option, it felt wrong, how I felt was something I didn't want to expose so I had to find a coping mechanism. And that came in the form of my 'rucksack'. This episode of my life threw me into the depths of darkness and my 'rucksack' was my saviour. A euphemism for my dark, messy subconscious mind, it was a place I could throw everything, bury it, but it's future misuse would have devastating consequences as I failed to understand that each time I threw something in my 'rucksack' I was throwing a piece of myself away.

CHAPTER 5

The 'Rucksack'

I went back to school approximately one week after the termination, and it was great to be back. I was laughing with my friends in the sports changing room, chatting with Mrs Bella about netball arrangements and generally feeling good about being back in my routine. It was like nothing had happened. I was in a dangerous state of denial, or maybe I was too young to grasp what had happened, I think it was probably the latter. My mother told the school that I had been suffering with bad periods hence my absence which led to a lecture from Mrs Bella on the best way to deal with this, going into graphic detail about how periods worked.

When I first saw Kane following the termination, he acted no different, it was like it never happened but why would I expect any different. I guess I hoped he may have at least asked about my welfare but I didn't understand at that time that narcissists have no empathy, he didn't care, it was always all about him. The incident was never discussed, he never mentioned it and I was too afraid to and within no time he wanted me to stay with him at his house so I had to tackle this with my mother. Following the termination, she had mentioned something about me going on the birth control pill but it didn't seem to go any further than that, just a mention, so it came as a surprise when she didn't stop me from staying at Kane's even though this hadn't been sorted. I don't know what I thought of this decision but at least it meant I was pleasing Kane, and pleasing Kane had become priority, he frightened me so if he was happy, I felt safe. And Kane's controlling was in full flight as was his insane jealousy so when I decided to gingerly approach the subject of the birth control pill, his response was priceless. He said there was no way I was going on the pill as it gave me free reign to sleep with anyone, and I was crushed. What do I do now? Should I do it without him knowing? But what if he found out? If I did and he did find out, I was sure he would kill me. I dropped my head hoping he would sympathise but that was never going to happen. He was standing there, arms folded, smirking with more than a hint of anger, looking down on me almost daring me to object. Of course, I didn't, I didn't want the consequences of an objection so I simply kept quiet, the fear running through my body, the confusion engulfing me, none of which were externally visible. So, being 'careful' became our form of contraception, this was Kane's rule, he even had control of that.

I look back on this in horror. Knowing now the path I was about to take it makes me shudder and it's one of those moments during the writing of this book that I found difficult. At just fifteen years old so much had happened but nothing that I wanted to remember, so I buried it. I can see now how destructive burying everything was but it was all I knew. It's so unfortunate that I didn't know any other way, had no idea how to speak up, express myself which is quite the opposite to how I manage my life today but for now, this is what it was and this chapter outlines how unhealthy these type of relationships can become to those who are particularly vulnerable.

So, were there any happy times with Kane? I guess there were but I only remember them being when Kane decided and only if he had chosen to be in a good mood, but this was also his form of control. He decided when the good times would be but he also decided on the bad times, when he felt the need to flex, to show me who was boss and little by little I became petrified of him. I simply didn't know what to say or how to behave in order to keep myself from either mental or physical abuse, both of which had increased with great ferocity. I simply didn't know where to go for help but at the same time I shied away from help. By this time, I was so frightened, worried and fearful of the consequences of Kane's actions that all I did was work on expertly saving face whilst silently trying to save myself and that was very hard but I did have my outlet, netball. Thank God I was still playing, thank God Kane had agreed. I needed this escape more than I realised, it was my time, a little glimpse of freedom. When I played it felt great but there was definitely an aggressive edge to me which I now know was the frustrations of my personal life being played out on court. Trying to play, keep the peace with Kane, cover up incidences I thought would make him mad however futile they were, make excuses to friends if there was something I wasn't allowed to do, it was all so exhausting. And I did it all with a smile on my face, I was the great pretender, the masked performer and this all became the norm for me, this is who I was and I got dangerously used to it. Or should I say, I simply got good at it, very good.

And then I felt a glimpse of hope. Kane's parents decided to move to Chadwell St Mary, they were doing a council exchange with somebody they knew and I saw this as a possible way out of always staying at Kane's as it was a bus ride from Tilbury and maybe, just maybe I could spend more time at home. Kane's parents hadn't said much to Kane about the move, it had just been mentioned in passing which Kane had dismissed as I don't think he thought it was a good idea plus he wanted to stay where he was. I do believe Kane's parents were a little fearful of him as he always tried to rule the home as he did me and could be quite abusive to his parents, particularly his mother. So, Kane's parents knew he didn't want to move which is why I believe they kept it low key, to save any backlash. That was, until the day of the move. I met Kane at his home in Tilbury and there were already very heated arguments going on, mostly between Kane and his mother but Kane, realising he had no option but to go, started gathering his bits and placing them in the removal van. He was very angry, I was very scared, but was told we were getting the bus to his new home so off we went. Once arriving in Chadwell St Mary it was about a ten-to-fifteen-minute walk to their new home from the bus stop so off we went. Kane's angry face was ever present, in fact his whole demeanour screamed angry as he marched his way to his new home whilst I concentrated on keeping up with him, always seeming to be a few steps behind. When we reached their new home, we walked in and suddenly all hell broke loose. Kane said he thought it was a dump whilst looking around in disgust, he demanded to know why his parents moved there, what were they thinking, why leave a great home for this. There was so much shouting and arguing going on between Kane and his parents that I felt lost in the background just standing there completely silent and embarrassed but I knew if I got involved it meant trouble. Anyway, Kane stomped upstairs to his new bedroom with me following him and then he decided to go for a walk and I obviously had to go with him. We returned sometime later.

Kane stomped out of the lounge and made his way to his new bedroom. He still had his angry face on and demanded I follow him, which I did. He hated his bedroom, nothing was going to change how he felt but, in my innocence, I think I said something along the lines of 'it's not too bad' or 'you'll get used to it once everything's unpacked and in order.' Not the right thing to say apparently, whack! I was struck around the head and landed on the bed, there was much shouting but only from Kane, his face right up to mine whilst pinning me down, screaming insults and voicing phrases such as 'what the hell do you know?' or 'don't insult me' or 'shut the fuck up', I was pushed, punched and pulled around and then he decided he had to get out and I was to go with him. I quickly pulled myself together and followed him down the stairs and out of the front door, his march still difficult to keep up with, I was struggling, not just physically but mentally, all I could do was keep silent and keep following. I don't remember where we walked to all I know was he kept shouting and scaring me, I was frightened and embarrassed, I didn't want anyone to see or hear us but if we did pass anyone, I immediately put my 'normal' face on so as not to give anything away. At some point we ended up back at the new home and I was ordered to follow him upstairs, his mood mellowed slightly, maybe the walk had done him good, made him calm down but I don't think it was either of these. A pattern had emerged where after he went through one of these incidences he would mellow and look at me with wanting eyes, smiling, but differently, it was a sorry look and although the word 'sorry' didn't exist in the dictionary of Kane it was the closest I was going to get. But it really had nothing to do with sorry and he knew exactly what he was going to do … he fucked me. And I did the only thing I knew. I threw the whole incident into my 'rucksack'.

I use the words 'fucked me' because they're the only words I can come up with if it followed an abusive incident. And the only one who benefits from this is the abuser, it's very empowering for them and all part of their control. It's dreadful looking back knowing what I know now but coupled with my dreadful insecurities we must remember, this was the seventies and much surrounding abusive behaviour simply wasn't spoken about, it was hidden. This type of behaviour today has a much-improved attitude and incidents of this kind now have labels such as 'date rape'. But I cannot call it that, we didn't know what that was so 'fucked me' is what I feel a very appropriate choice of words for what was happening to me at that time. I am all for us as a society opening up and understanding more about physical abuse, mental abuse, date rape, gaslighting, narcissistic behaviour, grooming, we have to recognise that these things really happen, they did then and they still do now. And although our current attitude and laws are very much improved it still means the victim has to feel safe enough and protected enough to expose their abuser, and that is the hard part. So, as a victim of such behaviours, I do feel we need to keep it in context. It takes a lot for a true victim to come forward so let's not lessen the courage it takes to do this by using situations to gain attention, money or social media hits, this only belittles the seriousness of it all. However, I digress, I have strong beliefs surrounding this subject so for now, I'll leave it there.

Life was now a little bit different. To see Kane, I had to get the bus which went from the end of my road and although I had hopes of spending more time at home, this simply didn't happen. Most of the time it was me going to see him, I would get home from school, change, walk up the road, get on the bus and walk the fifteen minutes to his house. We'd spend the evening doing whatever he'd decided then he would walk me to the bus stop later that evening. However, on route home, he would persuade me to call my mother from the phone box we passed and tell her I had missed the last bus and that I wouldn't be home. I remember my mother's voice, she knew I was lying and I hated hearing her response which, although was in agreement, her words were coated with disappointment and I felt terrible. And there was Kane, looking like he'd won again, got his own way, knowing I was too afraid to say no, too afraid to fight him. I hated these times when I felt torn but he always won and I tried never to show any signs of disappointment or fear, I simply smiled and put my feelings in my new place of escape, my 'rucksack'. The bus rides became a normal activity, we used the buses almost daily, toing and froing between Tilbury and Chadwell St Mary. However, sometimes when we met, I might be told that instead of the bus we were going to walk which thankfully I didn't mind. So, on this particular day we had walked from Kane's house to mine and decided that later we would get the bus back. It was a warm day and it was a Sunday so fewer buses and

Kane decided that instead of getting the bus back, we would walk. So off we went.

It was a Sunday so not many people around as Sundays back then really were rest days. After leaving my house and making our way to the bus stop in Tilbury to get the bus to Chadwell St Mary an argument ensued. I can't remember what the argument was about but I'm not sure I ever understood what any of our arguments were about. All I know is, a lot of it centred around jealousy, I was apparently always looking at other men, if we passed any males or I came across members of the opposite sex I was always accused of looking at them and fancying them. This always led to a beating but mostly mental abuse so maybe that's what happened on this day, it's a bit of a blur. Anyway, there was Kane and I, standing in a shop doorway waiting for the bus, him shouting and grabbing my arms, me frightened and embarrassed. Then suddenly he threw me around against a large pane of glass that formed part of the shop front and the whole thing came crashing down whilst I was still pinned against it and I froze. I do remember a male walking past on the opposite side of the road who shouted 'that was clever' and carried on walking. Kane's response in a cocky tone was 'yes it was!' I said nothing, I had no idea what to do, glass surrounded me, large fragments and small shards, I didn't even know if I was hurt but that didn't seem to be important. Kane told me to walk away, he was already walking so I did as he said whilst the sound of broken glass continued to fall and crunch under my feet. I have no idea how I escaped unhurt but by some miracle I did, someone must have been looking after me that day. Kane had made the decision to walk back to Chadwell St Mary following this incident leaving the chaos behind, well he certainly wasn't going to hang around, and it was a very long silent walk. The only thing I could hear was my heart pounding. What had just happened? And the next day this incident was the talk of my school. One of my classmates happened to have a little job in the shop and she was telling everyone about the attempted robbery, at least that's what they thought it was. But it seemed nothing was taken so there was some confusion as to why it had happened. One theory was that the robbers had been disturbed and I listened to this with utter shame, I felt absolutely dreadful but I joined in with gasps of disbelief, after all, nobody would ever know I was part of this, I was far too good at covering up plus we didn't have CCTV back then so no evidence. I sometimes wish we did have CCTV as evidence of what had really happened may have been beneficial to me but we didn't so I threw the whole incident in my 'rucksack'.

If I could remember and put together every incident with Kane, I could probably write a book on that alone. But the truth is, there are too many to remember, it was just my life and although today I have dug deep and worked on my healing, there are still things that elude me. So, instead, I have picked out a few incidences to give the reader some idea of what was going on and to help you get a feel for the situation, which I hope it does.

At this point I was floating through this strange life, juggling all the balls, keeping the peace and pleasing everyone, except myself, I didn't know how to do that. I spent most of my spare time at Kane's, under orders, whilst still making appearances at home and this pattern continued until I got to school leaving age. I'd been with Kane for approximately eighteen months when the time came to leave school and find a job. It was normal to simply leave school and find work so that's what I set about doing. I didn't really know what I was going to do but a lady I knew from Tilbury (her daughter played netball which is how I knew her) approached me about a junior role in a shipping office in Tilbury. I was delighted and arranged to see the manager and was so excited when I was offered the job which I accepted there and then knowing that life for me would change a little. I was sixteen, almost seventeen, pretty naive and really nervous about going to work but they said they would train me in the world of shipping, show me the ropes and they did exactly that and once I got over my nervousness, I actually started to enjoy it. This was a new phase for me, I was working, meeting and interacting with new people and earning a wage which should have been a great time but there was Kane, always in the background, bringing me down and the only thing this new phase seemed to do was add fuel to Kane's already burning fire. I worked with both men and women and of course Kane was particularly interested in the men and no matter how much I played everything down in order to keep the peace he still questioned and bullied me, insisting I fancied the men and no matter how carefully I trod on those eggshells they always seemed to crack. However, I went to work each day with a smile on my face acting like everything was ok, even if I had received a beating or a torrent of verbal abuse the night before so like my netball, work had become a place to escape, another outlet, somewhere I could almost talk freely, laugh, interact with people and learn. When I say 'almost talk freely' that is how I felt, I had become so afraid of Kane that even when he wasn't present, in my head he was still around, listening and controlling so there was still a part of me I held back but I guess this was the closest I would get to a little bit of freedom so I took it. There was anything between six and ten people at any one time in the office, some locals, some Londoners and we were like a little family, it was fun and as much as I struggled initially, once I settled, I loved it. This was also the time Mrs Bella and I parted ways, I can't really remember how it happened, I just remember a feeling of relief but I didn't really know why. My netball was going really well and still providing an escape so I had both work and netball as my outlets, and my God I needed them, it gave me a glimpse of sanity.

Day-to-day life continued, I was still travelling to and from Kane's house, going home after work, changing, going off to get the bus. Pretty much the same pattern I had when I was still at school. My escapes were still work and netball, even though they were challenging at times with constant interrogation from Kane. It was very difficult to enjoy anything fully but I didn't want this to show and I was happy that nobody suspected anything was wrong. I didn't want anyone to know how I was living, I felt ashamed, I felt a failure and even though there were times I just wanted to end it all I just kept smiling. Yes, suicide had entered my mind and once that door opened it only ever stayed ajar, it never closed, the thought often there. Sometimes in my daydreams I imagined telling someone, anyone, but I never really knew who that person could be and I wish I never felt like that as this would lead to my dark thoughts. However, suicide in my opinion takes a lot of courage which is something I didn't have and no matter how often I thought about it I simply wasn't brave enough to follow it through. I know some people reading this will say, 'why didn't you tell me?' 'I was here.' 'I would have helped.' And although some of those people for various reasons I would never have gone to, today I absolutely know that there were people who could have helped but the person I am today is not the person I was then. I didn't know how to reach out, I was petrified of Kane, I knew he could harm me as he had done many times so all I wanted to do was continue hiding and smiling. In my mind I had it under control, I knew what to do and I didn't think it could get any worse.

I was not very good at attending social events with Kane as they often ended in chaos, mostly due to his jealousy, so if I could avoid them, I did. However, one I couldn't avoid and one I remember was a party we were invited to by someone Kane knew which was to be held at a local hall in Chadwell St Mary, so a walk from Kane's house. I can't remember what the occasion was, maybe a birthday, but I was told we were going so when the time came, we got ready and off we went but only if he approved of what I was wearing and, on this occasion, I was lucky, he did. We arrived and

I was by his side hoping that nobody talked to me (particularly anyone of the opposite sex). He mingled a little whilst I mostly looked on. I had developed this method of not engaging to any great extent, holding back in order to discourage conversation, keeping it to a minimum so as not to anger Kane. I always felt that, if a conversation with anyone had, in his eyes, gone on too long, he would intervene and take over in order to keep me out of it and keep the whole situation under his control. I always tried to keep everyone at arm's length and approximately two hours into the occasion I was winning and all was well. The evening continued, everyone thought we were having a good time, we looked like a couple enjoying ourselves and I guess we were, based on what a good time was for us. And then we had to leave, abruptly. I think we said our goodbyes, I can't really remember. All I know is we left, leaving them all to continue their evening believing we'd had a good time.

Towards the end of the evening Kane decided to dance with a female which left me alone. I don't remember who the female was but it was always OK for Kane to interact with women, family, friends or otherwise but in his way of thinking, the same didn't apply to me. And then to my horror somebody came to keep me company. It was a man but his company wasn't in a flirtatious manner, far from it, in fact, if my memory serves me well his partner was the one dancing with Kane and I think he just didn't want me standing there alone. I think they were both acquaintances of Kane but I knew that would not make any difference to Kane even though this man's intentions were kind and polite. I immediately saw Kane looking at me, he always had his eyes on me, they would burn into my skull and frighten my mind causing stomach flips and palpitations. I knew this look too well and I knew it meant trouble. The song finished and Kane made his way back to me his whole demeanour screaming trouble. My heart was racing, I was kind of smiling trying to make it look like nothing was wrong but I knew it was. His anger towards me showed, his cockiness had increased, he puffed his chest and he had that look that scared the shit out of me. My God, I was in trouble, I knew this behaviour well. Shortly after this I was told we were leaving which was just before the evening finished so it didn't look too suspicious. We left and headed back to Kane's and the bomb exploded. Once outside, I was immediately accused of fancying this man, Kane was screaming at me, arms flying everywhere, face close to mine, fire in his eyes and then he started pulling and pushing me around. The more I cowered the worse it got and a short walk on we came to a field we had to cross. Kane was in full flight, he pulled me to the ground and then all I remember was being dragged back to Kane's by my hair, the field which was about 100 yards, maybe more, whatever it was it was quite a long way under the circumstances. I was petrified, I was crying but trying not to be too loud for fear of attracting someone. I was broken, I had no idea what to do but wait until it was over. We arrived at Kane's home, his parents were in bed, they must have heard us but as was the case on many previous occasions they never got involved, Kane was actually controlling the whole household so he could do what he liked. I was a mess, my head was sore, my mind in pieces and my soul broken but this meant nothing to Kane, he had control and that was always the aim. I end up in his bedroom as I was staying there, the control continued but it had flipped, he was now sorry, he loved me, he didn't mean it, all part of the control, and I knew what was coming. Once calmed I saw that look, a look I hated but I knew what it meant ... and then he fucked me. It's so fucked up, I knew it was wrong but I was scared and I did the only thing I knew, my coping mechanism, I threw it in my 'rucksack'. My head was so sore the next day but fortunately it wasn't in a place you could see but that was one of Kane's specialities. But, however sore, I put my mask on and smiled.

The truth was hidden, but behind my smiles something else had developed and it crept up on me during my time with Kane. I started to realise that I had a very unhealthy association with food. Kane looked after himself very well, he was always immaculately dressed and used weights in order to keep himself in shape and he was also very careful with his diet. I have to say, his method worked but he would put pressure on me to do the same as he wanted me to keep in shape. So now I started feeling a little self-conscious although I can now see this was another control method but this wasn't obvious to me at that time. I had always been conscious of the way I presented myself and being heavily engaged in sport, this helped keep my weight down but now it felt different. I started to almost fear food, it had become the enemy and before long I found myself skipping meals but this would then be followed by complete gorging of anything I could get my hands on. It was very ugly and the guilt after a gorge was intolerable so my first thought was how to get rid of everything I had eaten. I tried throwing up, assisted with my fingers down my throat but I just couldn't get on with this method so I resorted to the next method, laxatives. It started small but as time went by, I was virtually taking them daily. I have never had an eating disorder diagnosed but it's really not difficult to work out and I believe I was suffering with the condition bulimia nervosa which stayed with me for many, many years. Some therapists say it's a form of self-abuse, some say it's common in people who are abused as it makes them feel their controlling something, even if it's bad. I think I can relate to both of these diagnoses. It is the most awful thing to live with, your mind feels under constant pressure about what and when to eat. You go to bed thinking about breakfast, at breakfast time you're thinking about lunch, at lunch time you're thinking about dinner and then there's all those times in between, the circle continues, day in, day out, every bloody day and its absolute hell to live with. But I had no idea how to change it, I'm not even sure I wanted to. I didn't really know why I was doing it but it was my thing, my secret, my control and you can guess where it all went, it made its way to my 'rucksack'. I had also developed another obsessive disorder. I was exceptionally organised and tidy, things had to be in order, straight lines, everything facing the right way, nothing out of place which I think was me subconsciously trying to take control or make everything right. I was, and still am, accused of having obsessive compulsive disorder by a few, maybe they're right but I don't believe I'm that bad, I have seen bad cases of this disorder and I don't compare but I was possibly borderline. However, this has lessened as I've got older but I did make use of it at different times during my life, particularly at work, it was good to be organised. So, at work I found it very easy to hide my eating disorder, I don't believe anyone suspected but being very good at hiding things generally probably helped. Day-to-day life at work continued, I was learning a lot and I enjoyed my interaction with my work colleagues, it helped me grow and understand life outside of what I knew. However, once out of work I was immediately brought back down to earth, back to the life with Kane, back to Kane's slave, Kane's punch bag, Kane's outlet for his own anger and control. I was living two lives which is very confusing and pretty exhausting mentally. And men in the office became an increasing problem for me due to Kane's jealousy. It became another constant battle that nobody was aware of.

I caught the bus after work to Chadwell St Mary to go to Kane's but when I arrived, I knew Kane was in a bad mood. We went upstairs to his bedroom where he started questioning me, as he often did, about my interactions with the men in the office. I hated the look in his eyes, his posture, his cockiness and I knew what was coming, I had been through this so many times it was now easy to identify. An almighty argument ensued which led to him slapping, punching and pushing me around coupled with the usual torrent of verbal abuse. I didn't know which was worse, the physical or the verbal abuse, I had got so used to both it seemed one simply complemented the other. But then he did something I had no idea how to handle. He went over to the bedroom window, opened it, sat on the windowsill, one leg in, one leg out and told me to say I loved him or he would jump. Now Kane didn't live in a bungalow so this was pretty terrifying, he's hanging out of the bedroom window making threats to kill himself whilst demanding I express my love for him. Control at it's very best but I did as he asked, begging him to come back inside. He stayed there for a while, torturing me for as long as he felt necessary, making me say over and over again that I loved him. I was sobbing at this point but I can see now this was his intention, to have me in the palm of his hands, to have complete control, to feed his own insecurities. He eventually got back inside and then the look changed, he had that half smile in his face, he'd achieved what he set out to achieve, well almost because … then he fucked me. And off it all went into my 'rucksack'.

I went to work the next day smiling, like nothing had happened. I had no intention of exposing my life. I was doing well at work and I felt like a little part of me had let my guard down and there was a hint of change in me. I started to laugh more and have a little fun and although I didn't have Kane watching my every move, he was always in the back of my mind. I sometimes felt guilty when I enjoyed myself and developed very mixed feelings about having fun. Was it right to have fun with others? Was it allowed? What was fun? Could I have fun without repercussions? I was so confused and simply muddled through each day trying to establish myself, trying to understand who I was, what I liked, what I disliked, what was right, what was wrong. What I didn't realise is the tools required to answer these questions I simply didn't have and the damage was far too deep for me to understand. So, each day was a challenge and the relationships I established with work colleagues were not always healthy, not wanting to upset anyone and lacking the ability to establish my own boundaries being a real problem which extended through every aspect of my life, with friends, associates, in fact, anyone I came across in life. And talking of friends, once leaving school and starting work, the friendships from school naturally change, people move on and of the few friends I had I probably keep in touch with only a couple, the rest are only through social media. As for my cousins, they were also moving on having met boyfriends and starting to plan their futures which was also the case for Astra so life was changing. My netball friends remained close as we shared our common interest which meant I saw them the most but that aside, I wanted to be closer to my friends than I was allowed but my ties to Kane restricted this so I always held back. Fortunately, some have remained close and today I can share the true me with them which means those friendships are now authentic, no holding back, and it's wonderful. But for me to get to this point took an awful lot of work and all I knew at this stage was, that tiny hint of change at work I was feeling, I had to hang on to, it felt like a little lifeline, maybe the slow road to change. I really hoped so.

One of my work colleagues whose name was Heath I really liked, he was about four years older than me, liked sport, was tall, attractive and liked a laugh. Heath seemed so easy to talk to and over time I looked forward to seeing him at work, he made me feel comfortable and relaxed, something I warmed to. There was also another male colleague called Snoopy, who was my immediate manager and I believe around thirteen years my senior but my relationship with him was very different. He looked out for me, was patient and supported me in the early years whilst I was learning but I felt different towards Snoopy, he was kind but I wasn't as comfortable with him. Both Heath and Snoopy lived in London and both were married, Heath having the odd moan about 'the wife' whilst Snoopy not holding back on how argumentative he and his wife were and we often laughed at some of the stories he would relay to us about the previous night's events. It was a very toxic marriage but Snoopy was not really the argumentative type, quite the opposite, so it seemed he just went along with everything and maybe relaying stories to us and laughing was his outlet. I worked with some very nice ladies also and although I'm still acquainted with some of them, there is one I still actually see, her name is Neve and like me, she played netball. We actually ended up having a small lunchtime league in Tilbury docks where we played together which was great fun and for me, another escape. I actually knew Neve prior to her coming to work with us through the Thurrock netball league, we both played in this league but at this point for different teams. When I look back, Neve in particular is someone I could have confided in and I so wish I could have said something but the fear, the shame, the disgust, the lack of self-esteem, the lack of confidence stopped me, as it did with any of my friends. I think I almost told myself it wasn't happening, especially when I was at work or playing netball. It was at these times I left everything in my 'rucksack', throwing it all where I couldn't see it, where it was expelled, or so I thought. One of the saddest things is, when you feel so bad about yourself and you lack self-esteem, you unintentionally look for things to make you feel better and one particular thing is compliments or attention, particularly from the opposite sex. This meant I was drawn towards men rather than women, fishing for compliments, trying to find a way to feel good about myself without realising how unhealthy this was. Today, as previously mentioned, I have female friends who I adore, I cannot put into words the value of having good girl friends, it just took a very long time for me to find out and now, I wouldn't be without them. Anyway, the attention I was getting from Snoopy had become troublesome, I was confused as he clearly liked me which I saw as a compliment but at the same time it felt a little uncomfortable. I wasn't sure why I felt like this but even if I did know I had neither the confidence or ability to know what to do. I could never tackle issues with people without feeling sorry for the offender, I would rather suffer and see them OK in order to avoid any confrontation causing so many problems in my life as I became an easy target which is exactly what I was to Kane, and now Snoopy, but in a different way. As for Heath, working with him, getting on well with him and having a mutual attraction led to a little flirting here and there in the office and sometimes I had to go out to Tilbury docks with him to drop off and pick up paperwork. I loved these times, I felt fantastic when I was with him, he seemed so grown up and, in my head, he was a real man. I don't think I knew what that was but all I know is, it felt good. Needless to say, I never spoke of the trips to the dock to Kane, I just tried to enjoy these times and neither did I expose the other problem I was having with Snoopy. I wasn't sure Snoopy liked Heath and I being out together so sometimes Snoopy would request my company to the docks and on one occasion he kind of warned me off of Heath saying, 'you know that silly fool loves his wife.' I didn't know how to respond so I just shrugged my shoulders, he clearly thought something was going on which it wasn't so I just let it go. However, Heath decided to leave the company and I secretly thought Snoopy was happy but for me it was devastating. I was seventeen years old and I was losing Heath's company. He was going and I would miss him. I remember the feeling so well, like my little hint of change and happiness had disappeared.

So, Heath was gone and as for Snoopy, he and his family eventually moved from London to a location closer to the office and Snoopy's new journey to and from work now passed Kane's house and for me this became a real problem. It was whilst standing at the bus stop to make my journey to Kane's that Snoopy would conveniently appear and ask if I wanted a lift. When this first happened, I was grateful but worried as I didn't know what

Kane would think of it but how could I say no without good reason and without exposing my real fears and why wait for a bus when you can get a lift? So, I accepted his offers, voicing my thanks when he dropped me off. These times were never spoken about, never arranged, they just happened and the mornings at work following each lift were just pretty normal with the usual banter between us all and Snoopy telling us about his evening's events. But of course, I never exposed my real events of the nights following one of Snoopy's lifts.

After Snoopy dropped me off I made my way across the path to Kane's, I knew I had to tell him I had accepted a lift from Snoopy because if I didn't and he found out things would be much worse. I was damned if I did and damned if I didn't, so I went for it. Oh my, I had an idea it would be bad but as ever, I lived in hope. Kane asked me why I accepted the lift, his demeanour as usual was cocky, standing tall, eyes staring at me. I shrugged my shoulders and tentatively said, 'why not, it's easier.' Whack, I felt the blow around my head followed by a torrent of abuse. I was accused of fancying him, wanting to fuck him, wanting to be with him and so it went on. This particular event went on for some time, there was a lot of punching but the verbal abuse was dreadful. I was a tart, I was a whore, I just wanted to fuck other guys. He was close to my face, pulling me around whilst I tried to defend myself, I was pushed against the bedroom door which slammed shut and although it made an enormous noise neither of Kane's parents, who were both downstairs at the time, reacted to this. They must have heard all the commotion that was going on but they never did react, such was the extent of Kane's control in the house. Anyway, at some point I tried to make a run for it, I grabbed the bedroom door handle, opened the door and made a dash for it but I wasn't quick enough. Kane

grabbed my hair and dragged me back into the bedroom, he then
grabbed my clothes ripping the arm of the blouse I was wearing. I
just sobbed, I had no way out, I was beaten once again. And then
Kane changed, mission accomplished, well almost because … then
he fucked me. Of course, I had to get rid of it, the whole incident,
the fear, the shame, the confusion, the pain, so off it popped into my
'rucksack'.

And there I was the following day engaging in all the various activities and chit-chat, how bizarre. It pains me to say this but, this happened on several occasions due to me getting a lift from Snoopy. I was stuck. I couldn't say no to Snoopy for fear of exposing the reason yet I knew what it meant if I said yes. I was between a rock and a hard place, at least that's how it felt to me. But then Snoopy started appearing at the bus stop far too often and seemed to make it his mission to find me. The times he appeared could not have always been a coincidence, I even changed the bus times but still he appeared. He used to wait for me, drive around until he saw me, it was like a game of cat and mouse but I always got caught. Snoopy was creating a whole new problem for me, one I simply didn't know how to handle and one that would go on for many years to come.

The time came for me to learn to drive so I could use the company car and go to the docks on my own, dropping off and collecting paperwork, so lessons were arranged. Snoopy told me he would pay for the lessons from the office petty cash which was great although I'm not sure it was quite legit, just something he decided to do to help me. I started lessons and longed for the day I passed my test so I could get about on my own, longing for my own car and freedom from the bus stop dodging. Fortunately, my lessons went very well and after a few months I applied for my test which was confirmed for July 1978, and I was ready. The day came as did the nerves but off I went to give it my best shot. It went very well, so well in fact that I passed and

I was delighted. I had taken it on a week day and had gone from work so I headed straight back to the office to announce the good news and I was beaming from ear to ear. Everyone was delighted and congratulated me, it felt nice but the whole thing was tainted, I was hiding a dreadful secret.

I remember such sad days when, after Kane and I had sex, I would lay in the bath and draw water up inside myself thinking that if he hadn't been careful, I could flush it all away. Such a naive and desperate action but I had to do something. I was always petrified after sex and lived for the moment my period came. When it did, I felt like a million dollars, I was safe, I'd got away with it. But one day my period never came and I can't even explain in writing how I felt, scared does not even cut it, suicidal would be closer. I remember sitting on the toilet willing blood to appear and as every day went by it was becoming apparent that I was in trouble so I took a pregnancy test, which were now available to buy in chemists and yes, I was pregnant. It was July 1978, the same time I took my driving test, I was seventeen years old and I now had to face Kane. I picked my moment and announced very sheepishly that I was pregnant and with his cocky attitude and unsupportive manner he said, 'so what the fuck are you going to do about it?' I was crushed, I just wanted to die, I was sobbing but to Kane it meant nothing, it was all just an inconvenience. It was clear I was alone this time, I couldn't tell my mother, maybe it was because I felt alone there too, I had nowhere safe to go, nowhere without exposing what was really going on so I took steps to deal with it. I think the emotions surrounding this had already made their way to my 'rucksack', I had detached myself. I think sadly, I disconnected from what was inside my body. It's hard to explain but maybe somebody reading this will understand, I simply couldn't connect, I subconsciously didn't allow myself to do that. I couldn't have a baby, it would be Kane's and that thought made me want to die so I almost pretended it wasn't happening, thinking it would go away but eventually I had to set about the process of dealing with it, a termination was necessary, it's so fucked up. Private was the only way to deal with this and I remember rushing to telephone boxes to make calls to appropriate clinics to explain my situation and seek advice, these were the loneliest times of all but somehow, I found the strength to organise everything. What was really difficult was, whilst in the middle of organising this I was at home preparing something to eat when my mother looked at me and said, 'have you had your period?' I said nothing. 'If you haven't, we need to do something, don't just leave it.' I could have burst into tears but I held it all back and the following week pretended I had my period, I'm not sure if she ever believed me but it didn't matter, everyone was happy and I could get on with things. So, the date was organised and the termination took place but later that day I had to be moved to a different unit as I was bleeding quite heavily. It was noted by the doctor that I was fourteen weeks pregnant and that terminations are always better in the first twelve weeks so I was moved in order to be monitored. Fortunately, the bleeding got under control and after an overnight stay I was released. The overnight stay was so easy to do because I stayed out from home a lot so nobody knew any different and Kane's parents never questioned anything so nobody knew where I was … except Kane. This is going to sound quite perverse but, once the termination was over, I felt this incredible joy, relief, elation, everything could go back to normal now, well, my normal. Strange feelings to have under the circumstances and very sad but I think my ability to detached myself simply took over. I was very good at it and it was just a matter of going through the process, so cold, so sad yet so necessary. As for Kane, absolutely nothing, no questions, no emotion, no comment, life just carried on.

So yes, I was pregnant when I passed my driving test, not my proudest moment after all. And of course, I threw the whole incident into my 'rucksack'.

I was still living with bulimia, I was taking laxatives daily but somehow managed to hide it from everyone, I'm not sure how as I spent a lot of time in the toilet with diarrhoea. It was awful but I didn't know how to stop it nor did I know why I did it. The eggshells were still cracking no matter how carefully I trod but it had all become so normal. It's very hard to explain how this happens, how such an awful existence becomes normal, something I understand now but had no idea then. I was just existing in a world of fear and a world I hated. I had no idea who I was and I always seemed to do everything wrong, a thought that had been ground into me by Kane. Because of this, I thought others saw me this way which led to me putting a lot of pressure on myself to get everything right which is an absolute recipe for disaster. Nobody gets everything right, failures are part of life, part of learning but my mindset could not comprehend this. I didn't understand this way of thinking, it simply didn't exist for me so if I did get things wrong, I felt such a failure and so embarrassed and very emotional. I could have cried every time something didn't work out and, on many occasions, I did, but I never let anyone know. I even got emotional when others were in difficulty, I wanted to help anyone I felt needed it but what I was actually doing was putting more pressure on myself. I took on others' problems in order to make them right, I felt sorry for them, I wanted them to feel OK, I almost felt their pain. Or did I? I think what I was really feeling was my pain, I didn't know the difference, I just wanted everything to be right, no room for errors, a perfect world. What an enormous amount of pressure to put on oneself and this pressure extended to sport. In netball matches, if we lost, I could have burst into tears, if someone made an error, I felt the need to comfort them, tell them it was OK. My emotions were totally out of control and it seemed I dealt with this and the instability in my life mostly on the netball court where I let my feelings run wild. It was the only place I could let off steam and deal with the confusion I lived with.

I remember Snoopy sometimes turning up to watch the odd game of netball, particularly if we were playing in his area of residence. I thought this a little strange but could never address it and this is something I never revealed to Kane. Snoopy's interest in me grew and grew which made me so uncomfortable, it was so weird. But, as weird and awkward as it was, looking back, I wonder if his interest in me almost made me feel warm and needed even though it was extremely unhealthy. Was I enjoying his attention? I think subconsciously I was but this was definitely not a conscious thought, I had never had so much attention paid to me and I think I was confusing attention with his infatuation. But whatever was going on in my head, Snoopy was a predator, a married man, my boss, who's actions were entirely inappropriate. I hadn't got my own car yet so the daily game of cat and mouse at the bus stop continued. I continued trying to get the bus at different times or saying I wasn't sure if I was going to Kane's that evening, but no matter what I said he always appeared. I knew he watched me. I also knew he had started driving down my street late at night as I now knew the sound if his car and I would go to the bedroom window if I heard him and see him. One time I woke up to the familiar car sound, looked out of the window and saw him walking along my street. At that moment he looked up, saw me, waved and carried on, it was around 1 am. The next day in the office he simply said he felt better once he had seen me and went home. Fucking odd I know but I said nothing as I had no idea what to say or how to deal with it. I think Snoopy had developed a strange infatuation with me but I never saw any danger in it, I just saw a sad man who perhaps needed help but that was my downfall, I couldn't see the bad in anyone and I think Snoopy knew that. So, he still gave me lifts to Kane's when he caught me and the battles with Kane continued every time I arrived at his house and revealed I'd managed to get a lift. Sometimes I would risk it and say I'd got the bus but the fear was incredible and I worried continuously at the thought of getting caught. I started to not say anything unless asked, that way I felt I didn't have to lie and if not questioned all I could think was, phew, I got away with it. Well, not always.

I arrived at Kane's, he called me upstairs and as I entered the bedroom, I saw he'd laid out a little table and had made some food for us. He was smiling, it was like he had done something wonderful and I should be grateful. He did not question my means of transport to his house so I simply smiled, took off my coat and sat down to eat thinking I'd got away with it. We started eating and I think I was only two mouthfuls in when the dreaded question came, 'how did you get here?' My stomach flipped my head was buzzing with fear but I was afraid to lie in case he found out so I said, 'Snoopy.' Well, that was the end of that meal. He stood up, grabbed me, threw me on the bed, pinned my arms down and blasted a torrent of abuse at me. The table got tipped aside with food going everywhere. I was sobbing, I was afraid, his violence continued but this time he hit the side of my face and for the first time ever marked me in a place that was visible to all. My first worry was, how am I going to explain this, what am I going to say, I had to think of something. The abuse continued, verbally and physically until Kane decided it was enough. A short time elapsed, time for him to change course, and then he started with the 'I'm sorry' and 'I love you' … and then he fucked me.

The following day we were going on a coach trip to Cheddar

Gorge but during the argument Kane had decided we weren't going. However, he changed his mind once he had gained control, which was all part of his game, and said we were going so the next day we went off to pick up the coach. I felt dreadful but Kane was full of smiles so I played along, pretending to be excited about the day. It was always difficult to understand how, after such an episode, Kane could act like nothing had happened, he played dreadful mind games, something I kept quiet about and never understood. Anyway, I still had a mark on my face but I came up with a plan. There's an attraction in Cheddar Gorge called Jacob's Ladder, it's many steps that lead to a beautiful view and we decided to climb them. Perfect, I fell up the steps and marked my face. It worked, nobody questioned it and I had managed to pull off another lie, a hidden secret, I had saved the shame of what really happened and I had protected Kane. Why would I want to protect him? Because everything had to be perfect, no mess, no failures, I was brainwashed, I was borderline OCD, I was bulimic and I wanted to die.

Quick, my 'rucksack', I need to rid myself of all this. And off it all went.

I'm sure for many readers this will all be difficult to grasp unless, of course, you have an understanding of abuse. I must admit, as an abuse survivor, even I shake my head as I write this but I think that's because, the place I'm in today is so far removed from the past that it's hard to grasp that this even happened, that I even went through it. At this point so much had happened and I was still only seventeen years old but I guess I had some sort of life around all the chaos, it just wasn't a life I wanted and I'd often daydream about a better life, what I called a normal life, like my sisters and my friends. Those daydreams kept me going, my mind would drift off to a better place where I questioned what life was all about. I couldn't answer that question,

I had no idea but I didn't lose the need to find out, I always felt there was more, I just thought it was out of reach but I clung to the hope that maybe, just maybe, one day I would find out. Unfortunately for me, it took a very long time but maybe the hope I felt helped me make it. Never lose hope or determination, you'll be surprised how powerful it can be. So, as I strive on, me and my hope, let's explore what happened next.

Eventually I bought myself a little car, it was great to be able to get around and it meant no more bus stop dodging from Snoopy, no more explaining myself to Kane, I felt like I could put this behind me. But it didn't really make much difference, Kane would just find something else to abuse me about, I never seemed to do anything right. I can see his face now so close to mine, shouting, screaming, bearing down on me, my mind broken, my body a punch bag, my soul lost. And it didn't really matter if we were in company, there were many occasions when we were out with friends or at a work function when Kane decided I had been looking at someone and felt the need to react. He would get that look on his face, half angry, half cocky and strut around, maybe to the bar, maybe outside and I would follow him in a desperate attempt to calm everything down and keep it away from everyone else. The embarrassment crucified me, I didn't want anyone to know. If he went outside, I felt like it was a result as nobody could see us. His jealousy was on another level, he was jealous of everyone, friends, family, work colleagues, male or female, the less people I interacted with the better, it was all part of the control. So, in an effort to keep episodes to a minimum, if we were walking along the street I would keep my eyes permanently down, too afraid to look up in case I was accused of looking at anyone, flirting, as he called it. In fact, if we were out anywhere, I made a very conscious effort to avoid any form of eye contact or communication in order to keep the peace. But it didn't always work, if he was in the mood, he would create a problem in order to show me who was boss, to put me down, to put me in my place. And I remember an incident when we were at a function in Tilbury and he blew up about something, I can't remember what it was but he stormed out and I chased after him in order to keep it from everyone. And nobody knew what happened.

We were outside Tilbury Community Centre and he was throwing a torrent of abuse at me and I just wanted to get away as my family and friends were inside. We started to walk towards my house which meant we had to walk through an alley at the back of Tilbury police station. Kane was really shouting, calling me a cunt over and over again. It was so loud that a police officer appeared, he had jumped over a wall which ran alongside the alley asking if everything was OK, he must have heard the commotion. I wanted to run to him, I wanted rescuing but it felt like I had lead boots on and then Kane replied, 'no, no, no, we're fine' whilst waving an arm around and dismissing him in his cocky way. 'Are you sure?' said the policeman, 'we're good' said Kane, still dismissing him and walking away. I was following and we were now at the top of my street, I guess the policeman thought it was just another domestic that would all be forgotten about in the morning. If only he knew, if only I could have said but he disappeared which gave Kane further opportunity to continue his abuse. I can still feel his face so close to mine shouting, 'you're a cunt, you're a cunt' and all I wanted to do was get away from my street otherwise the whole neighbourhood would have heard. He walked away thankfully, I was told to follow and as it was so late and there were no buses, we walked to his house in Chadwell St Mary. Well, I say walk, it was more like a march as Kane still had his angry head on and this is what he used to do, he liked the thought of me being a little lap dog trying to keep up.

It was soon my eighteenth birthday and I wish I could remember what I did. It seems to have come and gone because, as hard as I try, I have no recollection of it. The one thing I remember that I think was around this time and maybe where I celebrated, was a netball dance we went to. It was a yearly thing where various prizes were awarded and Kane and I were attending along with my netball colleagues and their spouses or partners and on this particular occasion, some work colleagues which included Snoopy. There were many people, it was a busy night and all was going well, music was playing, some people were dancing some were eating from the buffet, people were drinking and generally having fun. I sat quietly with our little crowd making polite conversation, trying not to upset Kane. It seemed I spent all my life trying not to upset him but it had become normal to do this, all I was aiming for was a night with no episodes and so far, I had achieved this. Then the time came for the prize giving so the music stopped and, I can't remember who but, a couple of people took to the stage. A speech was made and the presentations began. They moved through the different divisions of our netball league until it came to ours and the first announcement was player of the season, and then I heard my name. I knew I was close but this was the confirmation, I'd achieved player of the season. I put my head on the table, I was delighted, I think I probably shed a tear and then went to collect my trophy and when I got back to our table my work colleagues had bought a bottle of champagne. They all knew, everyone knew, they were all in on it but were sworn to secrecy. I was very happy and quite proud of my achievement and the rest of the evening went without a hitch whilst I harboured a little secret.

I was sitting on the bed at Kane's and all I could see was Kane standing upright looking down on me shouting. I have no recollection of the cause of this argument but my guess is, he found something to argue about because he had an ulterior motive. It was about a week prior to the netball dance and I was sitting there, heart racing, mind scrambled, not knowing what I had done when suddenly he said, 'and all this rubbish about keeping it a secret that you got player of the season.' I looked up, I wasn't excited, I was horrified and had no idea what to say. I put my head down as he continued, 'people ringing me telling me what was going to happen, saying I must not say anything.' And as I looked up, he said, 'so now you know, and that's why we have to go to YOUR fucking netball dance.' He was shouting as usual and looking at me for a reaction but I just lowered my head. What a mean thing to do, he just couldn't bear the thought if me having any attention or achievements so he decided to spoil everything. I pretended I never heard his words. This is not what I wanted so I just buried it.

So, the night of the netball dance I had to pretend I didn't know about my award, I had to act surprised and I vividly remember Kane's face. He had a very smug look, he was enjoying this, he felt he had won, I wasn't the winner, he was. I should have won my prize for best actress, not player of the season because acting was all I was doing, I felt such a fake. I wanted to be happy but Kane had made sure I wasn't going to be and he so enjoyed it, he'd achieved what he'd set out to do and that's probably why there was no drama on the night. Mission was already accomplished. So, I threw away this moment and it was the perfect shot, it landed straight in my 'rucksack'.

Isn't it awful the depths a narcissist will go to, anything to ensure you have no joy in life, no fun, no attention, no freedom. It's quite incredible the way their brains are wired, they have zero empathy are self-indulgent and see people as products, it's all about what they can get from you. They do not understand love and will replace this with obsession just so you can't be around anyone else and will use you for control, money, sex, anything to serve their fragile ego. And they have such a grandiose idea of themselves believing their own bullshit and believing others believe it too. And they love to bring you down, to destroy you which I think is their greatest kick, to watch you break knowing they did this. Of course, on reflection and some years on, I understand this now, I can see the pattern, I studied it a little as part of my healing and concluded that it's extremely difficult for a narcissist to change, in fact it's almost impossible so think hard if you're in the hands of a narcissist as the chances of things changing are virtually zero. But, right now, at this time in my life I didn't have the strength or knowledge to know what to do and so life continued in the only way I knew.

I so often wanted to end my life but that was only ever in my head. It takes too much courage to carry out such an act and courage was something I didn't have. However, I knew my life wasn't normal and I knew it wasn't normal to have these dark thoughts but I only saw two choices, die or stay as you are. I never saw an alternative. I was trapped in a life that to me was my only option, it was my bubble, I couldn't run, I couldn't tell anyone and I couldn't burst my bubble for fear of what was on the other side and what might happen. And even if I did try to escape, Kane would search me out, find me and probably kill me, I truly believed this. I was so afraid of Kane, I lived in constant fear but I had work and netball and they continued to be my escape. My father was now heavily involved in my netball to the point where he had become an umpire and I think he thoroughly enjoyed it. I was definitely a big part of my father's life but I never felt I could confide in him for fear of disappointing him. Our relationship wasn't on an emotional level but he wasn't an outwardly emotional man. He was a simple man with working class values. He went to work, earned the money and gave his weekly wages to my mother for her to manage. My mother complained a lot about the fact that he did not take responsibility and often relayed stories of his incompetence to Aline, Jet and I. I don't think my father saw it this way. His mindset was, as long as he went to work, job done, his simplicity almost removing himself from my mother's requirements. An interesting combination.

It was around the time, when I was eighteen, my youngest sister Aline met a boy and they had become very close. My eldest sister Jet was already in a very steady relationship with a boy she had met from the days we used to hang around the alley. So now, we were all in relationships and it was Jet who was the first to get engaged, I believe she was nineteen years old and it was a happy occasion. Aline was the next to get engaged and again, a happy occasion. Their lives seemed to be so different from mine and nobody would have known how often I observed them, thinking about how odd my life was and how odd I felt. To me, they were what I classed as normal but that aside, with all the engagement activities going on all I could think was, please don't let me be next but more of that later, I had bigger things to worry about.

I was nineteen years old with fear utterly consuming me. I had discovered once again that I was pregnant. I went through the usual thoughts in my head, planning when I would tell Kane but still living in hope that the test was wrong. But it wasn't and I had to tell him. I don't think I ever accepted that I was pregnant, even when tests had proved I was, and this may sound strange but it's incredible what the mind can do when under so much pressure and in such difficult circumstances. It was like I had an illness and took medicine to cure it, the only difference was, I went somewhere for the cure. This is the only way I can describe how I felt and writing about it now makes me realise how bloody awful it was, how the situation I was in so affected my mind, it was simply horrid and I find it so, so sad. So, I had switched off the pregnancy, it would go away, I would have to make it go away. Kane's response once again was 'what the fuck you going to do about it?' whilst shrugging his shoulders and accompanied by the usual cocky stance and the half smile on his face, I can see it so clearly. Once again, I got everything organised, I used telephone boxes to make calls for appointments and organised everything on a weekend so I didn't have to have time off work. I distinctly remember the day I went in, I went by train to London, I was alone, it was very, very cold, it had been snowing but I was on autopilot and just went through the motions. I remember seeing a young girl in there, she must have been five months pregnant, she was really showing and she was with an older woman who I assumed to be her mother. She was showing signs of stress, anxiety and nerves whilst fighting back tears and I just wanted to hug her, tell her everything would be OK. I couldn't stop watching her or the older woman who showed no signs of sympathy, in fact, it was quite the opposite, she was very hard and tough and had this constant look of disgust on her face. She reminded me of Kane, heartless. Maybe I saw myself in this young girl and my need to hug her was born from my own desires, needing somebody who would say it's OK, somebody who could help me but of course that would never happen because I had no idea how to let anyone in. Once the young girl disappeared, I couldn't stop thinking about her, I felt helpless and she has always stayed in my mind often wondering if life turned out well for her. I met another young girl in there and we started chatting, she was on her second termination which she was happy to share with me but I kept quiet which made her assume this was my first. She started telling me not to worry, it's OK and that I wouldn't know anything. She proceeded to tell me how, once you're anaesthetised you slip away and then you wake up and it's all over. I felt like she wanted to comfort me, it felt nice but it had gone too far for me to disclose my story so I remained quiet. We were *assigned our beds and it just so happened I was in a room with this girl so we settled in and continued to chat until our time came. And then it was over. I would describe it as almost like a conveyor belt, one after the other, you're just a number for their records which in many ways I could handle as it helped me switch off. The girl and I continued to make conversation and then a doctor appeared, stood at the end of my bed and asked in a loud voice, 'when was your last termination?' I answered. He then said, 'and the one before that?' I answered and he left. I wanted to die, the girl now knew this wasn't my first, I felt so ashamed especially when she turned to me and said, 'I thought this was your first?' I felt like I had lied and I said something along the lines of 'it's my first here,' which was true but I'm sure the shame showed on my face. I just wanted to get out of this place. And as luck would have it, I was released that night. It is possible to be in for just one day unless there are complications and as I was OK, I took off. It was dark and cold with snow and ice everywhere, I was in Brixton, I was alone, I even remember the long tan leather coat I was wearing. I dashed for the train, I was scared and wanted to get back to familiar ground and soon I did, following a couple of train journeys and a bus. I had made it back to Kane's. Of course, he was his usual self, it wasn't talked about, no emotions and life just carried on like nothing had happened. Quite incredible.*

Another sad moment for the 'rucksack'.

The lack of emotion in all this was quite incredible, almost unbelievable but I couldn't allow my emotions to take over, I think they were lost in my rucksack, the only place I knew where to put them and soon life was back on some kind of track. Holidays had become a thing Kane wanted to do and following some short discussions it was decided that we would go on a skiing holiday. I'm not totally sure how this was decided but the holiday chosen meant we were to go by coach to a resort in the Pyrenees, on the French side so when the time came, we made our way to London to meet the coach. Once we had all boarded and equipment and luggage dealt with, we headed off spending the next twenty-four hours travelling which was extremely tough and as you can imagine, I spoke to nobody except Kane during the whole time. But finally, we arrived and I was so relieved, not just because we had made it and could get off of the coach but also because it was a nice little resort. It was quite pretty, very scenic and it had the usual ski lodges for accommodation and a communal eating/entertainment area catering for between forty to sixty people. We were met by our rep and allocated our rooms, quickly settling in before making our way to the communal area to go through our itinerary and the following day we were up and ready for action. Neither of us had skied before so lessons from a ski instructor were a must so we booked them, went into our group and began our daily lessons. We were joined by some of our fellow travellers and it seemed a fun group and of course there was much laughter as there always is with beginners. There was much fumbling around, people trying to stay up, the inability to stop and heading off in the wrong direction, sometimes into the paths of others and if you've ever experienced this you will probably agree that those first ski lessons are the best and often the funniest. Anyway, the week went on and our group improved and there was much discussion at dinner each night about the day's events, and soon it was time to come home. We made our twenty-four-hour journey home which was even more difficult than our journey out and I vowed from that day I would never travel that long by coach again, and I never have. I went back to work extremely tired but gushed to everyone about my first skiing holiday, minus the coach trip!

We arrived at the ski resort, settled in, and gathered up the next morning for our first lesson. It was exciting and our group seemed good fun and soon we were all laughing and trying to adjust to life on skis which was much talked about that evening at dinner. The following day we were up and ready for our next lesson and during the day I noticed Kane talking to a young lady from our group with their conversation continuing at dinner that evening, I was very aware of this and also aware of the fact that she looked pretty besotted. This was repeated the following day and night so when we eventually retired that evening, I mentioned this lady in conversation which was pretty much dismissed. Kane had brushed it off, he'd looked at me like I was crazy and it was all accompanied by his cocky stance. However, it clearly hadn't gone unnoticed as the following morning an argument erupted, I tried to get away by heading for the shower but as I reached the shower cubicle, he was right behind me shouting obscenities and accusing me of eyeing up the ski instructor. He pushed me into the cubicle and tried to slam the cubicle door which caught me full on, he grabbed my hair and punched me in the side and back calling me a whore and telling me I fancied the instructor. I had no idea what to do, I just wanted him to leave me alone so I cowered in the corner which seemed to work as he left the room leaving me to shower and got ready for the day ahead. Of course, I hadn't eyed up the instructor and to this day I have no idea what he even looked like but I spent the rest of the holiday avoiding any eye contact with him and just listening to instructions with my eyes down. The same can't be said for Kane though, he had put me in my place so he could enjoy the rest of the week interacting with the instructor and, of course, the young lady in question which became quite intolerable but I was too afraid to say anything. He had also made friends with one of the coach drivers who seemed to be encouraging the whole situation and I have never felt so invisible, it was like I wasn't there, I was a nuisance, I was spoiling their fun and I couldn't believe this was going on given what he had done to me. Then, the night before we were due to come home, we were all in the communal area having a few drinks but I noticed Kane had gone missing. I left it for some time before heading outside to find him, and there he was, in a very quiet place cosied up on a bench with the young lady in question. She saw me first and made nervous eye contact with Kane, she was clearly warning him and his response was to turn around quickly, stand up and walk towards me. It was pretty clear what was going on but I was too afraid to say anything, I knew what it meant if I did and I didn't want to go through that again. I just wanted to get home so I remained silent. During the rest of the evening Kane seemed to be on a high, chatting with his new friend, the coach driver, and organising to meet up when they got home which I found odd as he lived in Kent, but who else lived in Kent? Yes, the young lady, what a coincidence. We retired for the evening and were all packed and ready for an early start the following day, Kane didn't say too much that night but at least he left me alone, and the biggest bonus … he didn't fuck me.

We all met the following morning at our designated spot, clambered onto the coach and headed home. The coach trip was difficult, I still felt invisible and Kane and the young lady stole glances at each other during the journey. I felt so ashamed with myself for not doing anything but at the same time I felt I had no choice. I knew the consequences if I spoke up so I just let it go. We arrived home and a few days later the coach driver contacted Kane to arrange to meet up, reading between the lines they were going to meet at a nightclub in Kent and the young lady was going *to be present. Of course, it never happened, Kane had had his moment, he had proved to himself what he was capable of, acting like a single man and impressing those who fell for it. Control was always his aim along with feeding his ego, the same needs just different circumstances and for people like Kane, it was mission accomplished. I was never part of the mission, I was just a spare but can you imagine if the boot had been on the other foot, doesn't bear thinking about.*

So, the ski slopes left their mark, but I now wonder what else I was expecting, it was never going to go well, Kane would make sure of that, how dare I try and enjoy myself. But, of course, that was then, a different time and I can safely say that today, I would never land myself in this situation. But, for now, the whole holiday and its activities had to be buried, sloping nicely into my 'rucksack'.

Sometimes I have to take a breath, shake my head and take in the enormity of the life I was living. I wonder now how I did it, how I held up, how I survived. Maybe the fear triggered not just suicidal thoughts but sheer determination and I'm glad the latter came out stronger. I wanted to be here, I wanted to be happy, just like my sisters, cousins and my friend Astra but it just seemed out of reach. All I had was my own thoughts, my daydreams and the belief that one day I would make it and I hung on to that belief. In the meantime, I was still having issues with Snoopy, his strange infatuation for me growing making me feel more and more uncomfortable around him and making things more and more difficult with Kane. I was able to keep a lot of it away from Kane as it was mostly in the office. Snoopy's strange comments, looks and his unending kindness bordered on creepy. He was still appearing at strange times in strange places and I still laughed it off with no clue what to do about it which I can see now encouraged him, I wasn't tackling this, it was like I was giving him free reign which was not what I intended so continue he did. One thing that was going well at this point was my netball, I was still playing in the local league, mostly evening games but I had also made it to County level and was representing Thurrock. I was delighted to have made the selection and loved the idea of representing my County, it made me feel proud and for me, important. I was part of the under twenty-one squad and we had a coach allocated to us who not only trained us for physical strength and cardio but also for the technical side, both of which seemed to help calm me down slightly, I enjoyed the structure. County meant I had to train at weekends and play games up and down the country but mostly these were day trips so no issue with Kane. I absolutely loved to escape at these times, I loved to dream, I loved to take my mind elsewhere apart from in the clutches of Kane, I loved the escapism and I would like to say, I loved being me. The only issue here was, I didn't really understand who me was. Me was someone I didn't particularly like so I often battled with myself, not understanding my actions or reactions. I think the me I had become was very damaged so even though I loved my times away from Kane and I felt somewhat free, my damaged mind came with me and most of the time I didn't know how to manage this. However, I loved a lot of my netball friends and even though I struggled with female friendships, there were some I warmed to and through it all, to this day, I still remain very good friends with a handful of them. For me, it's wonderful to now know how to enjoy female friendships, to understand what it can bring and how much fun and laughter it can be and this goes for all my female friends I have made along the way. It's great to enjoy the company of fellow females and to have great trust and support in each other. But I digress, back to netball. Playing in the league and playing and training for the County kept me busy and surprisingly enough it didn't seem to set Kane off. Yes, there was the odd comment, a frightening moment, maybe some abuse but overall, he didn't really get involved and it was a relief. But then the time came for a big event, it was the Inter County Tournament when all Counties got together over a weekend and played netball solid for two days. We were all asked who would be available and I believe most of the squad were, me included. I was so excited and more so because it was to be held in Jersey. I couldn't believe it, what a great opportunity which we were all really looking forward to. The plan was to fly on the Friday, play Saturday and Sunday and fly home Monday so we would be away for three nights, four days. Some had never flown before so there was a lot of teasing and banter about having to flap your arms to get the plane off the ground, it was fun, we laughed a lot and it felt good. There was much discussion about the trip and our training continued in preparation. We had a few months before the event so there was plenty of time to plan but it all came together and eventually the time arrived, we were off.

Kane and I were in Romford shopping, it was a Saturday and I had been desperately trying to find the right time to ask him if I could go to Jersey. I had already confirmed to the County coach and all the other players that I was going, how could I not? I couldn't say 'I'll have to ask Kane first', that would expose too much so my mission was to catch Kane at the right time. How bloody naive of me, there was never a right time but it had to happen soon as plans were being put in place. Romford was a good shopping centre in those days, it had most of the usual high street shops plus a good market. Markets were a much bigger thing back then, we all liked to mooch around a good market looking for a bargain, sadly not the case today as there are very few left. However, during this shopping trip I kept trying to find the right moment to ask my question but I kept putting it off, should I say it casually when shopping? Should I say it when we stopped for lunch? Should I say it on the bus home? Of course no time would be a good time but I think I probably picked the worst time ever. We had stopped at a jewellery shop and were admiring the window display when suddenly Kane turned to me and asked if I liked a particular engagement ring. It was a beautiful ring but I was horrified, what was going on?! He said he wanted to buy it for me, he wanted us to get engaged and, in that moment, looking at his smiling, controlling, daring face I blurted out, 'can I go to Jersey for a weekend with the County netball team?' My heart was racing like you could never imagine, my stomach turning like a rollercoaster, the panic in my whole being must have been visible. And his face spoke a million words, and this was not a good face, it was one I knew, the change was frightening and I knew I was in trouble. He proceeded to shout at me face to face outside the shop which was so embarrassing and then stormed off. I don't remember what he said but now he was marching, long strides, chest out with a 'don't fuck with me' attitude. His cockiness combined with his anger was soaring. I quickly followed, trying to keep up, it must have been so obvious to onlookers which made me even more afraid, I didn't need anyone getting involved, that would make the situation worse so I behaved like nothing was wrong. I followed Kane around most of Romford and every now and then he would blurt out some kind of abuse. I was trying not to cry, I just wanted to go home, to get away from any observers and although I knew home, being Kane's home, wasn't safe, at least nobody could see what was inevitably going to happen. We didn't do any more shopping that day, we marched to the bus stop and got the bus back to Kane's and then the fun began. Here we were again, I sat there, head down just hoping he would agree, that he would see sense, how stupid and naive of me, and then it began. According to Kane I wanted to go so I could fuck someone, he asked if I thought he was some kind of mug, his voice getting louder as he grabbed me and pushed me down on the bed pinning me down as he usually did, grabbing my hair whilst *delivering a torrent of abuse. He accused me of wanting to go away rather than have an engagement ring, he was turning it all around so it looked like I was at fault which I now understand as gaslighting. The truth is, I didn't want an engagement ring but I was now saying I did, I'd say anything to calm everything down and to go to Jersey, anything to keep the peace. Kane won the day by saying I could go but not without a scene, he had shown his authority and his power and I felt I was right back to that fifteen-year-old girl being asked to choose between netball and Kane and I hated it. However, I could now relax about the trip but I still didn't talk about it with too much excitement for fear of upsetting Kane, I was going and that was the result I wanted. I went to work the following Monday able to speak about it more freely and at netball training I could relax a little and get more involved in the discussions about the plans for the trip and it felt good even if it was tinged with sadness and fear. What I had to go through to get there was unbelievable and I wished I could stop it.*

The following weekend I was taken to a jewellery shop in Grays and had to select a ring. I did as I was told and that was it, we were engaged and I have never felt such a wave of embarrassment as I did then. I was embarrassed to say I was engaged to Kane but who would understand why? I simply played along but hated showing the ring to anyone, it was a fake engagement and only I knew that, but still I smiled.

I mentally threw that ring into my 'rucksack' along with all the drama surrounding Jersey, it was the only place for it.

Jersey is a lovely little place and during our time there we managed to fit in a tour of the island and it was beautiful plus, considering it was May, it was exceptionally hot, more like the middle of summer, and it stayed like that for the whole weekend. We had a couple of nights out while we were there which I did my best to enjoy. It felt strange being out and being free, nobody looking at me, watching my every move. There was nobody to upset, nobody to fight with so I did my best to just have fun which to a degree I accomplished, and it felt good. We didn't win the tournament but we'd given it our best, we were simply out played but it was a great experience for everyone and I think we all came home sporting a suntan. A weekend to always be remembered with a smile.

Another event around this time was my eldest sister Jet, who was now twenty-one, got married to her childhood sweetheart. Yes, she married the boy from the alley and they had set up home in Tilbury. My youngest sister Aline and her beau followed, they had been staying with us for some time until they could buy their own house which they eventually did. Their house was in Grays and they moved there when I was around twenty-two. So, at this point both sisters were married and had left the family home and as I didn't spend much time there my parents were mostly on their own. It was around this time that I had my suspicions that all was not well with my parents' marriage, particularly with my mother. She just didn't seem happy and when my twenty-first birthday came around, it coincided with my parents' twenty-fifth wedding anniversary so us three sisters decided to throw a surprise party for them. Was it the right thing to do? I guess so and at least it took the limelight off of me. The party was held at Jet's house where we all gathered, surprising them on their arrival and presenting a gift we had all contributed to. It went without a hitch, everyone seemed to enjoy themselves but I knew something wasn't right with my parents. The signs of tension and the pretending to be happy from my mother I could absolutely see, maybe because I had done it for so long myself, I noticed the signs. I wasn't totally sure but for now I kept my thoughts to myself.

It seemed everyone was getting married. My cousin Jolene had married as had her two sisters and my friend Astra had also married. Jolene and

Astra had both married boys they had met at the Chadwell club where they frequented and on the odd occasion, I would join them. I'm really not sure how I managed this but mostly it was when Kane and I had argued and he had gone silent or when the argument had resulted in a split. Well, I call it a split, I was never free of him, I just waited for him to appear again, and he always did. Anyway, I was bridesmaid at both my sisters' weddings and Astra's and with everyone getting married, I wondered how I had escaped such an event. I was petrified that Kane would start talking 'weddings' but he didn't, but he did however talk about buying a house together. It was in Tilbury and he went ahead, getting all the details, talking mortgages etc. etc. and I said nothing, all I could do was pray for a miracle. Please God let this pass. And it did. I had no desire to understand why it passed, I asked no questions and silently cried with happiness. I had escaped.

And then, a very poignant moment in my life happened which I can now see was a game-changer.

I don't remember exactly when this episode happened, all I remember is, it was after Jersey and after our engagement. I was at Kane's, we had just arrived and we went upstairs. Kane was disgruntled about something, or nothing, hard to work out how his mind functioned. I was in my usual position, sitting on the edge of the bed and he was in his usual position standing in front of me, looking down on me. His shoulders were back, his stance was cocky and his look was devilish, something was about to happen. And as he stood there, he came out with the most perverse fucking statement yet which was 'I can't have children.' I looked at him not knowing how to react, I really didn't know what to say so I said nothing and he continued, 'I've had a test, I can't father children so who the fuck have you been sleeping with?' What was he doing? He was the only man I'd ever slept with, why was he playing with my mind like this, why, why, why? He knew exactly what had happened in the past, the pregnancies, even if he had always dismissed them each time. There was only one reason he would do this, to try and catch me out, to confess to sleeping around. How low can somebody go? I'm shaking my head as I write this, it's simply disgusting. I was abused, I was fucked, all by the same man, nobody else, I was petrified I would not get my period every month, it was living hell, and now this. They were his fucking babies, a statement I'm not proud of, he revolted me and at this point I felt so low they needed a new word for low. I needed to end everything. Please let me find the courage. He walked away and never mentioned it again but it stayed with me always, it's in your head, it's in everything you do, it's fucking sick. And that night … he fucked me but this time I really did feel different. The feeling of nothing now included all the pent up hate I felt for him and my life in general and on reflection I believe this was the start of the end, the disgust was too much to ignore. But in the meantime, this latest episode all made its way to my 'rucksack' but with a little fragment remaining with me, a fragment I hung on to. At this point I had endured so many episodes, too many to write about, that I'm surprised there was any room left in that 'rucksack'. But it's amazing what your mind can do to protect yourself but was mine about to change?

I felt different, I still had no control of my life but something was happening. I had coping mechanisms by way of my 'rucksack' plus the OCD tendencies and the eating disorder, none of which were healthy but they were all I knew. But, these things aside, something was stirring, I thought more and more about life without Kane and also Snoopy. I didn't want these problems anymore and I started to daydream about life without complications but I struggled with two things, what did I really want and how would I get it. I really had no idea, I didn't really know anything different but I felt determined to find something better after all, it couldn't be worse than the situation I was in. I secretly hung on to these thoughts trying to work out what to do, how could I escape? At this stage I didn't know but at least the thought was there and I hung onto it. And then I hit a brick wall, I was devastated, words fail me, this was exceptionally hard, I even considered leaving it out but if I did, I would feel like I was cheating or being dishonest. And what message would that send to the reader, and myself, that I hadn't moved on? I hadn't listened to myself? My little hint of healing? Healing has to include honesty, as hard as it may be, I know this now so I had to remind myself of this when I reached this stage of writing. I think the difficulty comes from still having a little bit of shame and even though I no longer blame myself it can still be difficult from time to time. You can never erase events, good or bad, it's how we deal with them that's the important part. And I am going to deal with this next part.

I was nearing the age of twenty-two and in a slightly different place since the episode with Kane regarding his fertility. What does it take for someone to think up such a thing, what kind of person does that? I didn't know but, although I was physically in the same place, mentally I wasn't and it confused me and for all that Kane had done in the past, the fertility game he tried to play seemed to hit me harder than anything. And then, I found myself in a place where suicide seemed to be the only option. My period was due and like every month I was desperately looking for signs but as each day passed, I became more and more desperate. Eventually I had to face the music and do a test and yes, I was pregnant again. I just cried, I couldn't stop Kane from fucking me and my desperate attempts not to get pregnant, my naive actions, were in vain. Lord almighty help me, please take me away from all this, give me the strength to end it all. But I was weak, I didn't have the strength and once again, I had to pick my moment to tell Kane and once again, the response was the same without any mention of his so-called infertility and once again, I started the process to terminate. I went into clockwork mode, clearing everything up, eliminating any emotions, organising, planning, just like I always did. There, I said it, and I know it was right to include it.

Of course, I had to somehow deal with this episode and I took the only route I knew and tossed it all into my 'rucksack'. What a fucking mess. Secretly I was dying, full of shame, full of guilt, full of confusion but I tried not to let these feelings dampen my hopes of escape. I was clinging to hope, it was all I had, I simply couldn't put myself through this any longer. I think the guilt engulfed me more than anything, my inability to stop this hung over me like a black cloud, I was still blaming myself, I never understood how not to. And because of that guilt I can only end this part by saying, RIP my babies, I know you are safe and protected from the monster. And may I find the strength one day to make my escape both physically and mentally.

Life continued in some sort of fashion and even though something had changed in me, nothing had changed in Kane. Life was the same torrent of bullying, abuse and eggshell treading. And then there was Snoopy, I was still dealing with him who's strange obsession with me had gained momentum and had become even more unnerving. I wish I had had the nerve to tell Snoopy that his skulking around was unacceptable but that kind of thinking didn't exist in me, I only thought how bad he might feel if I said something. Ironically, I was protecting him, a sure sign of my lack of self-worth and boundary setting. He once said he had a song for me, it was 'Ain't No Mountain High Enough' by Diana Ross which might give you an idea of what I was trying to deal with but when he told me I just smiled, I had no words. Nowadays when I hear that song, it takes me right back to that time but it's easy for me to simply shake my head and laugh, as an endorsement to my healing. I sometimes wonder what would have happened if Kane knew all about this, he had no idea as to the extent of Snoopy's actions but my guess, he would have blamed me, I would have been the reason, encouraging Snoopy. I don't think it takes much to answer that question and shows what a coward Kane was, I was the easier target. Fortunately, I was not too much of a target where netball was concerned, Kane was still letting me free to play netball, not taking much notice which I liked as it allowed me the time to let my mind leave him behind. By this time, I had been part of the creation of a new team in the Thurrock league which was made up of some younger County players and some more experienced and mature players. The team I played for prior to that were made up of mostly young County players which on paper should have whooped the arses of a lot of their opponents. But we didn't, it just didn't work well enough. Maybe we were too young, too reckless or lacked experience to know what was needed but whatever it was, we disbanded. And that's when the new team was born and we went by the name of Flight. I enjoyed playing for Flight, I liked the combination of people, I liked the experienced players, it somehow made me feel comfortable and safe, like I had found my netball family and I loved it. I was still playing for Thurrock County which meant I still had my netball family as most of us were involved, so we all spent a lot of time together. And then another netball tournament was announced, I was around the age of twenty-two and I cannot recall the location but it was far enough for us to have to stay away for three nights, and so the battle with Kane began. I went through the usual, picking my moment to ask if I could go, getting the moment wrong, being abused until he felt he had complete control and then and only then would he agree to me going. But I didn't care anymore, I didn't like what I had to go through to get the result

I wanted but, I was going and that's all that mattered. Bizarrely enough, I felt like I'd won.

The weekend of the tournament arrived, it was Thurrock County we were representing and apart from netball there were various other sports included. Lots of different people from around Thurrock area were there playing various different sports and from the moment we arrived, there was a definite buzz about the place and it felt good. We played some great netball on our first day and it felt quite euphoric, I don't know what it was about the place or this tournament but there was a real sense of fun, excitement and camaraderie and for me, I had never felt so good away from Kane and I loved it. On the second night a disco had been arranged for us all, so once our games were over and we'd been fed, we scuttled off to our rooms to put on our glad rags and with much excitement made our way to the hall where the party was taking place. There were already a lot of people there, music was playing, people were laughing and having fun and I felt alive for the first time in years. I have no idea why I felt so good on this particular occasion but I decided to just soak it all up. Maybe it was because I felt safe, free, alive but, whatever it was, I was not going to let it pass me by. We quickly hooked up with a local football team who were known in our area for being pretty talented and soon we were all dancing and laughing together and my feeling of fun and excitement heightened. There was one particular footballer who was paying me attention and for someone as insecure as I was, it made me feel like a queen. We were laughing, dancing, drinking and I felt like I was on planet 'happy', could life really be this much fun? This night was a real turning point in my life and I wanted more, I was getting a glimpse of freedom and I didn't want it to end. It was like I was another person, maybe I was but whoever this person was, at this point in time, I loved her. And then I took it to a whole new level. I ended up getting very close to my admirer, we started kissing, we were laughing together and I wondered if this was how relationships should be. And then I slept with him. Oh my god, how did this happen? Well I know how, because I wanted it to, I wanted to experience someone who made me feel this good even if it was only in the moment. I got up the following morning and was on a confused cloud nine. I don't think I really understood the enormity of what had happened, it was all based on completely unstable emotions but I couldn't take it back, it was done and now I had to face the consequences. Kane.

I arrived back from the weekend and went home, Kane had already called so I called him back and played down the whole weekend, we agreed to meet the following evening. I felt strange, different, happy, petrified, excited, confused, a whole host of emotions were crawling through my head and I had to establish how to deal with them but as I didn't know what to do, I did nothing. I went to work the next day and gushed about the weekend and one of my work colleagues took an educated guess that something had happened, I was different and she noticed. After work I went to Kane's which was OK, he didn't really ask me much about the weekend, his interest was minimal, he was just his usual arrogant, cocky self but I just couldn't be the same and he noticed. It was about a week later that he questioned me seriously about a change he had noticed in me since my weekend away, I was sitting in the lounge at my house and he was standing over me. I can still picture the scene very clearly in my head. He asked me what was wrong. Had something happened. Why was I distant and I remember a tear falling down my cheek as he asked if I'd slept with someone and with all I had in my body I said yes. I was flabbergasted at my honesty given Kane's history but in the back of my mind I was hoping it would be the straw that broke the camel's back, that he would punish me and end it all, maybe that's why I did it. But it wasn't my lucky day, he simply said, 'well, once in eight years, I guess it could be worse.' I could have punched him and I would have if I knew I wouldn't get worse back. That is not what I wanted to hear. Could I ever get rid of him? Over the following week I was questioned, Kane the

Gestapo, me the prisoner, and he would not rest until I told him who I had committed my infidelity with, so I spilled the beans. To this day I have no idea what he did with that information, whether he acted on it, hunted him down, who knows? What I do know is it was thrown in my face time and time again but I still didn't understand why we were together, why he had accepted my infidelity, this is not what I was expecting and certainly not what I wanted but stay with me he did, something I understand more today than I did then. I was desperate to seek out my fling, after all, I had spent the night with him, surely that is what he wanted, to see me again. But of course, that would not be the case and I had a very emotional lesson in one-night stands, another episode for my 'rucksack'. However, something had changed in Kane, the mental abuse continued but the physical abuse had become so much less, why? I didn't know, I was just confused and waited for the backlash. It never came.

Life was different. I was different. Kane was different. Everything seemed different and although Kane's mental abuse remained, the physical abuse continued to be so much less. And then I had another lift when around this time Heath got in touch with the office, I was beyond excited and so glad I still worked there. I had been with this company for around five years, my first job, near home and I never found any reason to move on, maybe it was my little bit of steady but, whatever it was, right now, I was glad I was there. Heath had been talking to Snoopy who relayed the conversations to the rest of the office telling us how he was and I found myself hanging on to every word. It seemed he had two children by now who were quite young, the youngest only a few months old which was unfortunate as the news came back that he had split from his wife. But that aside, it was great to hear from him. Shortly after that he visited the office and how lovely it was to see him. We interacted and I felt like an excited schoolgirl even though he seemed a little subdued but he had gone through some personal stuff so I guess it was to be expected. Around the same time my mother's unhappiness had increased, she had changed and I don't want this to sound derogatory but it was like she only had time for herself, her focus had shifted and it was difficult to understand why. Being the last child at home, with Aline and Jet living their married lives in their own homes, I became more aware of the changes but failed to understand why. But all would become clear.

My mother at this point was working at the local supermarket and often talked about a man she worked with who was really good fun and she would enjoy sharing his stories and jokes with me when she got home. To be honest, he sounded like a great guy and someone fun to work with. But there was another man, his name was Raffa and he would prove to have much more of an impact on my mother. He was a customer at her shop, he came in regularly and one day she started telling me about how he was paying her attention. The next thing she told me was that he had asked her out which was quickly followed by claims that she had refused. But there was a shift in her personality and her behaviour which I believe was down to a few things. Firstly, the work colleague who made her laugh had showed her a bit of fun which she seemed to always be lacking in her life, secondly, she felt good that someone was paying her attention, she enjoyed the excitement of it all and thirdly, she had started her menopause. Now, I'm not making any excuses when I mention the menopause but I know it can have a massive impact on some women's lives and I think my mother was one of them. She was very young when she lost her parents, very young when she married and had had us three girls by the age of twenty-five so I think she felt she had missed out a bit on life and was experiencing something new which was both fun and flattering and she was enjoying it. I think her feelings for my father had long gone, she never really seemed satisfied or happy with her situation, I simply don't think their personalities matched. They may have matched in their early days, there clearly must have been something there but over the years something had died and my mother began speaking derogatorily about my father. Jet, Aline and I heard stories of his incompetence and how difficult life had been. I'm not sure my father would have seen it the same way as, as I've mentioned previously, he was a simple man with simple views but overall, pretty harmless. My personal opinion is, she was seventeen, alone, no parents and living in an era where you married and had children young and that's where my father came in. I think he was her saviour, her only option maybe but, of course, like many marriages, this can be dangerous later in life and this is the stage I believe my mother was at.

At work, I started speaking to Heath quite regularly, we were agents for the company he worked for so there were reasons to speak with Snoopy always earwigging our conversations. I knew Snoopy didn't like the relationship I had with Heath, it was pretty obvious, he made me feel so uncomfortable whenever Heath and I were interacting or if his name was mentioned and he clearly saw him as competition. It seemed so much was going on in my life, Kane was different, my mother was different, I was different, Heath was having an impact and Snoopy, well he was being Snoopy. Everything felt different which mostly stemmed back to my one-night stand, or maybe before but following the one-night stand was when I really felt a shift, that's when I became very unsettled and strangely enough it coincided with Kane's change of behaviour. It's easy for me to understand this now, narcissists hate to feel like their losing control and so they change their behaviour in order to get you back on track. Some do something called love-bombing, making you feel special, flowers, chocolates, making you believe they've changed but the ulterior motive is only to get you back under their control and when they do, they slip right back into their true selves, unable to keep up the facade. But this is not something I knew and as the months passed, things were pretty much the same until one day Kane and I had had an almighty argument. I think Kane's facade had slipped and he was once again showing his true colours but I have no idea what the argument was about. He had no knowledge of my excitement when I spoke to Heath so it couldn't be him so my suspicion is, it related to Snoopy. And this time, in my current state of mind, I felt different, I was truly at the end of my tether with Kane and all his attempts to threaten me. He said he was going to crash his car, to attempt suicide and although I was crying, I don't think I really cared, he was simply trying to get control again, to have me begging and although he scared me, deep down I knew he wouldn't do it, at least not to the extent of killing himself, he was too conceited to carry out such an act. So, off he sped, Kane and his anger, trying his best to scare the shit out of me, and he did, but this time I just let it go. I stayed away from Kane for a day or so and then he called, and acting like nothing had happened he asked me to go and see him that evening. The next word from me was a milestone, with a pounding heart, shaking hands and a dizzy, sick feeling that made me feel like I wanted to pass out, I said, 'NO!' I waited for the backlash, every muscle in my body was tense and his response was 'OK, well what do you want, a few days?' I could only think of one answer, 'yes,' and again I waited, but all he said was 'OK, I'll call you in a few days' and the relief flooded over me, I had a bit of time but I had no idea what I was going to do with it. I was extremely frightened and wondered what Kane would do, he wasn't the type to do nothing, he would want to gain back control and I believe I suffered from dreadful anxiety during this time. I hid my car by parking in another street so Kane would think I was out if he drove by and I had the most surreal feelings, it was like I wasn't here, I was floating through space. And then, a few days later he called and once again asked me to go and see him and with all I had in my body I said that word again, 'NO!' I was shaking but he, once again, said he would leave it a few days, phew, I had bought myself a bit more time.

The anxiety and surreal feelings continued so I spoke to my very dear friend Astra who lived a couple of streets away with her husband Jason. It's strange but this was the Astra who pointed Kane out to me right at the beginning, yes, the one who fancied him. But, despite it all, our friendship remained and I always joke to her that I'd done her a favour although I know she would have handled him completely differently, she certainly would have put him in his place. Anyway, she told me to go see her and Jason so I went to their house and Jason kindly opened a bottle of vodka. My god I needed a drink and I think Jason knew this. So, Jason and I had a few vodkas but poor Astra couldn't join us as she was very, very heavily pregnant with their first child, or should I say children as they were expecting twins who, by the way, were imminent. I felt like I needed to drown my sorrows, to relax, to try and forget and to a degree it helped, I felt safe at Astra's, Kane wouldn't find me there, I was hiding and I could pretend and fantasise about the future. The time came to retire, Jason and I had drunk copious amounts of vodka, my head was spinning but Jason was like a cool cucumber, like he hadn't even had a drink, maybe he didn't indulge as much as I thought which proved to be a blessing as that evening Astra's waters broke and she went into labour and I had no idea what to do. I was in a bit of a panic, feeling helpless so Astra told me to stay at her house while Jason drove her to the hospital. Astra and Jason knew what to do, they were organised and ready for this moment. They grabbed some bags, got in the car and went to the hospital whilst I lay on the sofa resting, waiting for some news. Jason called early that morning to tell me she had given birth to two beautiful girls and although they were a little poorly, they were doing OK but she wouldn't be bringing them home straight away as they needed medical attention. Eventually, they were able to come home, much to the relief of Astra and Jason and now they were a family of four. I couldn't even imagine how you dealt with this, all I knew was life would be very different for them, a major change confronted them. But they would handle it, they had to and by default, they already were. And I would just mention at this point that, these weren't the first babies to arrive within the friends and family circle as by this time my eldest sister Jet had given birth to my first niece, the first grandchild and from both sisters, more would follow.

But for now it was back to reality and besides all the excitement I still had Kane to deal with. He was leaving me alone but I still had anxiety about the whole thing, something that Heath picked up on during a telephone call at work. He asked me what was wrong but I was too nervous to say anything so I just kept quiet for a bit until eventually he coaxed it out of me. He was very kind and understanding and offered me a break from Tilbury by going to visit him in Kent. He said he would take me to dinner and I didn't hesitate to provide a one-word answer but this time the word was 'YES!' I felt relief run through my body, I was getting away and I couldn't wait and a day or so later I was on my way and I felt like I was leaving everything bad behind. Almost nine years of control by a complete narcissist. The physical abuse, the mental abuse, the gaslighting, the date rape, the bulimia I was suffering from, I was leaving it all behind. I was running at breakneck speed and I didn't look back. Words cannot describe how I felt, it's indescribable. I still shake my head, was I really getting away, surely not? But I was and at this point, and this was not a conscious act, I closed my 'rucksack', zipped it up and locked it with no understanding of what the consequences of that act really meant.

In conclusion to this difficult chapter, there are no doubt going to be people who understand but there will also be those that feel the need to judge. I cannot control how you feel, all I know is, my story and my journey have helped me eliminate judgement of people as we never know their story and until we do and have walked in their shoes, we really shouldn't try and tie their laces. The shame of my life was part of why I never spoke to anyone, not friends, not family, nobody knew anything but I shouldn't have felt like this and over time I had to search for reasons why I did. But for now, I was about to embark on a new chapter, I felt I had reached my breaking point which I guess came from a build-up of years of abuse. Nobody knows when that breaking point will come, if ever, but if you feel you're at that point, find the strength to act, it's your only hope of finding yourself even if your new journey is frightening. For me, I welcomed my breaking point, I wanted change, I wanted freedom, I wanted happiness and even though I had no idea what lay ahead, all I knew was, it couldn't be worse than what I was leaving behind.

CHAPTER 6

The Runaway

I chose my outfit carefully which I had purchased from a little boutique in Civic Square, Tilbury, just underneath where my work office was. I had chosen white trousers, a red top and a small heeled court shoe and I put my best effort into hair and make-up and I felt good, I felt alive but most of all, freer than I had ever felt in my life and to top it all, I was meeting Heath. I can see now these feelings were totally inflated but that wasn't something I understood, I just went with them and soaked up the moment. I drove to meet Heath in Kent, not far from where he lived and when he arrived, I felt a little nervous, but in a good way. It was so nice seeing Heath again, looking back I think I saw him as my saviour, someone to rescue me, someone to look after me, someone to escape with, someone to have fun with and someone to laugh with. In comparison to what I had known, Heath seemed so grown up, a gentleman, something I had never experienced which made me feel warm and fuzzy. When we organised our date, the plan was to watch Heath play football that afternoon so, after exchanging a few pleasantries, we made our way to the venue. Heath handed me his car keys to look after which for some reason made me feel important, part of his life, trustworthy. Such a small act that, for me, said so much. So, there I was, on the sideline feeling very excited watching the game, only missing a small part for a break to the ladies' room. It was a cold day but I felt warm, a dull day but I felt bright, I was somewhere safe and everything felt so perfect. When the game ended, Heath went to change and then came to meet me at his car where he asked for the car keys. Oh dear, I couldn't find them, I had lost them, what had I done with them? I had no idea so there we were thinking where they could be but the good thing was, in between the panic, we were laughing and it felt good not to be berated for making a mistake. Anyway, the ladies' room was the only place I had gone so off I went and low and behold, there they were, on the floor. I think in my dizzy state I stopped thinking logically, excitement overtook but there was no harm done, we just laughed, and laughed about it for many years to come but I'm not sure he ever trusted me with his car keys again! So now, with keys in hand, we got in the car and he drove me to his house as we had agreed that I would change there before leaving for the restaurant, it also meant Heath could get ready. We spoke about various things, work, life, home and eventually made our way to the restaurant Heath had booked which was a steak house in Greenwich and so obviously called The Greenwich Steak House. It was lovely and as Heath was known in the restaurant we were greeted warmly and following some polite conversation from Heath, we were shown to our table. I thought this was all pretty cool and I felt like a princess, albeit a shy one. I had nothing to compare this with, this was all new to me but I liked it so I did my best to soak it all up and enjoy it, trying not to feel bewildered. Heath surely was my real-life knight in shining armour, at least that's how it felt. We talked more about work, his life, my life and enjoyed some fun moments in between. He paid me compliments, it made me blush, I didn't really understand compliments, it wasn't something I could relate to but it felt nice. I didn't talk deeply about my life with Kane, I didn't want to, after all, I had left that in Tilbury, I only spoke a little about his jealousy and that it wasn't a good life. I didn't go home that night but he was the complete gentleman. It seemed so romantic, we hugged and talked and eventually fell asleep. I had run to a safe place and I was sure this was where I wanted to be. The next day, we said our goodbyes and I drove home with us both promising we would see each other again and the anticipation of our next meet was almost too much to bear but I was brought right back down to earth when I arrived back home in Tilbury. My mother told me Kane had called and had asked me to call him back when I was home and I felt the anxiety crawl all over my body. My stomach churned and I started to drown in my thoughts with all the niceties of the previous night slipping away. I felt like I was back in that dark hole and all I wanted to do was run but it's these times where you have to find some inner strength, to believe in yourself and focus on your goal. Wanting to run back to Kent, to Heath, was foremost in my mind but this was not an option so after a very long delay I decided to make that call. Kane answered, I took a deep breath, I was shaking, I felt like my whole body had pins and needles. He didn't know where I had been and I had no intentions of telling him so I waited for him to say something and when he did, his words were 'how are you?' to which I replied 'OK.' He was chirpy and upbeat as he continued, 'fancy coming to Petticoat Lane?' It was Sunday, a great day for Petticoat Lane market. The anxiety increased, my mind struggled but eventually that word came out again, 'NO!' Kane became very soft, gentle and dare I say, passive. I didn't understand, I was waiting for the explosion, anything I could relate to but it was like he'd given in and deep down knew it was over. He simply said, 'do you need a few days?' 'YES,' I responded knowing I never wanted to go back to him, I just had to find a way to ensure that didn't happen and all I could think was, if he stays like this it will be much easier. The conversation ended, and whether he accepted it or not, for me, it was over and all I needed to do now was find some strength and stay focused and safe.

Kane stayed quiet, accepting that I needed some time which bought me some breathing space. A couple of weeks passed and eventually we did speak and once again, Kane was gentle. I think at this point acceptance it was coming to an end was definitely on Kane's mind as he was in his love-bombing stage, something narcissists turn to when they feel like their losing control. But I knew this now, I had seen it so many times and let me tell you, don't be fooled because the minute you give in and go back, they turn straight back into the abuser they are, they simply can't help themselves. Anyway, we spoke about some money we had saved, it was in a joint account and we decided the best approach would be to split it between us. This gave me further hope, a step closer to freedom but it meant we had to meet and although this was the last thing I wanted, I knew I had to do it as I had something for him that needed returning. After discussing the finer details, we organised to meet at a cafe in Grays town centre where we would have a coffee and then go to the building society together as we both had to authorise the transfer. I think what helped and gave me strength was, I had already seen Heath a couple of more times and it was going extremely well so beneath all the anxiety, I felt like a little warrior, strong and determined, ready for a fight that only I was going to win. I was approaching this with all the hate I had for Kane and all the strength I had to do battle even though, beneath it all, there was still fear. I approached our meeting place, it was the agreed time and my god my nerves had kicked in, what was he going to do, how would he be? I had no idea, I just tried to stay strong and focus on my new life. And there he was, soft and smiley, greeting me gently, making polite conversation and being kind, I think he even paid for the coffee. What the hell was going on, was he going to remain in his love-bombing stage? I was ready for confrontation, I was ready to defend myself but I wasn't getting the reception I was expecting and all I wanted to do was get away so I kept everything short and wasted no time in providing the final proof that for me, it was all over. I slowly went to my coat pocket producing my engagement ring and slid it across the table towards him, he was shaking his head saying, 'don't do this,' trying to hold my hand and stop me but my determination was unbreakable and all I said was 'I don't want it and I need to go.' I find it hard to explain how I felt at this point, mainly because of Kane's reaction, he looked like a broken man and he was playing the part well. He kept shaking his head in disbelief and I remember thinking, is this how you react when I stand up to you!? I spent years living in fear and this is all I had to do!? The money was sorted and I felt elated that it was now final but so bitter at his reaction, I felt robbed of all the years I spent with him when escaping could have been easy. I walked away and all I could mumble to myself, which were the only words that felt fitting, was 'you fucking cunt!'

I was spending more and more time at Heath's, he made me feel safe and each time I went to see him I felt like I was going to my happy place. I was spending so much time there that I was virtually living there but that's exactly what we wanted, both of us, we loved being together. I had heard nothing from Kane since our meet, I think he must have finally realised it was over, that I had meant it and that he would have to accept defeat. He really had no choice but I didn't really care, he was gone as far as I was concerned, no more Kane, well, at least physically. At this point, I loved Welling in Kent where Heath lived but running parallel with that was my absolute hate for Tilbury and everything it stood for. For me it was where everything bad happened, I didn't feel any connection with the place and the less time I spent there the better. And then my dream came true, I moved in permanently with Heath and I was so, so happy. However, someone who wasn't so happy was Snoopy. Once Snoopy heard the news you could tell he was a little put out, even Heath noticed a difference in his tone when he spoke to him on the telephone but, even with this knowledge, it didn't stop Snoopy's unhealthy interest in my life. But the bonus was, I didn't live in Tilbury anymore, I only worked there, so it was easier to avoid him which I saw as a one of the benefits of running away.

With Heath I felt like I had grown up overnight, I had never been treated well and it was a wonderful feeling, I had freedom, I wasn't questioned about anything I wore, anything I did or anywhere I went except from the perspective of being interested, it was such a different life and I got totally immersed. Heath and I seemed very well matched, we liked similar things, we were both sporty, I still played netball and Heath played football. We loved going out, mostly to restaurants but sometimes to our local where we would meet Heath's friends, who were a great bunch, and I could have fun with them without being questioned or berated. Heath worked hard and often long hours but we always had time for each other and our dinner dates were often in Greenwich, a place I came to love and still do. He even took me to one of his work functions in London, it was Christmas time and I had such fun picking an outfit, ensuring I looked my best, hoping to make him feel proud to be with me. But I also felt the need to look good as Heath had told me a lady from work who he used to date, who had struggled to accept they weren't an item anymore, would be there. Well, there is no bigger reason to look good than a bit of competition, especially if you're insecure yourself, hence a new outfit, I simply HAD to look my best. Of course, I had to know who this lady was so during the evening Heath pointed her out to me and I thought no more of it as we continued to enjoy our evening. At this point I had been living with Heath for about three months and for me it still felt like the honeymoon period, things were ticking along nicely and Kane had left me completely alone which was a real bonus but then something changed. Heath was working late more and more and we were getting telephone calls at home where nobody said anything. Heath's response was to simply shrug his shoulders but then one Sunday morning there was a knock on the front door, it was quite early so we were both intrigued and when Heath went to answer it, he could tell by looking through the glass that it was the lady he had dated from work. She lived in North London and had made the trip to his house for reasons unknown to me. Heath refused to answer the door saying he didn't know what she wanted but she was very persistent and after about an hour and with her still standing at the front door, we agreed that he should talk to her so he answered the door and sat on a wall outside with her in an effort to understand why she had made the trip. They were there for about an hour whilst I waited patiently inside until Heath returned and when he did, he was smiling and shaking his head saying she was crazy and wouldn't accept that their relationship was over. I smiled with him believing every word, after all, nothing could break us, we were in love, weren't we?

Even though I was living with Heath I still spent the odd night at home, sometimes because I was seeing friends, sometimes due to netball and sometimes to sort out more of my own things I still had there. I was travelling from Kent to Essex and back every day for work so a break from the drive was sometimes welcomed but it's fair to say, I always felt odd and uncomfortable back in Tilbury and was always glad to get back to Kent. Then one day while I was at Heath's alone, I received a telephone call, it was Heath's ex, the one who had paid us a visit and she wanted me to meet with her. She said there were things I should know claiming that she had just left Heath and that they had been out together. Now I was under the impression that Heath was working so now I was intrigued so I agreed to meet her the following evening at a pub near London Bridge. When I arrived, I scanned the room and there she was, I recognised her so I wandered over and said hello. She was very calm, she said hello and looking back, she probably knew exactly what she was going to say. We ordered drinks and she proceeded to tell me she had never stopped seeing Heath and that when I was back home in Tilbury she had stayed at his house. Apparently, Heath had told her I didn't live there but when she stayed, she said she looked in the wardrobe and given the amount of clothes of mine that were there, to her it was obvious I had moved in so she felt she should tell me what was going on. It turns out, the work function Heath took me to was the first she had known about me as up until that time they were an item so seeing me walk in with him was somewhat of a surprise to her. I didn't want to believe her but part of me knew she was telling the truth, it all made sense, Heath working when sometimes I couldn't reach him, her turning up at his house, who does that? Only some sort of crazy, jealous lady and she didn't come across like that and by the time we parted I was in tears. I didn't want to cry but I was so upset, so emotional, my bubble had burst and with very little confidence and self-esteem, it hit me hard. She was quite cold and non-emotional when I cried and we parted with her saying, 'don't say I didn't warn you.'

I drove back and went straight to our local pub where some of Heath's friends were. We always had fun at our local but, on this occasion, I wasn't in the mood for fun. It became obvious to all that something was wrong, I was a highly emotional person and found it difficult to keep my feelings under wraps so when Heath walked in my face said it all and when he asked what was wrong, I looked at him with such hurt and bitterness and said, 'I've just met with her.' There was no explanation needed, he knew who I meant and after a short while we went home and then the argument started. Heath denied they were sleeping together but did say they had shared drinks on the odd occasion but I was too emotional to believe anything and the next day I packed a few things and went back to Tilbury. I felt broken, hurt and humiliated and being so emotional and unstable, I found it hard to deal with such an incident. I couldn't eat, I couldn't sleep, I felt terribly betrayed and it knocked my confidence and self-esteem, not that I had much to begin with. Of course, it wasn't a problem going back home, my bedroom was still the same and I just slotted back in, telling my mother the reason for my return. I can't remember her reaction but it seems she had more on her mind than Heath and I. My father was still at home but he never asked any questions so no explanation needed there. I was feeling terrible so I just did what I knew, carried on regardless but not long after returning home, my mother confided in me that she had secretly met with Raffa, the guy from the supermarket, on more than one occasion and she seemed quite besotted with him. He was several years younger than her, he was new, he was fun, he was exciting but he was also married, as was she, two big issues my mother seemed to have overlooked. So, I sat and heard about everything that had gone on in the past weeks and had no idea what to do with this information, so I did nothing except listen and give the odd piece of advice. And suddenly it felt like the mother/daughter roles had reversed. I was a complete mess and didn't feel I could talk to her about my issues, but that wasn't unusual so I just supported her as best I could. I felt mean as my father was oblivious to all this but what could I do? I couldn't tell him as I would be deceiving my mother but by not telling him, I was deceiving my father, I was a real piggy in the middle, a situation I really didn't welcome and one that made me feel so bad and so confused. What should I do? I had no idea. I was struggling with my own demons and emotions whilst trying to be supportive to my mother. I had to do something, so I did the only thing I knew. I, hypothetically speaking, grabbed the keys to my 'rucksack', opened it up and threw the whole lot in. And there was me, thinking there was no more room.

In the meantime, Heath and I had been in contact and he reassured me his ex was lying. Apparently, she was just bitter and trying to ruin his life. I wanted to believe him, I wanted to go back, I missed him, I missed our life and in truth, I probably missed my escape. So, we met a few times, we talked and I felt so much love for him that I couldn't imagine being without him so eventually, I went back. We actually seemed to get past this whole incident and our life together continued, it was a good life but perhaps one I didn't know how to appreciate. I'd never been in a relationship with anyone that was like this so I was learning as I went along. Meanwhile, my mother was still seeing Raffa and I believe, that she believed, she was in love with him. Not that I was an expert on the subject but she lived for her times with him and loved it when he came into the shop. Then, one day, she asked me a favour. Would I say she was coming to stay with me in Kent for a couple of days so she could go away with Raffa. What could I say? She was my mother so how could I say no? I hated the situation but pretended I didn't and said, 'of course' and the guilt for my father gathered in my head. I tried to understand, I know she hadn't had the best life based on what she had shared with us three girls so part of me wanted to help. But should I? Even if the answer to that question was no, I didn't feel I could say no, I felt a little trapped, I felt like the child I was when I first met Kane. My god, I hated it but this situation happened on a couple of occasions and each time I had very mixed feelings about it with fear and guilt running through my body. It seems these times always took me back to how I felt with Kane which was very strange but nevertheless, I did it. And this feeling would be further fuelled as, once my mother had established her feelings for Raffa, for what she claimed to be love, she started to open up about her marriage to my father and told me intimate things I should never have heard. I listened but inside I closed myself down. I knew how to do this, I'd had a lot of training and right now, I was glad of it. My father was blamed for all the bad things that had happened during their twenty-seven plus years together and, to be honest, I sided with her and once my sisters were aware of this whole situation, they seemed to side with her also. I never really felt comfortable with this, my father was not a bad man, OK, he was one of those fathers who was just present and, in my opinion, didn't truly understand the husband and father responsibilities, but who does? He was absolutely harmless, I was probably the closest to him because of my sport so I felt torn, nothing felt right and I hated it. Maybe my mother shared a lot of information about him as a way of justifying her own actions. Was she was trying to be malicious? I really don't know but whatever her reasons, it had a huge impact on me. I really didn't want to hear some of the information and I didn't want to watch my mother changing, heading to the point of being unrecognisable, and I didn't want to watch my father being oblivious to it all. I think he definitely saw a change in her but believed it was simply her menopause and that it would pass. There was so much going on and for me, being someone with major issues of my own, I made a conscious decision to stay away from my family as much as possible and I only came to Tilbury to work, but once the day ended, I drove straight back to Kent, to my happy place, to Heath, my rescue home. I did my best to avoid any issues or confrontations or stories about my father as I did not have the tools to deal with it. Tilbury, for me, was already full of bad memories, feelings, fear, unhappiness, confusion and I didn't want to add to that so at this point, with my hate for the place growing, I almost cut myself off. Of course, it wasn't the place, it was the events but I really couldn't decipher between the two.

Cutting myself off from Tilbury and family was quite a sad thing to do but I had so many issues, many I still wasn't aware of, that I didn't want to deal with anything else and my family was a bit messy at this point and I simply didn't know how to handle them. During this time, weeks would go by where I never saw my mother, father or sisters nor did I speak to them and it felt wrong. However, things took a turn for the worse because, like most affairs, my mother's affair with Raffa ended. Of course, his claims of always going to leave his wife were complete nonsense which were proved when he ended the affair when things got to that sticky point. I think it must have lasted a year or so during which time my mother had become totally immersed so when it ended, she was beyond devastated and with my head buried in the proverbial sand in Kent, I don't think I saw the full extent of the outcome of this. I think Jet and Aline both had front seats to events that followed with my mother being so devastated she was inconsolable and my father running around trying to help, still believing it was her menopause. I did visit her once during this time and I have to say, she looked terrible. She wasn't eating or sleeping properly, she had love quotes stuck to her fridge which reflected her feelings at that time and I think it would be safe to say, she was broken-hearted and I had no idea what to do. I had never been able to talk deeply about anything with my mother, particularly about emotional matters, which I think was ingrained in me many years ago so the situation facing me now was very uncomfortable. I stayed for a while, made small talk and eventually left, fleeing back home to Kent. I didn't keep myself updated on the situation too much but things got pretty chaotic with my mother and father in the coming months, and it was difficult to ignore. I think, following her affair, my mother had glimpsed a different life, one she had never known and it seemed she wanted more, she'd tasted a kind of freedom, a life she had maybe secretly craved and one that was way outside of the one she had simply gone along with, the one she had with my father and us. I don't think she was ever totally happy and often betrayed herself as a victim, and maybe she was, it would be unfair of me to comment without knowing more about her life, something she didn't speak of much. And it's not as if I could have sat and discussed it all with my father, he would have been distraught, he liked his belief that this would all pass and I wasn't about to burst his bubble, he would never have taken it. I do think my mother was definitely showing signs of a mid-life crisis, these situations are not unheard of, she was like a runaway train, out of control without even realising it, needing to be herself without knowing who herself was. It's difficult feeling this way, of course, I know this, but I found it hard to sympathise, I needed to hold myself together, I hated the whole situation and just kept running home to Kent. It wasn't long before my mother started going out with a couple of friends, not unusual for some but very unusual for my mother. She started frequenting a couple of pubs, she was drinking more, she seemed to be having fun and had a new found confidence. It was a side of my mother neither Jet, Aline or I knew so I think, on the whole, we just stood aside, only dealing with incidences that directly affected us, hoping the storm would pass. I know Jet and Aline dealt with some very difficult times whilst I was hiding in Kent, things I found out much later and if I had had the ability to help, I would have but I had no tools for this, I had nothing to offer so running was my coping mechanism. Anyway, this went on for many months and there were some pretty embarrassing and hurtful moments, but she had exploded and nothing mattered except her need to have fun, her way of coping with the fallout of her broken heart and in my opinion, her menopause. However, the one most affected was my father, he had no idea what was going on, the complete change in my mother smacked him in the face full force and for him, it came from nowhere and then we saw a side of my father we'd never seen before. My father wasn't an emotional person, he never had been, or should I say, he had never shown emotion but suddenly he became an emotional wreck. He showed anger, confusion, obsessiveness, desperation, sadness all of which were very confusing. This wasn't my father, who was it? So now Jet, Aline and I had two unrecognisable parents both going through such difficult times but for different reasons and neither knowing how to, or feeling they could, communicate with each other. I remember my father calling my office and telling me my mother had been out again and he believed there was another man involved, in other words he thought she was carrying on with someone. To my knowledge he had never known about Raffa so trying to pacify him was very difficult with the knowledge I held in my head but it certainly showed how he would have reacted if he had known. He was crying, I had never seen or heard my father cry in my entire life, it was so confusing. His voice screamed desperation, he so didn't want to lose my mother but all I could do was listen and respond with the odd word every now and then. And the anger he showed led me to thinking, Raffa, you got off lightly, if my father had known about you, I think he would have done you harm and I truly believe that. There were many more episodes to come from both my mother and father, it was an awful time, not just for me but for Jet and Aline. We had parents we didn't recognise, parents we couldn't relate to, we were mere spectators of the show, a show that was about to drop another bombshell when my mother announced she wanted a divorce. I do wonder at this point if there was a slight acceptance from my father that this wasn't going the way he wanted.

I also think his next move was his way of maybe giving my mother the time alone he thought she needed. He was forever hopeful, he would have tried anything so when they agreed to separate my father organised to go and live with my nan, his mother, who lived alone in a three-bed house in Tilbury. I can't imagine what either of them were feeling but at a guess I would say one was devastated and the other relieved and it's not difficult to work out which emotion belonged to who. So that was how it would be but as they began their new lives there was another bombshell and this time from my father. My mother had told me, and probably my sisters also, that my father was not doing so well and she thought maybe he was depressed so she suggested he went to the doctor. He did but she then disclosed that he had told her he wanted to end his life and that he couldn't live without her and he was going to take an overdose. My mother spoke to the doctor who assured her he would be OK and that the fact that he was telling her was indeed a cry for help. I guess it was my father's attempt at breaking my mother down in a hope she would feel sorry for him and take him back, like an emotional blackmail, but that would never happen, my mother was in a place she wanted to be and I don't think anything could have changed that. I applaud her in some ways for finding the strength to stick to her guns, it's not easy when faced with a situation like this. I must admit, I panicked for some time when I was told this information about my father, would he really kill himself? We had been assured he wouldn't but I still called my mother regularly to make sure all was OK. And luckily, it was and it was indeed a cry for help, an emotional attempt at a reconciliation and as time went on, I felt comfortable with the fact that he would be here tomorrow, and the next day, and the next. And he was. Eventually they both settled into their new lives but neither would be without controversy for some time to come so I kept running.

Amongst all the chaos I was trying to get on with my life in Kent with Heath. I was somehow able to shut an awful lot out of my mind, or so I thought. Of course, all I was doing was burying it or slinging it into my 'rucksack' which kept making special appearances. However, I was enjoying my life, I enjoyed being with Heath, I enjoyed his company, we were good together and on the whole quite compatible. We enjoyed social events such as work functions or Masons' ladies' nights which were often black tie affairs and I have to say they were spectacular. I loved dressing up for these occasions and going to the grand venues, it made me feel special and it made me feel like I was a far cry from my days with Kane, it was such a contrast. Did it make me a better person? I thought so, but I really had no idea how to measure people or what being a better person meant. I'm working class and there's nothing wrong with that, I'm proud of my roots but it's fair to say I wasn't proud at this time in my life due to my association with Tilbury, the memories, the dark times and in my eyes these new people I was mixing with were better just because they were at a black-tie event which surely meant I was better too. It's easy to see now that I really had no idea, the grandiosity and pretentiousness of some of these events went right over my head but over time and much later in life, that would change and I would learn the real value of people and that, amongst all the black-tie bravado, there's low life in high places.

With Heath and I enjoying our lives, included in this were some great holidays together. Heath's father was Greek Cypriot (although he had already passed by the time I met Heath) so there were a lot of family in Cyprus and we had a few holidays there. These holidays always incorporated family visits and they were great at showing us around the island which was never too much trouble for them, they were lovely people and these holidays were very memorable. Cyprus is a beautiful island but you have to prepare yourself for the heat as it can get extremely hot. Some of Heath's relatives lived in the North of England so occasionally we would visit them at weekends. They were extremely hospitable, even if everything did evolve around food, we seemed to be always sitting around a table to eat which was much the same in Cyprus, they loved to feed you, it's just their way and it was rather rude to decline. This, of course, played havoc with my bad association with food and the bulimia but even at this stage I was still resorting to my simple answer, laxatives. The eating disorder was ever present, it never went away when I moved to Kent and I had no idea why or what to do so I did nothing, just kept taking the laxatives. Anyway, that aside, one of our other holidays was skiing. We went with a group of friends which was fun and it was a lovely place. Unfortunately, Heath had been unwell and he really wasn't well enough for a skiing holiday. Skiing holidays are pretty hard work and take up a lot of energy, something he didn't have at this time so sometimes I went out with other members of our group. It was fun but rather unfortunate that Heath was unwell. We also ventured to Florida and was unfortunate enough to get caught in a tropical storm. I was petrified, I had never seen rain and wind like it and I had this idea in my head that we would be evacuated to some safe place. Our plan was to go to Disney World which was looking doubtful and I kept an eye on the weather channel constantly. This probably made matters worse as, in the end, I said I wanted to go home, so Heath, after making sure this was what I wanted, changed our flights so we could travel in two days' time. However, the following day we woke up to sunshine, it was beautiful and all I could think was, maybe we will get to Disney World. I looked at Heath and he knew what was coming, 'shall we stay?' I said, and he turned to me and said, 'what DO YOU want to do?' The long and short of it is, Heath changed our flights back, we unpacked everything having packed it all for our return home, and started again. I think it's safe to say I might have tested his patience but we laughed at this event for some time to come and were glad we stayed as we did see Disney World and all the other attractions. Funnily enough, we never went back to America, maybe it was the storm, they're pretty ferocious, maybe it was the not so good memory overall but whatever it was, America was somewhere we never returned. We had, however, various other holidays and overall enjoyed a pretty full life which was a great distraction, all the nasty stuff stayed buried whilst I enjoyed living. Our time was also still filled with our sports, Heath still playing football locally whilst I was still playing netball back in Essex, travelling two and from Kent and our team, Flight, were doing really well in the league. I was also still playing for the County so my life with Heath, my work and my netball meant I kept busy, just how I wanted it. But, of course, you really should allow yourself some downtime, something I couldn't do but I understand the reasons for this more now. You see, when carrying issues, for some people, as soon as you have nothing to do, you simply find something, a distraction, anything to stop you thinking too deeply. I couldn't sit for long periods of time, I was like a whirlwind, working, keeping the home, socialising, playing netball, anything to occupy my mind. I hardly ever contacted my family during this time, I was struggling with that, I simply couldn't deal with everything that had gone on and was still going on. My ability to handle this was zero so I stayed away and kept busy.

When Heath and I had been living together for approximately four years, I was around the age of twenty-seven and at this time I started to find the courage to make a few changes to my life. The first was to leave my job in Tilbury and venture into London where the big wide world awaited and, at last, I could leave Snoopy behind. Oh yes, he was still stalking me but it was much less because of where I lived and, of course, who I lived with. Bye, bye Snoopy and because of my inability to deal with him, leaving my job was a great way of getting rid of him, so I thought. As Heath was already working in London we started travelling to work together by car, which was quite normal in the eighties, so we spent quite a lot of time together. These were great times, it was the yuppie years, the eighties, wine bars were opening everywhere, socialising at lunchtime was normal, people seemed happy and I incorporated myself into this life quite easily, it was fun with a capital 'F'. It was during these times that Heath bought me a brand-new car, it was a Ford Fiesta XR2i in bright red, it was a complete surprise and I loved it, it fitted with my new life which sounds quite pathetic now but at the time it was how I felt. But it got even better when, the following year, Heath upgraded it to a Ford Escort XR3i also in bright red and I felt like the bees knees. I'd never known such luxuries and I guess for me material things made me feel good, made me happy, made me feel like a better person and I didn't want my bubble to burst. In fact, in my ignorance, I never thought it would. The other change I made was to leave my netball team, Flight, in the Essex league and also leave the County. I decided to play in Kent and had established myself in a team in the North West Kent league and had also made the Kent County squad. The team worked out well and, like the ladies in Flight, I remain friends with some of them to this day. However, I really didn't enjoy the Kent County, needless to say, I said goodbye to that and just played in the league. Netball was so much easier with Heath, there were no difficult moments if I was away on a tournament, he was not the jealous type and completely understood the whole team camaraderie. I think he understood it as he also had his sport, so he got the whole team thing. Football was his passion for a lot of the time I was with him but neither of our sports were ever a problem, we simply understood each other. However, as much as we understood each other's lives, it was also around the age of twenty-seven that I started to realise I was somewhat confused about myself. I was highly emotional with very high or very low moods with nothing in the middle, the slightest mishap was met with outbursts that were completely irrational. I still had OCD tendencies, everything had to be perfect with little room for error and it exhausted me. I felt I couldn't make any mistakes so I worked hard at making sure I did everything right both at work and at home which, of course, is quite impossible but I simply couldn't see it. I also had a very critical attitude towards others, I was very detrimental and felt the need to point out others' faults and Heath was the one who took the brunt of this. I was also very

needy, thirsty for attention, I liked to be liked, to be everyone's friend, to
be the nice person, especially at work. I hated upsetting anyone, something
that remained with me from my younger days, my boundaries were simply
not in place, I didn't even know I needed them. And another extraordinary
thing was my attitude towards Heath when he was unwell. Unfortunately,
Heath suffered with colitis and at times was very ill, even spending time in
hospital but to me this was a complete inconvenience. Why can't he help
himself? I would say to myself, my discontent showing all over my face,
he just needed to get better. I had no empathy, a trait often portrayed by
narcissists, god forbid that I had adopted some of Kane's behaviour, was
that possible? But all these feelings were confusing and often contradictory
and I simply didn't understand and of course, running alongside all of this
was the bulimia, something was wrong but I didn't really know what it was.
Why was I like this? Why did I have such demons in my head when my
life was perfect? Why, why, why?! I didn't know so I carried on, what else
could I do? It was about a year later when I hit a crisis point, I was unhappy,
confused, anxious and it was affecting Heath and I. I wouldn't say we hit a
rocky patch but for me personally, I was definitely in a bad place, nothing
seemed right, I hated myself, I hated life and I felt I needed help so I went
to the doctor. I had to divulge some difficult information to the doctor
and following our conversation it was suggested that I might benefit from
counselling to which I agreed so I was put on the waiting list. Heath was
happy I had sought help but having waited and waited for an appointment,
it never materialised and during the wait, I had lifted myself out of this low
period so by the time I was offered help, which was some months later, I
said I was OK and didn't need it. I look back now and can only wish that I
had taken that appointment but counselling has to feel right and has to be
at the right time and this was not the time for me, quite unfortunate really
but it was simply not to be. So, life continued, my troubles increased and if
I'm honest, I was bloody lost but I carried on, forever smiling, portraying

an image of happiness. To the outside world Heath and I continued as the same happy couple but there had definitely been a shift in our relationship and not in the right direction. I'm really not sure if Heath understood the severity of our situation, particularly what was going on in my head, but in all fairness why would he know as, apart from the odd mood swings, I still smiled. My criticism of Heath did not cease and was mostly unfounded and I remember Heath mentioning about a song that was out at the time called 'Criticise', he said it summed up how he felt and I couldn't deny it, he was right but I didn't know what to do about it. I couldn't stop it because I didn't know why I was doing it, even though I hated being like it, it was so confusing. I think Heath dealt with this by staying away from home busying himself with work or his new hobby, golf. Heath had always been a borderline workaholic so coming home late was not abnormal for him but for me it suddenly meant I was being ignored. And then he would go off to golf at weekends which felt like another rejection, a rejection I struggled to deal with as I felt like I was being treated as second best. I had lived with Heath for four years before these issues started, I didn't know why and I didn't like them because up until this time, things had been great so why was I spoiling everything? I didn't know why but my thoughts and behaviour would take me to an inexcusable place and prove to be the start of a very difficult time.

Heath decided to take up another hobby, shooting, and with my feelings out of control, I saw this as another rejection. I didn't know how to communicate this to Heath, I seemed to lack the ability to have an adult conversation if one felt hurt or rejected, I just didn't know how to do that so when Heath immersed himself fully into shooting, and was away quite a lot, the feeling of rejection increased which was coupled with me feeling like I wasn't enough, both of which knocked my confidence and self-esteem. I do remember trying to throw myself into whatever hobby Heath was into at the time, which he wasn't unhappy about, but it didn't detract from the fact that his hobby came first and I needed to be number one. The shooting hobby gradually became quite a big thing for Heath, we had several guns in the house and Heath had gone from clay pigeon shooting to shooting wildlife. He knew someone through work who was into it big time and he often invited Heath to a shoot which Heath always attended. These events would take all day and sometimes he would attend the after-shoot dinner so it could run into the evening also. When I look back, I think we both had our issues, mine relating to self-worth and Heath's relating to being a people pleaser, neither of which are healthy and neither if which, when combined, make for a good recipe. I was really struggling but I was also very frustrated due to my lack of ability to talk about how I felt. Heath wasn't aware of my past, I didn't want to talk about it, I carried a lot of shame and chose to keep everything to myself but it was coming out in other ways, ways I didn't understand. I started to wish I'd taken the counselling option months previously, why hadn't I? I now know why and, as mentioned previously the time has to be right and this just wasn't my time so when offered help, I turned it down believing I would be OK. But, I wasn't OK and someone paying me attention at work around this time definitely spelt danger. I was working for a company in London, not far from Old Street, I enjoyed my job and the people I worked with, there were around twenty-five of us in the office, it was fun and sociable and somewhere I felt worthwhile. I so needed that feeling, I craved recognition from everyone, so someone paying me attention was always going to mean danger, not that it seemed dangerous at the time, I was flattered and excited and I got sucked in. It started with us just chatting at work, we would laugh, joke and flirt and then one day we ended up leaving a function at the same time and as we walked towards the train station, we ended up stopping in a side street and kissing. Everything in my body told me it was wrong but it didn't stop me, I had no idea how to say no, I had no boundaries but wasn't sure I even wanted any and considering he was married it was so very, very wrong. I now believe us ladies should never embark on an affair with a married man or indeed any man with a partner, that's just my humble opinion which mostly comes from the fact that I wouldn't like it done to me. I also think my respect for women has grown immensely over the years so doing this to a fellow female just feels wrong. And let's not forget that most of these men will never leave their wives or partners so I would see the whole thing as a disrespect to myself and other women and a complete waste of time. That aside, I was in a different place at this time in my life and instead of attempting to discuss with Heath how I felt, I ran in the other direction, finding answers in the arms of someone else. Of course, I was an easy target but I am in no way blaming the other party, he had his agenda and I fitted it but sadly I just couldn't see any of this at the time. However, the affair had begun and continued for about six to eight months, we met for drinks when we could and when we were on business, we had the convenience of hotel rooms. It was so seedy, so confusing but also for me, very exciting, something I seemed to need at the time. But then I made a big mistake, I used a female work colleague's name in order to get out for the evening, the terrible thing is, she didn't know I had done this. I had stooped so low, it was a terrible thing to do and wasn't fair to her but I didn't know what excuse I could use to see my affair and had to think of somebody Heath didn't know. What I didn't expect is for Heath to contact this work colleague and ask her where we had been as I had come home saying I enjoyed it and he wanted to take me back there. I was caught out, my colleague called me to say Heath had contacted her and all I could do was apologise, but I needed to think fast, I had to come up with a story, and I did. When Heath arrived home that evening, I could tell from his demeanour that he was going to hit me with it, and he did, so I fed him my story. Someone was paying me attention at work so I agreed to go for a drink just to put the record straight, which I had done. Heath looked at me in a very concerning way but as far as I know he bought it and I was off the hook but I had no idea what the impact of this would be and I certainly wasn't prepared for it. Within no time my affair was over, I somehow managed to end it. Was that a milestone for me? Was I making a decision that was best for me? Had I stood up for myself? I would like to think so but honestly, I think my decision was borne from the fact that I had been caught, nothing more, nothing less and it's no good pretending otherwise. Following this incident, Heath and I continued in our relationship but I think my story together with my constant criticising hit him hard, it was just too much and like me, he had his insecurities which I seemed to have touched on. We were actually like a car crash together at this point, as a couple we lacked substance and if you stripped all the material stuff away, I'm not sure what was left. I could now see we both had our issues and were both being tested but neither of us knew how to deal with this effectively. However, like me, Heath found a way and it knocked me sideways. First, I noticed he was paying particular attention to his appearance and on casual clothes day at work he made a real effort, he was different, distant, eager to leave the house and was spending more time shooting with his work pals which included a lot of dinners and late nights. I was suspicious, I knew something was up but I said nothing until the late nights turned into arriving home in the early hours of the following morning and then six or seven in the morning and at these times his mobile was always turned off. By this time, screaming matches had ensued, I was like a raging bull, but whatever I did it didn't stop so when he went off and was uncontactable, I found a way to try and deal with it by roaming the streets and this was when I started to think about being 'normal'. These days 'normal' is a word I find difficult to comprehend, what does it really mean anyway? But back then when I was roaming the streets and looking in people's windows seeing families sitting together watching TV with the two point four children, the dog and a Ford Mondeo on the drive (this was the eighties!), that's what I believed was 'normal' and that's what I thought I wanted. During these times I couldn't eat, I lost weight, I couldn't sleep, my emotions were out of control and this was probably the worst thing to happen to someone like me because I saw it as nothing more than utter rejection. I really couldn't handle it and I know I had no right to judge considering what I had done but it seemed to me that Heath was doing the same and he too did not know how to communicate on the level that was required and it was disastrous. I remember a time when he rolled in in the early hours, I had just got out of bed and was removing a loaf of bread from the freezer and as he walked through the door I threw the loaf at him. It flew down the hallway, he ducked and it crashed against the front door. This is how I dealt with my frustrations, with anger and violence which solved absolutely nothing. It seems funny now and once we got past this stage, we called it 'the flying loaf episode' although I'm not sure we ever really got past this stage of our lives together, it became a slippery slope. And then, there came a time when Heath fessed up, he told me that someone at work had paid him attention and he liked it, he said he had been spending time with her but they had never slept together and he didn't want to pursue anything with her and had told her it was over. Well, déjà vu, hadn't I been here before? Yes, I had, remember the ex when Heath and I first met? I had no idea what to believe but what could I say, I had been in exactly the same situation at work and done exactly the same thing, now we were even, not that that was the answer, it wasn't a contest and it just made things worse, it was a terrible mess created by two messy people.

Heath and I continued in some sort of fashion for a couple of years more, I was now twenty-nine years of age but I think the shift in our relationship was too great. Too much had happened, I was messy and so fucking confused, I felt so low and, once again, I didn't want to be here, my reactions and coping so dramatic. Heath and I had survived seven years together and it wasn't all bad but I think my runaway story had to come to an end, and it did. I was so fucked up, I had run away from my past, had a new man, a new area, a new life, a new home but for some reason

I wasn't satisfied and I couldn't work out why. So, what was I going to do? Well, one of Heath's friends knew we were having problems, his name was Loci, he was divorced, no children and had a three-bed house and said if it would help, I could have one of the spare rooms in order to give us some time to try and work things out. He said he was trying to help and maybe a little time apart might clear the way for a reconciliation. I stored this information just in case I needed it and low and behold, the day came when I did. Heath and I had had an argument, I have no idea what it was about but, in my rage, I called Loci asking him if the offer still stood and he confirmed it did so once Heath left the house to go shooting, I packed a suitcase with essential clothes and toiletries and went. I can't explain how I felt because I didn't know but I was so grateful to Loci who greeted me at his door on my arrival. He was very calm and I breathed a sigh of relief and all of a sudden, I started to feel like I had some space, somewhere to think, somewhere to hopefully be me. But who was I? I was hoping I would find out but being almost thirty and being single for the first time in my life with a very messy past would not make it easy. And guess what? Apart from the suitcase I took to Loci's, I also took another bag, that proverbial 'rucksack'. Yes, I was unknowingly still carrying it around.

This runaway stage of my life all happened in the eighties and what a great era it was. However, as much as I enjoyed most of it, I failed to understand what my past had done to me, and I guess it was pretty bad, so consequently I failed to understand how to deal with it. Back then I thought moving and starting a new life would be the cure but wherever you go, if there's a 'rucksack' involved, it will come with you, it does not disappear. Yes, we can bury our 'rucksack', we can pretend it doesn't exist but somehow it will emerge, in our behaviour, our reactions, our emotions, this is almost certain. As for Heath and I, I truly believe we were good together, there was a lot of good stuff but on a deeper level, we both lacked the ability to know how to handle our emotions and weaknesses and there was a lot of history, particularly on my part. It seems our meeting may just have been bad timing but it was over and I was about to embark on a journey of discovery.

CHAPTER 7

Who Am I?

I settled into Loci's home but I must admit there were many nights in the early days that I missed Heath. I felt lost and very alone so in order to sleep I found myself a teddy bear to keep in the bed. It seemed to work, it gave me comfort, maybe lots of people do this, I don't know but for now it helped me. But amongst the lonely feelings there was a big part of me that wanted to be alone, to live as I wanted, to be truly free for the first time and these thoughts encouraged me to get past the loneliness. But what I didn't understand was what being free truly meant, was it just being alone, pleasing oneself, having nobody to answer to? That's how I saw it but there's so much more to it than that. You have to free the mind to be truly free, to unload that rucksack, to discover who you are and what makes you happy, to deal with your demons, to become aware, all things I began to discover during my next journey.

Following my split from Heath, I started having real issue with him. Me leaving and going to Loci's was something he had not expected and his reaction was very out of character. The first issue was, once I had settled into Loci's I went back to my house to gather up a few more things choosing a time I knew Heath would be out but when I tried to get in, I discovered Heath had changed the locks. I really wasn't expecting that, Heath was not a malicious man and it seemed so out of character so I called him but my efforts were in vain so I retreated back to Loci's. This seemed so childish, why play these silly games? I guess you never really know somebody or their capabilities until they're faced with certain situations, a bit like people where money's concerned, a time when you really see some people's true colours. But this wasn't it, it gained momentum and was about to get worse as apart from changing the locks, Heath would not answer the door to any further attempts I made to gain access nor would he answer any of my attempts to call him. We jointly owned the house so I spoke to a good friend of mine who said it was illegal not to let me have access and if I broke in there was nothing he could do. Glad to say, I didn't take this route, I just waited, stressed about it a lot, talked about it a lot, dramatised about it a lot, all of which were the only ways I knew, whilst hoping he would see sense. And then, completely out of the blue, I received a letter from a solicitor Heath had hired, it was quite lengthy but ultimately it was saying that I had threatened to smash the house up which is why the locks were changed and I couldn't be trusted. I was distraught, was this really happening? I had not expected such a cruel act, I didn't know this side of Heath but it seemed he would do anything not to allow me access, but why? I just didn't know, neither did I know what to do. So I did the only thing I did know, which was nothing except dramatise about it again and tell anyone who cared to listen. While all this was happening, I had started to live life as a singleton having no idea what I was doing and definitely on shaky ground. I started to go out more, I was still playing netball but only in Kent so with work, my friends plus netball friends, I managed to keep myself busy. However, it was during one of my weaker moments that I agreed to meet with Heath, he had been in touch and wanted to talk. We agreed a date and time and he picked me up and took me to one of our favourite restaurants within the vicinity of us both and although I had always enjoyed it there, I felt a little uncomfortable. We had chatted on a few occasions previously and our conversations had always centred around me returning home. Heath wanted me to go back but I had no idea how to react so I agreed to discuss it over dinner. We ate, we drank, we chatted and I really felt cornered as Heath was putting an awful lot of pressure on me to go back home. I felt so nervous, so out of my depth and not having an awful lot of strength, I agreed even though it felt so wrong but for some reason I went along with the decision and we made plans for my return home. Heath dropped me back at Loci's, our plans in place and I think Heath was the first to tell Loci the 'good' news but after Heath left, Loci and I chatted and I expressed my concerns saying it didn't feel right and I wasn't sure I was doing the right thing. Loci was impartial which was understandable, the only thing he said was that I should do what feels right and I should try not to be led and I should be true to myself. I took these words on board, I thought hard about it, having a couple of sleepless nights but in the end, being true to myself was exactly what I did and I told Heath I didn't want to come back. I felt terrible, I was very nervous, my stomach was churning, I didn't want to upset Heath but if I didn't, I would upset myself and I was trying very hard not to do that. Anyway, I did it, I made a decision, I hoped I would stick to it which would be my own battle but it was what I wanted so I would have to work at it. I knew it was right but mostly, I knew it was right for me. Heath wasn't very pleased when I told him but he had to accept it, it was what I wanted, my decision was made and once again I set about living life on my own. I didn't however tackle the subject of the house, it would need to be sorted but I just let it ride, I guessed one day it would have to be dealt with but it simply wasn't top of my agenda. In the meantime, Loci and I had become great friends and it was good for me to have a fun friendship. We laughed a lot which is always healthy and when Loci had to attend some business dinners, I would sometimes accompany him, at his request, and these were always good fun. Loci also had friends who were part of the Round Table, an organisation that used to hold ladies' nights, just like the Freemasons nights, so when the next one came along Loci asked me if I wanted to go, to which I agreed. I still loved evenings of this type, dressing up, getting hair and make-up done, enjoying the glitz and glamour. Oh, they were fun and Loci was great company, we got on well and as two single people we could accompany each other to events we didn't want to go alone to, and it worked well.

My job at this time was great for the situation I was in personally. I was working in Aldwych in the West End of London for a very well-known American oil company. There were approximately 2,500 people in the building which meant it was a very sociable place and it would not be unheard of to have birthday, promotion, leaving or business celebrations several times a week. There always seemed to be a reason (or excuse) to go to Covent Garden to eat, drink and have fun. I also had a boss who enjoyed socialising which meant even more times out including lunches and business trips away. In some ways I couldn't have been in a better place, I needed distractions, I had no idea who I was so I drifted into this lifestyle unaided, I just went along with everything, muddling my way through. I remember one of my first nights out as a singleton in a local pub near our office in Aldwych, there were quite a few people there and the drink was flowing and I felt great. At some time during the evening, I distinctly remember turning to a work colleague and in my drunken state saying, 'I'm single for the first time in my adult life and I have no idea what to do, how do you be single?' Her response was 'just go and enjoy yourself,' which was just what I wanted to hear and then the George Michael song 'Freedom! '90' started playing which I sung at the top of my voice incorporating several dance moves just to get the point across. I had my fist in the air while jumping up and down, head going from side to side, I had it all going on, or so I thought. Pretty hilarious now when I think about it and yes, as I write, I'm shaking my head whilst smiling. When I look back I distinctly remember the look on my colleague's face when I asked about what to do as a singleton, it was a look of confusion with a hint of sympathy and pity all mixed up with a big dose of boredom but of course I couldn't see this at the time, all I heard was, enjoy yourself and that was my focus. As for the song 'Freedom! '90', I still love it today and play it often, not because of that crazy night but simply because it is a great song. However, this song was around at a pivotal moment in my life and, not realising it, I had started to unravel. My thirty and single lifestyle was in full flight and I was out almost five nights a week, either with work or friends back home, and I was still playing netball. I have no idea how I managed this but when you're in it you simply don't see it. It became normal to run for the last train or not make it home, crash somewhere and go to work the next day in the same clothes. I do believe many people have experienced this but not usually in their thirties as this lifestyle is commonly associated with the younger generation. But for me, I found myself living out the years I felt I had missed, my teens, I was like an old teenager and looking back I can see what a car crash it was but, in the moment, all I could see was me living the life I thought I wanted. So, with this wonderful, crazy, single life going on why, deep down inside, wasn't I happy? I couldn't answer that so I simply carried on having fun, covering those feelings with good times, alcohol and promiscuity. Yes, this time of my life was quite promiscuous, I had many dates, looking for love without knowing what that word meant, thinking that if someone loved me it made me important, loveable, liked, all the things I couldn't seem to give myself. This is one of the problems if you lack self-love, you search for it elsewhere and you have a tendency to believe that sex is the tool that enables you to find it, but I can categorically tell you that this is not the case, sex and love are two very different things but I simply couldn't distinguish between the two. It was a disaster and what I often thought was a loving relationship ended in nothing and very quickly which I didn't understand causing, sadness, guilt and depression to set in. But after a short while I would bounce back and try my luck again, all the time failing to understand that losing your self-respect was certainly not the way to find love. But, why did I want love, I thought I wanted freedom, a single life, it was all so confusing but I think the problem was I couldn't function on my own, I needed other people to make me feel good not realising that what I really needed was self-love. But I didn't know what that was, I didn't have it nor did I have any self-respect and didn't understand the effect the lack of these would have on my life. Today, I do understand, I'm happy to say I have this knowledge and my life's choices are very different compared to those days, and all in a good way. So, love yourself fully, I cannot emphasise how important this is and how it contributes immensely to a healthy mind and more stable life.

I continued to live with Loci and had been there for approximately six months when I was presented with an opportunity. The mother of one of my netball friends had a one-bed flat in Sidcup which was available to rent and the rent was very cheap which was all to do with tax reasons. I can't tell you how excited I was thinking how great it would be to have my own place and found it very hard to hide my enthusiasm and quickly made arrangements to go and view it. The flat in question was a Victorian style house that had been converted into two flats, the flat for rent being on the ground floor and when I saw it, I said I would take it without any hesitation. It wasn't quite ready, it was being repainted so I had to wait a few weeks but, in the meantime, I started planning my departure from Loci's, buying bits I would need and boxing up a few things. It was definitely the right time to leave Loci's as there had been a strange moment whilst we were out together at an event. We had an overnight stay, separate rooms, and Loci had had quite a bit to drink and made me feel a little uncomfortable with his advances. I eventually went to my room leaving him to sleep it off in his but the journey home the following day was a difficult one. We were unusually quiet with me making excuses that I was tired. It felt very awkward and you could have cut the atmosphere in the car with a knife, unspoken words just hanging there that neither of us wanted to tackle. I think Loci felt rejected, he really wasn't my type physically and we had never been close except on a friendship level so I was a little surprised at his advances. Maybe I had been naive and looking back, I probably was but for the time being I did what I did best, ignored it and waited patiently for the day to come when I moved out. And soon that day came and by the time it did, everything between Loci and I was fine and I put this silly moment from Loci down to an excess of alcohol, it happens, I told myself but I was too excited about my new home to think about it any further. My new home I saw as my little haven and I had such high expectations about this stage of my life, I had never lived on my own but I told myself this was right. I was looking forward to it, I was ready for this next phase, I was excited, so why, after I had settled in, did I find myself feeling thoughtful, sad and anxious? I ignored my feelings, mostly through my 'rucksack', and continued to live my life with a smile but not long after moving in and whilst sorting through some boxes, I found myself looking through some old photos. I didn't realise how tough I would find this, particularly those I came across that included pictures of Kane. Once I had gone through them, I went through them again, and again, until I had every photo that included Kane and after a short hesitation, I tore them into pieces and threw them in the bin. I don't know why I hesitated but it did feel like he was watching me and it frightened me probably resulting in the hesitation and all I could think was, would he know I did this? What would he do? And then I thought, he still controls me. I was crying, I had hoped that by living my life as I was and ridding myself of the photos I would rid myself of Kane and everything associated with him, I had hoped he would disappear from my mind, just like the photos had. But it didn't feel like that, so I cried some more, slept and started the following day afresh all in the hope that in time all the bad stuff would go away. I had some very deep thoughts once I started living alone and not of the happy variety, I think an awful lot hit me at this time but nothing I really understood. Nothing made sense, maybe it was because I had more time alone and didn't have as much distraction which is highly likely, but whatever it was, this move was not living up to my expectations. Don't get me wrong, I loved my little place, my home but it had unearthed something in me I didn't understand, something had started simmering but I didn't know what it was so I carried on with my life smiling as I always did. I distracted myself as much as I could with work, socialising, netball and dating but the dating was still nothing of any substance and I started to wonder if my life in general had any substance. What was I doing? Why was my life like this? I was experiencing extreme highs and lows, enjoying the highs but pretty desperate during the lows. Someone fucking help me understand! But who could help when nobody knew anything was wrong. The only one who knew was me, was I the only one who could help? Was I the answer? That thought unknowingly remained in my mind, like a planted seed waiting to grow.

So, while that seed was growing and my life continued around it, somehow, and I cannot remember how, Snoopy ended up back in my life. It's a bit of a mystery how but my guess is he had kept in touch with Heath and I until we separated and then kept in touch with me and my inability to tell him to take a hike had led to him knowing my whereabouts. So, he was back and yes, he started driving along my street and making odd appearances and the only way I knew how to react was with pleasantries. He came to Sidcup once, said he was in the area and even though every bone in my body knew this was unacceptable behaviour, I greeted him like an old friend even inviting him in for coffee. It was very strange but I acted normally ever afraid of tackling his unusual behaviour for fear of exposing him, hurting him when the only one I was hurting was me. I wasn't being honest with my gut feelings but then I never was, so I buried my anxieties about the situation, it was the only way I knew. He started his usual drive-by routine. It wasn't that often unless, of course, I never spotted every instance but when I did, I simply greeted him without questioning why he was around. It was so painful, why was I not questioning this man's actions?

I hated myself for it. Nevertheless, Snoopy was back and with my life remaining a circus, Snoopy was thrown back into the mix and I started to feel like the clown, the star of my own shitshow and it felt quite bizarre. I was still, at this point, working in Aldwych and there were people around me at this time who knew I was an easy target, the one who never stood up for herself, the one who never said no and in my work and personal life this attracted a lot of people that I would call users. I couldn't see it at the time as I was too engrossed in my need to surround myself with people, anyone who paid me attention, even my then boss would take advantage of me in more ways than one. And then my boss asked me to mentor one of our overseas colleagues and I had a sense of pride at being asked. The person in question was a gentleman from our offices in Nigeria who was planning a trip to the UK for a year's work experience and as part of my job involved dealing with Nigeria on a day-to-day basis, it made sense for me to be asked and I eagerly agreed. I was a little uneasy about this at first, wondering what he would be like, questioning if I could do it, not really understanding exactly what was required and thinking how I could make this a success. Many questions floating around in my head but when he arrived, I was so relieved. His name was Luan and much to my approval, he was an extremely approachable man, very easy to talk to, very pleasant with a kind looking face accompanied by the most incredible laugh, something we all commented on. He was very well presented, wearing sharp suits with fresh looking shirts and great ties. He was tall, at least six foot two, very lean and very likeable and I heaved a sigh of relief. So, my mentoring role began, spending every day with Luan, showing him how we operated in the UK, highlighting some of the struggles we encountered with shipments to Nigeria and he listened intently, trying to take in as much knowledge as possible whilst he was with us. And on the flip side, it seemed the arrival of Luan encouraged more socialising, my boss wanting him to join us on our nights out either drinking or dining, something Luan seemed to embrace and also wanting to show Luan the London sites which my boss tasked me with so I soon became Luan's tour guide. Over time we all became quite close to Luan, he was liked by us all and great to be around, his character and unforgettable laugh embraced our office and for me personally, it was a year of great experience. But that year quickly passed and soon it was time for Luan to start planning his return to Nigeria so we organised the date booking taxis, flights etc., ensuring everything was in place. It had been a great year from both a work and social perspective and I think I speak for all when I say, he was going to be missed. So, as a way of saying thank you, Luan asked me to join him for dinner a couple of days before he was due to leave and I gladly accepted. Everything was organised, we would meet at his apartment in Kensington that was being rented for him by the company and he was then going to take me to an Italian restaurant in Victoria. I was looking forward to it and arrived at his apartment at the agreed time without any expectations but when I arrived, my god, what a fab place. The lounge alone was bigger than the whole footprint of my flat and I couldn't even imagine what the rent was. However, when I arrived and Luan greeted me, I noticed he seemed a little on edge, unsettled, I wasn't afraid but this was not the Luan I knew but I put it down to the fact that his imminent plans to return home were on his mind. After a short while exchanging pleasantries, we made our way to the restaurant and when we arrived, I realised I had been here before and had really liked it so all good so far. The evening went well, we had a couple of drinks and a lovely meal and chatted about the previous year, sometimes serious, sometimes laughing, but during all the discussions and laughter I noticed a difference in Luan. He seemed a little distracted and he was looking at me differently and I couldn't make out what it was but my gut was telling me I had to prepare myself for something. And I'm so glad I did because the moment came when he cupped his face with his huge hands and fixed his eyes on mine saying he had something to ask me. I took a very brief moment before asking him to continue and the following words from Luan came as somewhat of a surprise. I could never have guessed what he was about to say but it went something like this, 'I would like you to be my European wife, would you do that for me?' For a moment I looked at him trying to understand what had just been asked of me, what did he mean, was he asking me to marry him? I already knew he was married and had four children, his wife and children all being back in Nigeria, information he had shared during his time with us but never really elaborated on it. I was confused and it must have shown on my face as Luan then went on to explain that it was quite normal for some Nigerians to have a second wife, preferably European, and he would love it if I would step into that role. He went on to say that if I accepted, whilst he was in Europe, he would spend time with me and when he was in Nigeria, he would spend time with his current wife and children. Now, we all know that, in reality and as much as you might want it to happen, the ground does not open and swallow you up but right now I really wished it would. Knowing this was impossible I had to think quick on my feet. I immediately came out with the old friend's speech explaining that we were friends and I didn't want that to change and changing our status could result in a loss of our friendship, it was the easy way out and one that I hoped wouldn't upset him. I felt anxious and now realised why he had seemed unsettled when we first met that evening at his apartment, he clearly had his agenda, one I wasn't expecting. My answer hung in the air, I felt so uncomfortable waiting for his response and after what seemed like a lifetime, he said he was disappointed but respected my answer. Well, as you can imagine, the evening quickly came to an end, not before encountering some awkward moments but we got through it and eventually parted ways and that was the last I ever saw or heard from Luan. It was the most bizarre situation and it caught me off guard but I think I came to realise that Luan always had a hidden agenda. I think he saw an opportunity that would fulfil his need for a European passport and there I was, early thirties, single, who maybe could be swayed into saying yes to the life he was offering. I often wonder if he saw the insecurities in me, he was smart and probably worked out that I was an easy target and of course, he would have been right so how did this insecure, fucked-up excuse for a female say no? I guess even I had my limits, which was nice to know. I often wondered if Luan ever did find his European wife but that's something I guess we'll never know. Bless him!

It was about a year, or maybe two, of living in Sidcup that I was having serious thoughts about my lifestyle and, more importantly, about the general feeling I had about myself. I had become aware of the fact that I was very erratic, I had no balance in my life, no direction, I was still having short bursts of highs quickly followed by incredible lows, I was bulimic and it was still questionable if I was borderline OCD. So, why was I like this? I had no idea but for some reason, unknown to me, I suddenly wanted answers. I always felt under so much pressure but this was mostly of my own making, social pressures, work pressures, situations I really had no idea how to handle except to compromise myself and I was beginning to really hate who I was. So, what could I do? I thought about it for a short while and realised I needed help but I also realised I would have to be responsible for getting this help, only I could make this happen. Maybe that little seed I had planted previously had decided to start growing, I really don't know but for some reason, I wanted to take action so I set about investigating what my options were. I thought about counselling but from previous experiences I knew the waiting list if I went through the doctor was a minimum of three months and this time, I didn't want to wait. I needed to do something now for fear of changing my mind so I looked up Relate who used to be the old marriage guidance councillors but had reformed and were now for all types of counselling. I called them, I was nervous but they were very sensitive, only asking a few questions but told me they could see me for an initial assessment the following week. I took the appointment without hesitation, ended the call and cried. It's difficult to explain how I felt, I don't really know why I cried, maybe I felt relieved that I had taken that step, maybe I felt it was the first step to a better life, I really don't know, it was a mixture of unknown emotions and ones I really hoped I would come to understand. Who am I? I was hopeful I was going to find out, it was a step, hopefully in the right direction but suddenly everything seemed to slow down and the week leading up to my appointment seemed to drag but I kept focused, counting the days and eventually it arrived. I really had no idea how this worked or what to expect, I just turned up, went to the little reception, said my name and time of my appointment and after a few seconds, I was asked to take a seat. It was the strangest feeling sitting and waiting to see a counsellor for the first time, I felt like everyone was looking at me in a knowing way but of course they weren't, I was simply paranoid, uneasy and I could feel my breathing was laboured. I was frightened, which heightened my emotions, but I sat quietly waiting for my next instruction. After a few minutes an hippie looking lady appeared, she called my name, I acknowledged, and she asked me to follow her into a nearby room. I sat down and waited for her to say something. It was a polite start, she introduced herself, explained what she did and confirmed her qualifications and how the process worked. She then turned to me and once again in a polite manner, asked me my name, age and address, well that was easy but then she said, 'so, what brings you hear today, Debra?' I don't think I have ever been in a situation where a question was so confusing or powerful. Why was I here? What should I say? Where do I start? How do I explain? But then I looked at her soft face and felt her relaxed yet confident demeanour fill the room and this hippie style lady suddenly made me feel like I was in a safe place, something I later discovered to be so important in counselling. At this point all I remember was breaking down in floods of tears and blurting out all sorts of things, some I remember, some I don't but I do remember whilst sobbing profusely saying, 'I was abused for several years and by the time I was twenty-one I had been subjected to four terminations.' I could barely make myself understood but this lady never reacted, she stayed calm and by the time I had calmed down she said that she felt from what she had heard that it would be beneficial for me to start counselling. A wave of relief washed over me, someone could help and I cried some more but my bubble burst when she said there was a three month wait with Relate and suddenly the bottom fell out of my world. I was mortified, my emotions were high and I just wanted to end my life there and then. I was ready for counselling, it had to be now and as I expressed this to the nice lady through much more sobbing, she threw me a lifeline. She explained that anything relating to the NHS, which Relate were, is a minimum of three months wait, however, I could choose to go private which would enable me to have an immediate appointment. I think I may have eagerly said yes prior to asking the cost as this didn't seem important but once I had come to my senses, I asked about the cost which we discussed and I agreed to go ahead. I didn't have loads of money at this point in my life but I had enough to socialise several times a week, that's where all my spare money went, so once we talked it through it was a pretty simple solution, give up one night socialising per week and use the money saved for counselling. It was a no-brainer in my book, it was worth the sacrifice so an appointment was made at a location in Erith for the following week with a lady called Sanu and the feeling when I walked out of there was simply indescribable.

Counselling can mean so many different things to so many different people, some see it as a place where someone will give them all the answers, some a place they don't really want to be but were advised to try it, some a safe place where they can hide from reality, some a place where they can compete and prove they didn't really need it in the first place, some a place where a genuine effort to change their lives was being attempted and I think I was probably a combination of most of these. But whatever I was, I was ready, an important factor in counselling and soon the time arrived for me to attend my first appointment with Sanu. I drove there feeling a little nervous, I arrived early so I sat in my car for a while thinking about what to expect and how I should behave. At this point I was extremely anxious and I started to wonder what Sanu was like and whether I would like her or whether she would like me but I guess I was about to find out as it was time to go in. I got out of my car, crossed the road and entered a small door. The set up was similar to the Relate office, when I walked in, they asked my name and asked me to sit in a small waiting area. I was told that Sanu would call me in a short while and a couple of minutes later Sanu appeared in a doorway asking me to follow her. I was then invited to sit in a very comfortable chair, it felt like a hug, part of the feeling comfortable process I guess but it was nice all the same. The room was very pleasant, it felt very calm and there was a glass of water placed on a table beside me and a box of tissues strategically placed within my reach. Sanu was a very pretty lady with long blonde hair, her age I found difficult to judge but I took a wild guess at early forties, she was quite petite and she was casually dressed but still looked very well presented. Initially she didn't feel as warm as the lady at Relate but I think if she was, I would have overlooked that fact as I was sizing her up, checking her out, something I did with most women as I always found them a threat or competition which inhibited my ability to be a good friend to any female. The session started in pretty much the same fashion as the one at Relate, Sanu told me a bit about herself, her qualifications and then explained the rules surrounding confidentiality and once I acknowledged I was happy with it all we moved on. She then asked some questions about me starting with the usual, full name, address, age, occupation and somehow this introduction started me talking but I don't think I was really making a lot of sense. I was trying to explain why I was there by cramming thirty years of my life into one minute jumping from one subject to another but Kane was always very prominent, he seemed to be the highlight of the show and the main reason I was there. I once again shed many tears at this session and all the time Sanu watched and listened, making the odd comment and although I initially felt uncertain about her, I was starting to feel her warmth, something I held on to. The time went very quickly and at the end of the session we discussed what we felt was the best arrangement for me and we concluded that I would benefit from weekly sessions in order to keep continuity. I was happy with this arrangement but had no idea how many weeks I would need but this was definitely a question that couldn't be answered, nobody really knows, it's impossible to say but it didn't seem important, the past two weeks had been a milestone for me and now I was here, ready to embrace it, whatever time it took.

These early counselling sessions proved to be very, very difficult, I had a myriad of emotions circling my mind and was completely unaware how tough it would be and it was agonising. I had no idea how to behave, my mind was still of the opinion that I had to please everyone and this included Sanu but she really wasn't interested in being pleased and in her professional capacity she started to work on who the real me was and why I was there. On the flip side, I felt the need to compete with her due to her being a female, and an attractive one at that, but Sanu knew this also and again, worked with me professionally to help me understand why I decided to start these sessions and to dig deep and help me get some answers. It's tough talking about painful past events but it had to be done, how else do you start to unravel the mess? It needs to be understood but the reliving of events is incredibly difficult and sometimes too much to bear. There were many occasions I didn't want to attend and had to force myself to go and there were some occasions I simply couldn't face it and cancelled, coming up with some feeble excuse. The times I cancelled I felt like I was bunking off school, it was the strangest feeling but you can be sure that all good counsellors know when you're having a wobble which often leads to conversations about the importance of keeping the sessions consistent. Consistency, I learned over time, is important, it's easier to remember something from a week ago and maybe pick up on it at the next session, but once you start skipping sessions you can lose the flow, you can even forget, or choose to forget if it's too painful, so it's good to stay focused and consistency certainly helps this. So, I worked on trying to ensure I attended every week and I can honestly say, I overcame the terror I felt some weeks and made sure I went. The strange thing is, when I didn't want to go, these sessions seemed to always be very productive and I remember leaving thinking, thank god I went, and that feeling is what kept me going when I had those difficult weeks. Of course, none of this made the sessions easy and what's really hard is still trying to live your day-to-day life whilst fathoming out who you are, particularly if you're tackling a tricky subject and you don't want to get out of bed, which sometimes happened. But, of course, you have to, you have to go to work, play netball, socialise, smile. Oh yes, those first few months were very, very tough indeed, sometimes they were hell, I felt like a baby trying to learn to take my first steps and in effect, I was. I was trying to work out who I was, why I was unhappy and confused which took a lot of delving deep into my past. And, remember that 'rucksack'? Well, it had almost become comfortable carrying that load around. Trauma is a very strange thing and sometimes, as bad as it is, it's all you know, it's your bubble and bursting that bubble can be very frightening as you have no idea what's on the other side. But some people make the choice to burst that bubble, unload their 'rucksack' and venture into the unknown hoping to find answers, a better life and a better understanding of oneself and I was one of those people. I did wonder at times what the alternative was and I concluded that it meant running away, just as I had run to Heath. But running does not answer your questions, no matter where you live or who you're with that 'rucksack' comes with you, like part of your luggage. But unlike the rest of your luggage, the 'rucksack' does not get unpacked. I truly believe that creating a distraction merely delays the inevitable, the car crash will happen. You can ignore the red flags, make excuses, live half a life, move to a new location whilst deep down knowing something is wrong. And that feeling deep down in your gut shouldn't be ignored, it's telling you something and it needs to be faced. Maybe telling yourself you deserve a better life will help.

So, the sessions continued and the months passed and all crazy manner of things started happening. Sometimes Sanu would provide suggestions, things to practise and I'm pleased to say I was a model student, I tried everything and to my surprise they often worked which encouraged me in my quest for normality. Now that's a great word, normality or normal. I remember during my early counselling days, and during emotional crying sessions, blurting out the words 'I just want to be normal', and I meant it because normal to me depicted, as mentioned previously, a nice house, two point four children, a dog and a Ford Mondeo on the drive where everyone lived happily ever after. Seems bloody ridiculous now and it makes me smile, after all, what the hell is normal, it's certainly not something you can pigeonhole. I actually don't like the word normal, what does it even mean? Is it simply an idea that's put into our heads that we feel obliged to follow, what society tells us? I believe so but that's just my theory and one I stick to today but, that aside, normal can mean so many different things to so many different people but it should always be what makes you happy. And as for my wonderful house, dog, car, kids theory, who says they're happy, nobody does and I've discovered that, in life, what you see is not always what you think it is, there's much more beneath the surface of many people, we just do that natural human thing, we judge. And we see this more often in today's competitive society, lives often being unrealistically portrayed, which is most prevalent on social media, creating enormous amounts of pressure, insecurities and self-doubt. But we should remember, this is not reality, it's mostly a case of how others want you to see them and I take most of it these days with a huge dollop of salt. It was quite a revelation having a better understanding of normal, it was liberating and along with other realities that started to emerge, I felt I was making progress and I could feel some shifts in my life emerging and one of them related to netball. I had suffered with a right knee problem for years but then my back started to get painful and my right shoulder had dislocated a few times leading to an operation, all of which contributed to my next decision but I think my decision related a lot to the first months of counselling, my progress, what I had learned and how I felt. I knew what I wanted to do so, at the end of one of our seasons with the team in the Kent league, I announced that I was going to retire and at the tender age of thirty-two and at the level I was playing, this was quite young. It seemed to shock a lot of people and I guess that's understandable as I hadn't made any indication that this was coming but what I did find unfair was being accused of retiring whilst on top of my game in order to ensure I'd be remembered as a good player. Now I had made some very good friends, a couple I still see today so I tried not to worry about the few who felt this way because only I knew the real reason which I couldn't share without exposing too much about my life. You see, it became apparent as my counselling sessions progressed that netball was my outlet which made total sense as I had used it as an escape when I was with Kane but as I became more aware of this and started to find myself, I simply didn't feel I needed it. Netball was most definitely an escape for me, my aggressive place, my place to offload but I was now doing a lot of this in counselling and starting to unravel my life. I was thinking about what I really wanted and I knew it wasn't to escape or run or hide. Don't get me wrong, I had some wonderful years playing netball and made some wonderful friends but I was changing, I was learning, I had started being more realistic, being more honest with myself, doing what I felt was right, making tough decisions. I had never done this before but somehow it felt right and my choice to finish playing netball would be the first of many changes I would make in the future. When I spoke about my netball decision to my counsellor, we worked through it and I felt like I had triumphed. It was something I had done for me, nobody else, just me, I wasn't trying to please anyone else and I didn't feel I had to, all I knew was it felt right and only I knew why. And what's more, I didn't feel the need to explain myself, I just walked away and it felt very empowering. I clearly remember, following my decision, one of the first weekends of the new netball season, I had just woken up, it was cold and it was raining and I turned over, snuggled back under my quilt and thought, 'thank god I don't have to go out and play in this weather', which I guess was another good reason to quit. I had no doubt in my mind that it was the right decision and it became a foundation for me to build on. And the strangest thing is, since quitting thirty-plus years ago, there has never been a day I've regretted my decision and I have never, ever missed it.

I felt like I had made a breakthrough, I had a long way to go but it was a start and there were moments I felt incredibly proud of my progress but it was often accompanied by some very dark times. Sanu and I were tackling so many issues and a lot of them, I learnt, were associated with my lack of self-esteem. I literally didn't have any nor did I have any self-worth, self-love or confidence which for the most part I could associate with my years with Kane. I found some discussions extremely difficult and as Sanu and I worked through various topics I started to dream a lot, unpleasant dreams, more like nightmares, incorporating times from my past. I found these dreams to be very complicated and difficult to understand and when I spoke to Sanu about them, she suggested that in order to try and make sense of them, I keep a notebook beside my bed and write them down the moment I remembered so they could be discussed at the next session which proved to be a very useful exercise. These dreams came at very random times but mostly prompted by something Sanu and I had been discussing, something that triggered me, something that tapped into my subconscious mind, my 'rucksack', so writing them down allowed me to talk about them at my next session to try and establish an association. It was during these times, and many others, that I had what I called light bulb or bell ringing moments where I felt a strong sense of understanding, where suddenly something made sense, like I had answered a deep-rooted question I didn't even know was there and by allowing my mind to open up, I took a different thought pattern, a new route leading to a new understanding. These were times I loved, mostly because I was learning and I enjoyed learning, working out the complexities of it all, I was like a sponge soaking up information, embracing new ways of thinking and these times are definitely the brighter side of counselling. My dream writing led me to writing so much more, suggested by Sanu. I had an A4 writing book and no matter what day or time it was, if a thought, feeling or memory came to me, whether angry, sad, happy or confused, whether it felt significant or not, I would write it down. This writing exercise is an extremely powerful tool, it's as if you're unloading from your mind, your 'rucksack', and putting it onto paper and it's surprising what this action can do. But it didn't stop there, we extended this to what is known as 'no send' letters where you write to a particular person detailing whatever you feel necessary never intending to send it. This is another powerful tool which gives you the opportunity to say exactly how you feel to whomever you feel you need to say it to without actually facing them. You can include anger, sorrow, questions, you can call them whatever you want, tell them how you feel about them, all manner of things and you can 'send' as many as you like, all in a safe environment. But what I found was, my first letters were not totally honest, they were mild and as most were addressed to Kane, it became apparent that I still carried a lot of fear for him. I was too afraid to say what I really felt, thinking he'd come and find me and punish me, it was like he still controlled me and if I'm honest, that is how it felt. So, after discussing my letters with Sanu, I would go away and have another go, and another, and maybe another until I was able to truly express my feelings. And the contrast between the first and last letters were incredible with the honesty starting to come through which meant I was making progress and unloading a pocket of my 'rucksack'. This was a very good feeling and over time it helped me gain a little confidence as I was saying exactly how I felt, leading to me feeling I was being honest with myself, which made me feel I had a little power and all in a safe environment and it was progress. The writing exercise is a tremendous tool, one I still use today which I have extended to writing poetry or drawing so if I am faced with any difficulties or uncertainties, which are far fewer these days, I sometimes turn to this exercise. It's a great tool, not to be underestimated as it can carry a lot of power. However, there was a topic where I struggled with any of the exercises, I couldn't make sense of it, nothing seemed to work, my mind simply shut down as if I was protecting my feelings and that subject was the terminations. Talking about this was a very tough time for me, whenever it arose in counselling sessions, the shame would envelop me. I would feel my cheeks flush with embarrassment and I would look at Sanu waiting for her reaction, anything that concurred with my feelings as I was sure she felt disgusted also. But that isn't what happened and it confused me. I wanted her to feel the same, to punish me, to tell me I should have known better, but she didn't. She calmly looked at me, made no judgement and sought about helping me work through this. Sharing this with Sanu was a breakthrough as I was the only one who knew, it was my dirty secret so it was a bit of a relief. You may argue that Kane knew but his attitude at the time didn't scream anything about caring, did he even remember? It was a pure inconvenience, an inconvenience he didn't want which resulted in his abusing and bullying me into a decision, the thought of which makes me shudder. But with Sanu's non-judgemental professional approach, I started to try and talk about this very difficult subject. I was having difficulty remembering dates, places, details of each event, it was as if I had tried to wipe it all from my mind. I think they were definitely at the bottom of my 'rucksack' which would take a lot of digging to find. I still felt a wave of embarrassment every time we discussed it but I had to fight through this, I needed to find peace with myself in order to move forward so, with Sanu's help, I soldiered through it. My dreams started to heighten during these times until eventually I started remembering details, dates, locations, even what I was wearing, all of which I had blanked out, thrown in my 'rucksack', and once the details started emerging, I knew I had to start writing. This was very, very tough but I knew it was necessary in order for me to take my notes along to my next session with Sanu where we would discuss what I had written and explore my feelings around it. During these discussions I would try very hard, between all the tears and the feelings of remorse and embarrassment, to talk about the events, what happened, how they came about, Kane's behaviour and attitude and it was absolute hell but I knew it had to be done, I had to deal with these feelings, I had to rid them from my 'rucksack', find a way to move on. I simply couldn't carry them around forever due to the devastating impact it would have on my future and although at times I didn't want a future I knew I had to fight for it. I had to stop blaming myself. I had to understand the whole situation so I worked hard, I focused, I tried everything Sanu suggested, I read books she suggested, I wrote down everything that came to my mind whether in dreams, whilst having coffee, whilst at work. It was bloody tough but I started to see the light, just a small one, but it was there and I learnt a lot about the subconscious mind during these times. I really had no idea how powerful the subconscious mind could be and the affect it can have on your everyday life and for me, this was progress as I realised the impact my 'rucksack' was having. I started to understand that all the bad stuff I threw in my 'rucksack' was emerging in my behaviour, the emotions, the highs, the lows, these were the result of blocking everything out and I realised, blocking painful memories doesn't mean it gets rid of it, quite the opposite, it emerges in many other ways and I needed to understand this in order to work towards being comfortable with who I was and finding my happy place. It just so happens that around this time I began to adopt a very analytical attitude. I thought about everything I did, the way I did it, how I managed my day-to-day life, how I dressed, why I chose certain outfits and what I was trying to portray, how I ate, how I sat, how I spoke and I even remember one day analysing how I buttered a slice of bread. I think I was trying to find associations with my behaviour and my subconscious mind and although it was agonising, for me it was necessary even though I wore myself out both physically and mentally. But my constant thinking and asking myself why I did certain things in certain ways started to help me understand where my actions were rooted and I can see now, I absolutely needed this in order to grow. However, I extended this analysing to other people. I found myself watching other people's behaviour, what they said, how they spoke, trying to see beyond what was in front of me and what was really going on in their minds and how I could fix it. I think I was trying to justify my own analysing, like I wanted to prove that we all had issues, that I wasn't alone and maybe I found comfort in this. But, trying to fix others is simply a diversion, something I didn't realise at the time but something I had to go through as part of my learning and healing and I guess I was probably quite irritating to anyone who got trapped in my 'I'll fix you' phase. But, thankfully, with a lot of hard work, I got through this and came to understand that you can't fix others, that is down to them and pulled the focus back on myself.

One thing that hadn't eluded me was my eating disorder, however it had improved, I had it more under control which ran parallel with my healing. It seemed the stronger I got, the better it was so of course I analysed why and concluded that food, and how much I consumed, was something I could control and this disorder started when I had no control and it made sense. I do also think it was a form of self-abuse, stuffing so much food to the point of feeling sick and then taking laxatives is not a way to take care of yourself. But this type of abuse was better than some of the alternatives, you can hide bulimia, nobody can see it so nobody knows but despite all this, I was definitely improving, I was learning more and more about myself every day and I had started to grow a little confidence and self-respect and it felt good. Around this time, I met a new friend, her name was Helsey and she lived opposite me. She was a bit younger than me and quite beautiful, something I don't think she truly saw in herself but that aside, we hit it off. Helsey was married to a man quite a bit older than her and although not married for long, it would be safe to say there were cracks in the marriage, something she disclosed to me during some of our 'girl' times together. Helsey would often wander over to me and we would sit and chat and laugh together and it was nice to have a friend nearby. We would also occasionally go out together, either local or to Greenwich, maybe to eat, maybe just for a drink but wherever we went, I noticed the attention Helsey received from the gentlemen within our vicinity. They noticed her beauty but also her innocence, she really had no idea how beautiful she was, something a lot of men find attractive. However, this scenario was a challenge for me as I had always viewed fellow females as competition, particularly attractive ones, but to my surprise, I embraced it, I enjoyed what was happening more than Helsey did and I enjoyed even more that I did not feel inferior. It was a breakthrough for me, I was in a different place, I was feeling more secure about myself and I was moving on. Someone else who lived opposite was a man called Cyd, he lived in the flat above Helsey and her husband and I didn't actually know Cyd until he put a letter through my door asking me out. I was a little flattered, it seemed a very proper way of doing things which felt good so I accepted his invitation. We went to our local pub and joined some of Cyd's friends and both Cyd and his friends were interesting and good company so it turned out to be a nice evening. However, during the evening I learned that Cyd was seven years younger than me which, for me, was a first so I was a little uncertain about the age gap. But Cyd wanted to see me again so I decided to overlook the age gap and give it a go, after all he knew my age which didn't seem to be an obstacle so we started dating. We did some fun things, socialising, walks, holidays to Cornwall, it was nice and for me, different. Cyd knew I was in counselling but we didn't speak about it much, it didn't seem important, we just got on with things. He made me feel relaxed, made me see life a little differently but there was one big contrast with us, family. Cyd's parents lived on the Kent coast and he made regular visits to them, often staying for a weekend, it was just what they did as a family which was lovely but not the kind of thing my family did. I had still kept myself pretty distant from my family, not out of any kind of hate but simply because of where I lived and what I had been going through, I needed to stay away from Tilbury so I rarely ventured there. However, after meeting Cyd's parents a few times I started going to the coast with him, staying for weekends and although it was nice, I sometimes felt a little uncomfortable in their company. Looking back, it's easy to see how different Cyd and I were, our upbringings were very different, Cyd's father was what you might call middle-class, the children were university educated, all of which was alien to me and it was apparent that our families were also very different and although I don't feel totally responsible for my uncomfortable feelings with them, it didn't help that I still carried a number of insecurities which led to me feeling inferior when I was with them. But, that aside, we managed a two-year relationship and towards the end of that two years and whilst out shopping, Cyd stopped at a jewellery shop and asked me to select an engagement ring. I was shocked but also overjoyed and went on to select a beautiful dark blue sapphire ring surrounded with diamonds and when we got back home, we happily shared our good news. Everybody congratulated us and, of course, we made plans to see Cyd's parents as soon as we could but it wouldn't be for a couple of weeks as we had plans for the immediate weekend. Our plan was to visit some friends of mine, a work colleague and his wife, who were cooking for us at their home in London which I was looking forward to but, disaster struck. Now, I cannot recall the reason but Cyd and I had an almighty argument the day prior to our dinner date. He went home that day and although he only lived opposite, I did not see him for three days. I had to tell my friends what had happened and that we wouldn't be coming to see them to which they showed sympathy and wished me all the best. Then I had to tackle Cyd. I was worried, I needed to talk to him but from the look of his maisonette opposite, he wasn't home as no lights had appeared so I tried calling his mobile but it was off. Second day, exactly the same, third day same again by which time I was losing my mind so I managed to get the home number of his parents and in desperation I called them as it was the obvious place that he would go. Cyd's father answered the telephone and when I asked to speak to Cyd his response was 'I'll see if he wants to talk to you,' rather heartless I thought but Cyd did come to the telephone. I explained how worried I had been to which he responded, 'I'll be back home tomorrow, we'll talk then,' and deep down I knew it wasn't good. Cyd kept his word and came to see me once he had arrived home and as suspected, it wasn't the news I wanted to hear, the engagement was off, it was all over. My engagement to Cyd had lasted all of one week and all I remember when he told me was how different he was, how distant, how cold, it was like speaking to a different person and I knew from this it was definitely over. On reflection I believe Cyd's decision was the right one, we really weren't right for each other, we were just two people experiencing something different but beneath it all, we really were polar opposites. The evening Cyd told me I contacted a male friend of mine and told him what had happened. He told me I could stay with him for a night or two just to get away and the following day he came to collect me. But before we left, I went over to Cyd and gave him the ring back, he seemed upset but I didn't hang around long enough to find out, once the ring was handed over, I fled. My friend and I spent a couple of nights chatting and drinking wine but I felt I really had to go home, I couldn't hide forever, so I returned after two days and started to get my life back on track even though I was uncertain what that track was. So, in order to help, I decided to put to use some of my learning from counselling by analysing my feelings and writing everything down, keeping a log of all the positives and negatives which all helped me understand and eventually lead to my comeback, I had bounced back and was ready to move on. During my time with Cyd I had remained friends with Helsey and her husband and Helsey and I would still occasionally hang out together but by the time Cyd and I had separated, Helsey and her husband had also separated and Helsey was living back in London with her parents. So, with Helsey and I finding ourselves single, we took the obvious route and started to see a lot more of each other, socialising together as often as possible. I also still went out occasionally with Loci, he was still around, we talked on the phone a lot and occasionally met up and everything seemed good there. And as for my family and friends back in Tilbury, I spoke to my mother from time to time, she had settled somewhat and was with a new man whose name was Joe. I had met Joe and he seemed OK and she seemed content. However, my father seemed to be going through his own mid-life crisis, working in the local pub, socialising, drinking, everything except finding a permanent lady in his life. He just didn't seem interested in settling down but I personally believe he never stopped loving my mother and his own mid-life crisis was his way of dealing with it. As for Jet and Aline, I saw them if I paid a visit to Tilbury, I tried to do the rounds if I went there, saying hello to all and heading back home. I also included Astra, Jason and their twins Kylie and Kensa in my rounds, sometimes leaving them until last and often staying over. These were the people from Tilbury I spent the most time with, we would socialise together and go on trips with the twins together. They knew a lot about my life, not everything but enough, and whilst not always approving, they listened to my stories giving the odd bit of advice whilst either shaking their heads or laughing, or both, it could go any way but they were there and went through a lot of my life with me. Back in Sidcup, I had other acquaintances to socialise with including a couple of the Kent netball girls so socially I could keep myself busy whilst still working on my personal progress. And of course, Snoopy was still making appearances but I started to feel a shift in my feelings about this, maybe because my confidence had started growing but, whatever it was, I began to truly wake up to his behaviour.

Back in counselling, I had been seeing Sanu for over two years and it had been one hell of a ride but I didn't feel I could leave her until about six months later. I had been thinking about leaving for a few weeks but I didn't know how to suggest it to Sanu but when I did, she simply accepted that it was my decision and we commenced our exit strategy. It was difficult, when you've been in counselling with the same person for two and a half years discussing all manner of things about your life, they almost become your crutch so you have to work on going it alone and saying goodbye. It wasn't easy, I had placed more trust in Sanu than anyone I knew, she was the only person who knew everything about my life, the only person I had opened up to, the only person who had guided me, without judgement, allowing me to develop into the person I had become and although I was very grateful, Sanu explained that the real work came from me. It's a fact that you can be in counselling and learn very little but this can be because of a number of things, you don't really want to be there, you don't feel a connection with your counsellor, you don't listen, you don't put the work in or maybe the counsellor is simply not that good. For me, I had none of these issues which led to a very successful two and a half years and as good as Sanu was, she was right, the real work came from me and I have a great sense of pride about that. I remember my last session with Sanu, we said our goodbyes and I walked out of the counselling room, went over to my car, got in and drove home. It was a very surreal feeling, it was like a terrible loss but we had talked about what might happen, how I might feel so part of me was expecting this and I was prepared for these feelings. But I also knew that Sanu was still going to be around and if I relapsed in any way I could always go and see her which was a great comfort to me. That aside,

I felt pretty good, I had learnt so much, I had started to forgive myself and I was feeling so much better. I was ready for the next chapter of my life. I was thirty-three years old and had no idea what lay ahead but for the first time I felt like I had some idea who I was and I felt more in control of my destiny. So, who am I? Well, to sum it up, this had been quite an episode in my life with counselling being the best decision I had ever made. It had helped me start to establish who I was and what I wanted and had helped me start to see life differently and with more positivity. I found I was a better manager at work, I had more confidence and although it was all work in progress, I was a fighter and it felt good and I felt ready. So, I would say I was somewhere I wanted to be, someone who understood themselves more and someone who carried a lot of hope for the future. For now.

CHAPTER 8

Reverse Progress

Feeling good, feeling ready to go it alone and feeling much more knowledgeable about myself made me feel somewhat invincible. I had learnt so much, particularly in relation to Kane and felt I no longer blamed myself for some of the horrific incidences. I was learning to forgive myself, an absolute must in order to move on and although it was an ongoing process, I was ready to put the new me into practice. Helsey and I started socialising in Greenwich as, apart from her day job, she was a barmaid at a local pub called The Greenwich Inn so if Helsey was working, I would go to the pub and spend the evening there chatting with Helsey and various other people. If Helsey wasn't working we often went out together socialising in pubs in and around Greenwich, sometimes watching live bands, and I remember these times fondly, they were fun and I enjoyed Helsey's company. At some point, Helsey started dating the guy who managed The Greenwich Inn who seemed nice enough, albeit quite a bit older than her but she seemed happy and it just meant we spent more time at The Greenwich Inn which I had no problem with as I'd got to know a few people in there. It was during one of the evenings at The Greenwich Inn that some people came in late for a drink, I didn't know them but learnt during the evening that amongst them was a man called Kyron. Helsey had told me his name, also disclosing that he had a pub, also in Greenwich, which was known for live music. The pub was called The White Swan and was actually on Blackheath Hill and I had passed it many times but never frequented it so I had no idea what it was like. During the late evening Kyron and I started talking which I was rather happy about as I found him quite easy on the eye. I discovered he was originally from Cork, Southern Ireland but had been in London for approximately fifteen years, and after further conversation, we discovered that we both occasionally played squash. He then said he was staying for a lock-in at the pub and they were ordering Indian food and would I like to stay and join them. I politely declined as it was a school night and I had work in the morning but I said I would like it if we could have a game of squash to which he agreed and telephone numbers were exchanged. I think I did the obligatory wait a few days before I contacted him and when I did, I asked if he fancied that game of squash to which he agreed and a day and time was set. When that day arrived, I drove to Kyron's pub to collect him as it was on the way and we then made our way to the squash centre. We made polite conversation en route, it all seemed OK and when we arrived, we got ourselves ready and headed for the court. We had a great game, it was fun, he seemed polite and well-mannered and all in all it was a good afternoon. Eventually we made our way back to Kyron's pub, going via Greenwich town centre, passing all the bars and restaurants and as we passed a particular Chinese restaurant Kyron commented that it was very good and asked if I would like to go there. Now I don't know why I did this but my next move was to say I would rather stick to squash for now, even though I liked Kyron. I wanted to go but wanted to get to know him better which was a new approach for me but it felt right so we arranged another couple of squash games and in the meantime, I visited his pub with Helsey and listened to the live bands. The music was centred around rock bands, some good, some not so good but however the music turned out, it was usually a fun evening. I liked Kyron, he seemed fun and polite, always taking care of Helsey and I when we ventured to The White Swan so after our next game of squash and whilst on our way back through Greenwich, I decided to be brave and ask him if he fancied that Chinese meal. My theory was, he'd already asked me and I rejected the invitation so the likelihood of him asking me again was pretty low so I went for it and luckily, he said yes and it was just the answer I wanted to hear. We agreed that we would go that evening and arranged a time with the restaurant so I headed home feeling rather excited at the prospect of our meal together, I was quite looking forward to it. When the time came, I got myself ready paying particular attention to my appearance, made my way back to Kyron's pub, parked my car and had a drink with him before walking to the restaurant. It was a lovely evening, one of those calm late summer balmy nights and it couldn't have felt better and the meal didn't disappoint either. Kyron recommended some dishes as he had frequented this restaurant previously, he also recommended the wine which also did not disappoint. As we drank and chatted, Kyron shared information about his life back in Cork and I was mesmerised by his beautiful soft Southern Irish accent which he still possessed even though he had lived in London for several years. At the end of the evening Kyron managed to pay the bill without me knowing, it was a lovely gesture and my efforts to go Dutch were dismissed to which I expressed my thanks and stated that the next time would be on me. We left the restaurant and walked towards the Cutty Sark where we sat on a bench for a while talking and watching the people ramble by, it was perfect and so began my relationship with Kyron.

Not being certain at this stage about how far this relationship would go, I didn't mention it to too many people, in fact there were only a handful of people who knew and I was happy to keep it that way. Someone I was seeing soon was Loci as we had tickets for a Jasper Carrott evening so I decided I would probably share the news with him when we met. In the meantime, I spent some nights at Kyron's pub, enjoying the live music and enjoying the attention he gave me. It felt good to be with him and I was enjoying the whole situation. At this point in my life, I was working in Barking, I had left the oil company a few years previously as they had closed the Aldwych office and relocated to Milton Keynes. I now had a more senior role with a large reputable shipping company which involved managing bigger teams, attending lots of meetings and occasionally having to visit clients and overall, it was a good role which I mostly enjoyed. So, whilst at work one day I had a call from Loci which I guessed was about our evening out and as it was my birthday, maybe he wanted to send me good wishes. Well, he did, his first words were happy birthday which I thanked him for which was followed by some general chit-chat about work, we were in the same business which made work discussions easy, and a few general pleasantries, but then he took me by complete surprise. Loci said he had something to ask me and I encouraged him to continue not having the slightest idea what was coming and of all the things it could have been, 'will you marry me?' was not one of them. Thoughts of my Nigerian friend Luan came flooding back with my reaction being the same which was one word, 'pardon?' Thinking I hadn't heard him right, Loci then repeated the words, providing me with the confirmation I needed, followed by 'you don't have to give me an answer now, have a think about it.' Well, I had no idea how to respond so I just said I would think about it and we'd talk later but what he did say following the big question was, remember what a good life we could have. Loci travelled overseas for his business and indicated that it would be great if I joined him on these trips, I think he was selling this whole marriage idea but I must confess, I was a bit confused. You see, Loci and I had never even shared a kiss, yes, we'd had some great times together but I had never seen him on a romantic level and didn't really think he had seen me that way either so where had this come from, had I missed something? Clearly, I had but here I was in this situation which had to be dealt with. It developed further when I got home that evening, I had had a delivery, my neighbour had taken it in and knocked on my door when I arrived home. Well, I could hardly see my neighbour, he was hidden by the biggest bouquet of flowers I had ever seen, they must have been two to three foot long, I had never seen a bouquet like it and yes, they were from Loci. I thanked my neighbour and proceeded to call Loci to thank him and show my appreciation telling him how beautiful they were. Loci was pleased that I liked them and gently reminded me to think about his earlier question to which I agreed. Why? I don't know. Was I protecting Loci, not wanting to hurt his feelings, it felt uncomfortable but I had to find a way of dealing with this, I simply didn't want to marry Loci and I had to tell him. A few weeks passed and when we did speak, we skirted around the obvious, well I did, with Loci always seeming quite relaxed. And then the time came for us to finally meet, it was at the Jasper Carrott evening and we'd arranged to have a light bite before we went in which is the place where we met. We greeted each other and sat down to order. It was awkward, uncomfortable and there was definitely an elephant in the room, one I had to tackle so I proceeded to tell Loci I had recently met someone and it was going well, which was my way of telling him I didn't want to marry him. Loci's face was a mixture of emotions, he seemed quite perplexed and suddenly the situation felt a whole lot worse. I was not handling this very well, I didn't know how to, so I was happy to finish our food and head to the show but the irony of it all was, our show was a comedy and nothing about this evening felt funny. Well, there wasn't a lot of laughing from our corner and if there was, it seemed forced so I was glad when the show was over and we said our goodbyes. Loci went quiet for a little while after this incident and I chose to leave him alone, I think I was hiding a bit but I knew it was for the best. We did however pick up on our friendship again after a short while but it just never seemed the same, how could it? We eventually parted ways but not before Loci found a nice lady who he later married and I'm pleased to say, I was invited to the wedding. I have no idea where Loci is now, the communication between us eventually stopped which I guess was always going to happen following his marriage but wherever he is, I sincerely hope he is happy.

Meanwhile I was still enjoying my time with Kyron and started spending more and more time with him. His life was a little crazy which I think goes hand in hand with running a pub, it didn't run in line with my work time frame but somehow, we worked it out. Kyron could be quite charming and attentive, often making me feel special, it felt good and I really fell for him but I did have quite an obstacle to tackle. Kyron had two children from a previous relationship, a daughter aged four and a son aged six which was alien territory for me but something I was prepared to tackle. I met them one weekend when they came to stay with him, they seemed OK and I did my best to make them comfortable which was not easy as my experience with young children was limited but we seemed to work it out, I wanted to, for Kyron, I wanted him to feel comfortable also. So, having got over that hurdle, it felt good as we had made a huge stride in the right direction and then one evening in his pub Kyron spoke about how he liked to go back home to Cork at least four times a year and then in his beautiful Southern Irish accent he asked if I would like to go with him next time. I was beaming, this was getting even better, I'd never been to Southern Ireland and without hesitation, I said yes and soon after we started planning our trip. But just before we went and about six months into our relationship, I had a night out with Helsey celebrating her birthday and as it was at The Greenwich Inn the plan was to go back to Kyron's afterwards and stay there the night. By the time I got back his pub had already closed so I let myself in and went upstairs where I found Kyron in bed, I was somewhat giggly and gushing about what a great evening we had had but his response was cold, making a few derogatory comments which took me by surprise but what surprised me more was it continued in the morning which I was struggling to understand. What was this all about? Had something else happened I was unaware of? Whatever it was he distanced himself and made me feel quite uncomfortable and it took a few days for it to wear off. I was baffled, this was all new behaviour from him but I found myself not being able to address it, instead I made excuses and decided that he must have had something on his mind. We moved on from this but I started to notice a pattern emerging involving that useless emotion called jealousy. He didn't like me going out with friends too much, in fact, he didn't like me socialising with many people at all and if I did, he made it difficult, his jealousy emerging creating unpleasant arguments. But I was sure we could overcome this and battled through it as I truly felt I had fallen in love with Kyron and was prepared to work at it. We eventually went on our trip to Cork and what a beautiful place it is, I literally fell in love with Southern Ireland and the lovely hospitality of the Irish people and looked forward to many more trips. I met Kyron's family, they were great, his parents lived in a beautiful little village set in a very rural area right by the sea. It was really nice and I could see why Kyron felt the need to return as many times as he did. We had a lovely weekend there, albeit filled with late nights, drinking and singing, a very typical weekend in Ireland I guess, but it was fun. I must admit, I was exhausted when I got home, my god they can party which I guess answered how Kyron could run the pub and endure a lot of late nights which was something I struggled with from time to time. So, I had met the children and now the family, all displays of a relationship heading in the right direction but despite this, I was still battling Kyron's jealousy and I had also noticed he often displayed signs of real anger, seeming to love an argument, and we started to have many. These times often caused us to split up but we always got back together and at the times we rekindled our relationship I saw the Kyron I fell in love with, someone who was warm, attentive, caring, fun but this side I only really saw following a split and reunion. It was like he enjoyed making an effort to get me back, drawing me in, but could not keep up the persona long term. I figured Kyron must have something going on in his mind, something from his past that created the jealousy and anger but my mistake here was thinking I could fix him, after all, I knew enough on this subject, didn't I? Didn't I fix myself? So, I set about helping him not realising how damaging this would be to me. This process went on for almost two years, jealousy, arguing, fighting from time to time, oh yes, we had physical fights, splitting up, Kyron being sorry, getting back together yet despite it all, I was still convinced we could be good together. But the reality was, I was spiralling downwards both physically and mentally, I just didn't want to acknowledge it, I tried so hard to understand what was happening to us and more importantly, what was happening to me and pondered regularly on how I could put this right, all the time knowing that the signs were there and Kyron was tapping into my insecurities and reminding me of Kane. So why was I unable to leave this situation? I couldn't answer that question so I just focused on making things work, I wanted to be with Kyron, I even fantasised about being his wife, surely if we were married that would fix things, he would feel more secure and everything would be great. By this time, Kyron was living in a rented flat in Deptford, I was still in my Sidcup flat where Kyron had stayed for a while but left following one of our arguments. I remember being out one evening near Deptford and we agreed that I would stay with Kyron that evening as the venue was close by. It was a music bar and we left the flat in good spirits, heading off to meet a group of friends there. We arrived and all was well, we had a few drinks and laughed together, it was one of those times I felt good with Kyron. There was a dance floor at this venue where some of our group had ventured to and towards the end of the evening, I ended up dancing with a few of these friends whilst Kyron was at the bar, a place where the dance floor was not visible. We were all having a laugh and then one of the friends, a young male, just happened to dance in front of me, holding his hands out gesturing for me to dance with him. It was completely innocent but just as it happened, Kyron put his head around the door, caught sight of it and immediately left. I hurried out to find him but he had disappeared and I had no idea what to do. I was worried, I was stranded on the outskirts of Deptford alone with no idea how to get home, it was around midnight and fear started to engulf me. I had to do something so I started walking in a hope to find a taxi as I didn't really know where I was or where I was heading but I did know this situation was dangerous, a female alone after midnight in South East London was not a good position to be in. I passed groups of people, some staring, some commenting but I kept my head down and just kept going. The rest is vague but I must have somehow got a taxi and got back to Kyron's, much to my relief and all I could think was, I'm safe but all I found on my return was Kyron in a rage, jealousy once again had overtaken him and he was shouting at me and showing not just jealousy but also so much anger. He did not seem bothered about the situation he had left me in, that clearly wasn't important, the only thing important it seemed, was that he got his point across in order to ensure it didn't happen again. It was his way of controlling me, but my mind was elsewhere, all I could think was, I made it back safely, knowing I was very lucky that evening. I had become quite afraid of Kyron but despite this, I soldiered on, trying to fix everything, I was even changing myself in order to try and please Kyron. I was already ignoring people so they wouldn't talk to me, particularly men, and I was also changing the way I dressed, being more conservative and losing myself in the process without realising it. And then there were work events, business trips, these were such an issue. If I had to visit clients with a male colleague, I found myself treading on eggshells trying to find the right time to tell him, it became tiring and his reactions became frightening. I remember once coming home from a quiz event and being questioned about male colleagues and when I left the room I heard a glass ashtray smash against the wall. He had hurled it in anger but this time I didn't react even though I was scared and to my surprise he immediately apologised. Maybe my lack of reaction had worked, maybe that was the way forward and would be part of my strategy. This was all part of my fixing everything plan, finding things that worked and to be honest, it was exhausting and all I was doing was damaging myself more and more but the best was yet to come.

Today I understand exactly what was happening here, Kyron displayed narcissistic traits, the love-bombing was always followed by jealousy, control, anger and physical and mental abuse and despite me learning all about this in therapy, for some reason I wasn't handling my situation with Kyron well, I was simply falling back into the same situation I was in with Kane. It would take me a while to understand why, to fathom it all out but I knew I would, I just had to find a way to get there and not be one of those people simply jumping from one sadistic relationship to another. I knew I could burst that bubble, I knew better, I just failed to understand how difficult it might be so I soldiered on trusting my own ability and working towards my own personal goals.

Following one of our splits, Kyron had called me late one night claiming to miss me and asking if we could meet up which we did the following day. He was being absolutely delightful, we talked about our future, he was understanding, charming, something he had perfected, and I kept falling for it but when we got back together this time, I decided I wanted more. I was thirty-six years old and felt I needed to settle which I can see now was simply an age thing but at the time I felt I had to take action. I shared my thoughts with Kyron but I did it subtly and then one evening whilst having an Indian meal in Greenwich he asked me to marry him. I knew I had forced this somewhat and can see now that marrying was not on the top of Kyron's priorities but at the time it was for me, I was happy, I could settle and marrying would be the ultimate fix. We decided we should tell Kyron's children which happened about a week before the wedding. Kyron took them to one side and delivered the news which all happened at an afternoon gathering with some friends of mine. Kyron had been drinking, I think he needed some courage to tell them but when he delivered the news, they seemed to be OK with it and eventually the time came to head home having tackled that hurdle. I was driving so everyone got in the car and we started our journey. It was getting late and Kyron had let the children's mother know that we would be later than planned which she seemed to be OK with but when we arrived at their home nobody was there and Kyron was fuming. He kept trying to call her but to no avail and this just made the situation a whole lot worse but then he saw her strolling along the road with her new man and you could almost see the anger pouring from his veins. At this point everything happened rather quickly, Kyron rushed up to her new man and punched him and a fight ensued. I told the children to get back in the car as the fight worsened. Both men ended up on the floor and Kyron was absolutely crazy, nothing could stop him. Both the children's mother and I were trying to separate them but it was a task that was beyond us. Eventually it stopped and the children, their mother and her boyfriend went inside their flat whilst threatening to call the police. There was a lot of verbal exchanges from both sides and Kyron would not let go, his anger increasing to a degree I had never seen and it was frightening. And then it worsened as once they were all out of sight Kyron felt the need to cause more damage so in his rage, he proceeded to smash the lights of the boyfriend's car by kicking his feet into them. I somehow think he was enjoying this but I just stared in disbelief and then out of nowhere the police arrived. They grabbed Kyron and then came to ask me questions and once I explained what had happened, they told me to go home but Kyron would not be joining me, they were taking him to the station for questioning. They put him in the van and I could still hear him shouting whilst kicking the inside of the van, it was so surreal, what an earth was this all about? I went home and ran a hot bath and just lay there staring at the ceiling. We were due to marry that week, everything was booked. We had decided to tell nobody and had arranged for two witnesses and it was all going to happen at Lewisham registry office. We had also booked a week in Ireland immediately after the wedding and all I could think whilst laying in the hot water was, how on earth can I back out now? I didn't even know if I wanted to despite everything and all I could think was how messy this all was. Kyron finally came home early the following morning having received a warning and, as usual, was full of charm and apologies hoping that the wedding was still on. It was quite amazing the change in Kyron, you wouldn't believe it was the same person from the night before and I struggled to understand how someone could have such different personalities. But, that aside, I fell for his charm and said yes, I still wanted to get married so it went ahead despite me feeling so desperately let down and so angry with myself for being so weak. On the actual day of the wedding, I sent a letter to my mum, my dad and my best friend Astra explaining what I had done and upon arriving in Ireland Kyron told his parents. I did notice that Kyron was very hesitant to tell his family, something I didn't understand but once he did, there wasn't much reaction from them, it was all a bit strange but maybe that was their way. As for the honeymoon itself, it was a disaster from day one. Kyron wanted to go out drinking with his family all the time which didn't feel much like a honeymoon to me, I couldn't understand why he didn't want to spend time with me, just the two of us, and when I tried to address this, it led to a lot of arguing and fighting. I hated Kyron when he drank, it made his anger worse so trying to reason with him at these times was impossible and I just ended up feeling afraid and defeated and always backed down. I really didn't enjoy our honeymoon as it really wasn't what I was expecting but somehow, we got through the week and were all smiles on our return home. But beneath the smiles I felt very confused as it seemed marriage hadn't changed anything so I convinced myself it needed more time and that I could make it work, a statement I can now see not to be the answer. But why had nothing changed? I didn't understand why and I was either being very naive or ignoring my true feelings but that aside, I did feel marrying Kyron would patch things and calm him down, I even thought it would calm his jealousy but it seemed I was wrong on all counts. Despite it all, I continued to try and make it work. By the time we were married I had left my Sidcup flat and moved in with Kyron in Deptford. It wasn't easy leaving my Sidcup flat, I had had some interesting times there and grown quite a lot so it was a mixture of happy and sad emotions mixed with anticipation. I knew I was taking a chance in every way but still I did it, I just wanted to be with Kyron, my husband, a word I started to enjoy saying. Maybe that in itself spoke volumes, did I just want to be married, to have a husband, to be settled? It didn't feel like that but looking back I think it was part of it, something I can only see through my eyes of today.

Our married life continued in some sort of fashion, nothing changed really, we just muddled along in the only way we knew how, a little bit of fun, arguments, fighting and me trying to adjust to Kyron's jealousy. It was so unstable and unhealthy but I insisted on fighting for it, for some reason I couldn't give in and let it all go so I battled on. I guess it was the nice times that kept me going, and there were some amongst all the chaos and one I particularly remember was a really lovely trip to Ireland. We booked our trip incorporating flights and car hire, first flying into Knock, hiring a car, travelling down the west coast with stops on the way and eventually flying back from Cork. It was so, so beautiful, it's a stunning country and my love for Ireland grew and, on the whole, despite a few of Kyron's jealous tantrums, we had quite a good holiday. This was one of the better times, the ones that kept me going, the ones that convinced me things were improving but I always seemed to be bought back down to earth, realising I couldn't judge my marriage on the odd good time when the bad times continued to dominate. And following one of those bad times, I remember feeling so low and so beaten that I spoke to my friend Helsey. Helsey was aware of our situation, not everything but she knew our marriage was troubled and during our conversation I expressed my need to leave Kyron in order to save my sanity, I was ready, I needed to get away and it seemed Helsey had a solution. Helsey's father, who was also a good friend of mine, was living in a large three-bed house in Plumstead, it was the house Helsey grew up in but her father was now alone following Helsey's mother's departure to Canada and he said he was happy for me to rent a room from him. I thought about his offer, I was nervous, was I really going to do this? I wanted to, I needed to and eventually I accepted his offer. We discussed the terms including the rent, so now I had to make my move and one weekend, I believe it followed an argument, Kyron went out and I simply left Deptford and moved to Plumstead taking a huge sigh of relief with me. I knew I needed some space, some time to breathe and this was where I could do it and for the first time in a long while, I felt a little peace sweep over me. Kyron and I stayed in touch during my time in Plumstead, we talked, he charmed, promising all types of changes until, about six months into my time there we agreed to give it another shot, to have yet another attempt at our marriage. We decided on a new start and moved back to Sidcup in a very nice flat above some shops. Sidcup was a place I liked and I can honestly say I was glad to be back there, I preferred it to Deptford as it was just outside London but not too far that we couldn't make trips there. I loved the flat, it was very spacious and we both set about making it our home with Kyron attending to all the paintwork whilst I concentrated on the soft furnishings. It felt good but very quickly I learnt that it makes no difference where you move to, where you decide to start again, unless you address the core root of your problems, you simply take them with you and soon the chaos started to emerge once again. Nothing had changed and I was hanging by my last thread, I had made the wrong decision and was more upset with myself for falling for it again and realising the place does not make the marriage and following another big fight, I loaded up my car and left. I had no idea where I was going, so I did something I thought I would never do, I called my mother and her partner Joe, who had been living together for some time now, and asked if I could stay there until I found somewhere to live and fortunately, they agreed. I was beginning to feel like a nomad, like I had no base and the more I thought about it the more I realised I needed my own home so I decided to do something positive and buy myself a little place. My mother and Joe were still living in Kelvin Road, Tilbury, they had stayed in the house we all grew up in, so I decided to look close by, staying in the

Thurrock area. It wasn't my most comfortable decision, being back in the area wasn't something I ever planned but I simply couldn't afford London prices and I needed a home of my own. Knowing I would not live back in Tilbury I started my search in surrounding areas with Astra alongside me for support. Astra and I made it our mission to find somewhere but after viewing a couple of places I was made aware by an old friend of a ground floor, two-bedroom maisonette that was going up for sale in Horndon-on-the-Hill. Horndon is about a ten-minute drive from Tilbury which I felt was far enough for me to feel comfortable so after viewing the maisonette, loving it and agreeing the price the buying process began with me obtaining a 100 per cent mortgage as I had no savings, a luxury not afforded by anyone today but it was my absolute saviour as I really didn't want to rent, I needed a bit of stability and I felt my own home would provide that. I should mention at this point that just before I left Kyron and our Sidcup flat, and in an attempt to understand my situation, I did go back to counselling. It was strange, the sessions were different, I was different, I wasn't responding well but I didn't understand why. I saw Sanu again for about six months but discontinued it once I left Sidcup. I don't think it was wasted time, I think, in fact, it saved me from disaster as, following a particularly difficult session, I walked along the river bank in Greenwich and just wanted to jump in, never to be seen again. It was the easy answer, or was it? Of course not, it's actually the more difficult answer and, once again and thinking about my discussions with Sanu, I realised it was something I simply couldn't do so I made my way back to the car, passing Sanu and her colleague on the way where we exchanged pleasantries. At my next session with Sanu, she expressed how she felt concerned when we passed each other on that particular evening and that she had, in her words, been worried about me. I guess I must have been giving off a vibe that evening that Sanu had tapped into but her concern made me feel warm even though I felt embarrassed about my dark thoughts. All I could think was, what must Sanu think of me, allowing myself to end up in this situation? A thought I later realised was a sure sign that my insecurities were prevalent. After all, therapists are not there to judge, the only person judging me, was me.

I think on reflection, I wasn't responding well to therapy because I felt somewhat ashamed of the fact that I had to go back and I was struggling to get past this. I had spent so long with Sanu that I now felt I had failed not only myself but also her and I really struggled with the idea of failure. I can now see that failure is nothing to be ashamed of, it's simply part of life and helps us grow and as for Sanu, I could have easily shared my thoughts with her but deep in the back of my mind I was doing something very damaging. I was protecting Kyron, something that's easy now for me to confess to but it wasn't back then. I had lost control and I was being controlled by Kyron and buying my own place was one way I thought I could get a part of myself back. However, what was really needed was to address why I kept going back, why I felt the need to keep trying at this marriage, why I thought I could fix it even after many failed attempts. I had reverted to my method of survival, I had run when what I really needed was to find answers, to understand and I definitely wasn't there yet.

Back to my move. Once everything was finalised, I got my moving date and with great anticipation, waited for the day. This was the first place I had bought on my own and it felt great and once I had moved in, I freshened the place up, with help from my mother's partner Joe, and made it my home with the little money I had. There were things that would need updating in the future but for now I did what I could to make it comfortable, buying most of the furniture second hand from the sellers. I was thirty-eight years of age and although I was very happy with my decision to buy this property and give myself a home, Kyron was still on my mind and I had no idea why. It would appear I still had a lot of work to do on myself, made obvious when Kyron contacted me during the time I was buying my maisonette and me not handling it very well. In fact, he came to see me in Horndon once I'd moved in and then he came again, and again and sometimes I went to see him back in London and before I knew it, we were back on. We continued as we had previously, not much had changed except I had a base to run to when we argued, my escape. But then, one evening, I got a telephone call from Kyron saying he was in trouble and that he was going back home to Ireland and wasn't sure when he was coming back, he was basically fleeing. Him and his brother had got into an altercation in New Cross and had been arrested and released pending trial, it all sounded pretty bad and he said he didn't want to risk the consequences. My first words were 'well, what about our marriage?' I don't know why I said this but I didn't know what else to say and I certainly didn't know what to do. He said he would contact me once he arrived in Ireland and that he was going to stay with his parents, he also said he had his daughter with him, using her as a distraction. My emotions were out of control, what was I supposed to do with this news? I was so worried but all I could do was wait for his call to say he was safely home in Ireland before I made my next move. When that call came, Kyron said he had contacted a solicitor and taken advice and at this point he wasn't sure what he was going to do but would love it if I could go and see him, so I did. Crazy I know but I needed to see him, I needed to understand his intentions and upon meeting I think his intentions were confirmed. Kyron was not coming back to England. He didn't want to risk the repercussions of his actions that night in New Cross. We discussed this at length and touched on the subject of me moving to Ireland, he said it was something he would love to happen so, after much thought, I said I would. What a crazy decision, I can see that now but I thought it would solve everything, I thought we could make it work if we were in Kyron's homeland, I thought he would be more settled. I thought, I thought, I thought. However, a plan for the next few months was made and I went back to Ireland at weekends as much as I could, taking a few personal things with me each time. By this time Kyron had found a house to rent so I handed in my notice at work but made a wise decision about my maisonette. I decided to keep it and rent it out, something my gut was telling me to do and one of the few times I trusted it. Kyron's daughter had returned to England on an assisted flight following a two-week stay but Kyron's son was having some issues so it was decided between Kyron and his son's mother that it would be best if he lived in Ireland for a while. His son arrived in Ireland a few weeks before me so he was already settling in to his new life which just left me, it was my turn to settle into my new life.

Now, it's probably relevant at this point to mention Snoopy. He had made some appearances but I started to feel a bit stronger about tackling his unusual behaviour, probably more out of fear of Kyron's reaction if I'm honest but whatever it was, it was stirring in me. I remember the day I moved into my maisonette in Horndon and between two trips to collect items from my mothers, I had a 'welcome to your new home' card put through my door by hand and it was from Snoopy. Now, he knew I was moving but this made me feel a little uncomfortable. He didn't live far from me so I wondered if he'd been watching, driving by trying to catch me there, I really didn't know. However, I did catch him slowly driving by on many occasions after I moved in so my suspicions were confirmed but given his track record, this was not unusual for Snoopy. However, this gave me ammunition when I was faced with a situation that needed my reaction, and react I most definitely did. After I moved into Horndon and to make my journey to work easier, I used to drive to my friend's house who lived nearby, park my car at her house and together we would walk to the train station and travel together to work. My friend's name was Kaci, we had met at work when she came to join my team and very soon a friendship blossomed. So, on this particular day whilst Kaci and I were strolling back from the station on our way home, we heard a car violently beeping his horn and waving at us. The driver was a young man who opened his window shouting, 'someone is watching you, when you passed him, he ducked down beneath the steering wheel, he's parked back there' pointing to the end of a cul-de-sac. Kaci and I looked at each other, both thinking the same as Kaci already had the low-down on Snoopy and we found ourselves saying in unison, 'I bet it's him.' We thanked the young man and explained we thought we knew who it was and that we would just carry on walking. The next thing, the violent beeping started again but this time the young man was tailing a car, pointing and mouthing to us 'it's him' and sure enough it was Snoopy. Snoopy at this point knew he had been caught so he pulled over and got out of the car saying, 'can we talk?' Now, I have no idea what came over me but I erupted. I was shouting, swearing, bringing up all the times he had crept about over the years and appeared at inappropriate places and times. Oh yes, I was on a roll and I did not stop and all he kept saying was 'please can we talk?' I think my last words to Snoopy were 'just fuck off', and I didn't feel an ounce of guilt, in fact it felt good to stand up to him and taking all the madness with Kyron aside, I must have learnt something, maybe I was getting stronger after all. I wish I knew the young man who made this happen, he's a hero, he had no idea what Snoopy was like and had unknowingly exposed him and helped me face the situation and for that I will be forever grateful. So, with Snoopy exposed, was it now dealt with? Could I now rest easy? Of course not.

I remember leaving work, there were tears and laughter, I had been at this company for seven years so had made some good friends and acquaintances, however, it was time to go, time to move on. I spent my last night at my maisonette having already loaded up my car and the following day headed to my mother and Joe's house in Tilbury, leaving the maisonette to my new tenants. I stored my car in a friends' garage just around the corner from my mother's house and early the following morning went to pick it up and start my journey to Pembrokeshire where I would catch the ferry to Rosslare and then drive down to Cork. Kyron and his son were to meet me at Rosslare so I could follow them to Cork and to my new home. I must admit, I felt very anxious and very tearful on the journey over plus

I was dealing with a lot of opinions about this move. I understood those opinions, most people thought they understood my life, this was just who I was but of course it wasn't. There was so much more than what everyone could see on the surface but how would they know? I'd never given anything away, I'd lived a lie and opinions were based on what everyone saw and that was down to me. So, comments like 'give it three months and she'll be back', did hurt but I myself knew this was a possibility but I also knew it was for different reasons and that if I didn't do this I would never know if this would have worked and always wondered what might have been. I needed to test whether this was right, after all I loved Ireland and with Kyron being back home, surely this was it. My new town and new home were lovely, Cork, being such a beautiful county, made me feel excited but my love for it depleted somewhat once I'd settled and found work. You see, visiting somewhere is quite different from living there, it's all about fantasy versus reality and for me reality kicked in very fast. I was quite excited that I had landed myself a job but the excitement was short lived as Kyron did not show the same enthusiasm, I think he was jealous of my achievement but this would not be the first time I had experienced this kind of reaction to anything I achieved so I simply buried it and prepared myself to start work. My first day arrived, both Kyron and I were getting ready to leave the house for work when he commented on my chosen attire. I always took pride in my appearance but I must say, since knowing Kyron I had become much more conservative. He complained about everything, it was too fitted, too low, too short, too accessible, the list went on and on, and on this particular morning he found fault. My response was to ignore it, I always dressed smart, nothing like he was suggesting but I became very conscious and tried very hard to please Kyron which made me lose my way with fashion, I had no idea how to dress any more, nothing seemed to be right. However, on this particular morning I left the house in trousers and jacket and headed to my new job hoping that things would settle in time.

I got to know my work colleagues and got stuck into the job in hand and soon I was flying through the work. I mostly worked with females, there was only one male and overall, they were a nice team and helped me settle in. I continued my daily battle of trying to dress correctly for work and when discussing work at home, I always focused on the females knowing Kyron would question me more about the male colleague. I found myself battling every day but battle I would, I wanted this to work so I continued to compromise myself hoping that was the answer. I tried desperately to make Kyron happy again, refusing to accept I was fighting a losing battle. My step-son was another victim of his father's controlling, aggressive ways, he was thirteen and adored his father but Kyron, in my humble opinion, had no idea what a good parent meant. My step-son went through an awful lot whilst in Ireland and I found myself trying to look out for him. I felt so sorry for him and often wondered how his life would end up given the amount of mental and verbal abuse he was receiving. Then one evening an enormous argument erupted, the cause of which I cannot remember, but my step-son was being hit with the most horrific verbal abuse and he was literally sobbing his heart out in the kitchen. I really wanted to comfort him but I knew that would make matters worse so I just sat and watched and listened in horror. When it eventually stopped, my step-son was sent to bed and Kyron turned to me asking if I thought he had been too hard and if I thought he had handled it correctly. I risked it, I gave my opinion which I knew would not be what Kyron wanted to hear but he had asked me so I replied as diplomatically as possible. Bad move, he may have asked me but he only wanted me to agree with him so another argument ensued, sharply ending with Kyron saying, 'what do you know, you don't have kids?' That was a step too far for me. My opinion is, just because you're a parent doesn't mean you know how to be a good one and on the flip side, just because you're not a parent, doesn't mean you can't have a valid opinion about parenting. However, this was all irrelevant and I responded with 'never ask for my opinion on this subject again.' There was silence and all the time I remained in Ireland he never did. The fact is, I simply didn't say what Kyron wanted to hear and that's the problem with narcissists, they ask your opinion almost as a dare, challenging you to disagree, shooting you down if you do. And I dared to give an honest answer, suffering the consequences.

There were constant daily battles, from dress code to how much money I was spending to having an opinion to worrying about my step-son, it just went on and pressure was building. In the meantime, I had managed to secure a better job but this brought about a new barrage of questions about who I worked with, how many men etc. etc. so this on top of everything else was starting to break me. I just wanted this new life to work and was doing what I could to help but it seemed to be all in vain. I was so lonely I only knew the people I worked with and some of Kyron's family but I had no friends and quite frankly Kyron liked it that way. However, I had one outlet at this stage, it was an old friend from London I was still in touch with, unbeknown to Kyron. I don't think it would have mattered if they were male or female if Kyron had known, just the fact I had a friend would have been enough to trigger his insecurities but it just so happens they were male. I had met him through Helsey, they had worked together in Greenwich, his name was Don and a few years previously we had dated. I was so glad I had someone to chat to, Don became my outlet, my go-to, my release, he was a grown up, a professional man and he spoke sense. I used to speak to him when I was at work so Kyron didn't know, it just helped release the pressure and my god I needed that release. At the same time, I was having extreme problems with my tenants back in England, they had turned out to be the tenants from hell and my neighbours were contacting me asking that I take action. I did my best but it was quite difficult dealing with it from Ireland so this coupled with my life in Ireland led me to be very upset, confused, sad and lonely and I cried an awful lot. I didn't know what to do and spoke to Don about it at length and although never telling me what I should do,

Don was very helpful. Then, one day whilst in conversation with him he said if I ever decided to leave Kyron, I was welcome to go and stay with him for a couple of weeks just to relax and rethink my life. He was an ex-pat in Dubai so it seemed like a great offer and one I held on to. Shortly after this Astra and my cousin Jolene came to visit, it was lovely to see them, it was a little glimpse of normality but still difficult with Kyron around but the three of us did get away one evening without him and I explained the whole situation and my offer of going to Dubai. I'm not sure what they thought but I was just glad to tell them and to spend time with them, it made me feel a little better but soon they were on their way home and I was left with my thoughts. I was so sad, so unhappy and desperate to do something positive. I was trying to understand how I had allowed myself back into this place, surrounded yet again by abuse and narcissistic behaviour. The loneliness was heart-breaking. I wasn't allowed friends, I was constantly questioned about work colleagues, I was constantly accused of flirting, I had no control over any money and was questioned about shopping bills. It was one argument after another and physical fights, nothing had changed. And then came the moment, one argument too many, the straw that broke the camel's back and I knew I needed to take action.

Following my offer to go to Dubai, I started to wonder if it would be the best option but that would only be for a couple of weeks, my biggest problem was, if I did this, where would I live if I came back to the UK? I couldn't go back to my home until my tenants were gone and the issues with them were mounting which I was finding difficult to deal with from Ireland so if I could find somewhere to live my plan was to swiftly deal with the tenants and move back in. Whilst this was all running around in my mind, I started to fantasise about my escape plan, how I would do it, when I would do it and I even went as far as writing letters to Kyron and my step-son saying I could not do this anymore and I was going home. I kept these letters at work tucked in a drawer but looking back, I think they meant something, I don't think they were fantasy letters, I think they were real, I think I knew, I was just too frightened to admit it for fear of being found out. And then one day my work colleagues invited me out, I cannot remember the occasion but I agreed to go knowing the battle I was going to be faced with when I told Kyron. And, I wasn't wrong as that evening when I picked my moment to break the news, the inevitable happened. Kyron made all kinds of accusations from fancying someone to wanting to fuck someone to being a tart, it just went on and on and I could not stop crying. I was a complete and utter mess and I was broken and I knew I had hit rock bottom in Ireland. I remember getting in my car and driving to the beach and just standing there watching the waves trying to calm myself down but when I got back home it just continued. I eventually got to bed and tried to get some sleep all the time thinking about what I needed to do knowing I needed to do something. Morning came and Kyron got up for work and as he walked across the bedroom to the en suite shower, I shuddered and at that point I fucking hated him. I then got myself up and started getting ready for work waiting for Kyron to leave and as soon as he was gone and I was alone, I called a friend of mine in Kent, another one I had been talking to about the whole situation and her name was Nyve. To my relief Nyve said if I came home, I could stay with her until I got myself sorted and I cried but these were tears of relief as it felt like a life-line. But I had no money, Kyron had stopped me having any but Nyve threw me another life-line and offered to purchase my ticket back home to England. I thanked her, feeling more relief, and then I made my way to the office knowing I was a little earlier than usual with a plan running around in my head. I was crying when I got there and went straight to my drawer and took out the letters and any other personal items I had. Nobody was there so I tried to slip back out but as I left one of my colleagues was on her way in and could see that I was upset. She asked what was wrong and if she could help but I just shook my head, I couldn't speak, I was still crying, I just waved my hand, left and I drove home to an empty house deciding to seize the moment. I immediately called Nyve who made enquiries for me about the ferry home. I told her there was one the following morning from Cork which meant I would have to find accommodation for the night, or one that evening from Rosslare which was a three-hour drive. I spoke to Don in Dubai and told him my plans and he gave me the best piece of advice possible. He said, if you find somewhere to stay tonight and get the ferry from Cork in the morning the chances of you getting on that ferry after a night alone with time to calm down are pretty slim. However, if this is really what you want to do, drive to Rosslare now, get on that ferry and be home tonight. I listened, I knew Don was right so I immediately called Nyve and asked her to purchase the ticket from Rosslare. That part completed, I then got on with loading my car and by the time I'd finished, it was packed to the brim. I took everything I possibly could, everything I needed and only left two things hanging in the wardrobe, a coat and my wedding outfit, the latter being a message to Kyron. I then took the letters I had written and retrieved from my work drawer, placing Kyron's on the kitchen table and my step-son's on his pillow in his bedroom. And then I bolted. I was on my way home, emotions running high, tears, relief, fear, sadness, a whole myriad of emotions. I had survived approximately four months in Ireland and most of it was hell. I felt I had reversed all my hard work in therapy but I knew what I wanted, to turn it back to strength, I just didn't anticipate how long it would take. Safe to say, it was a very long, thoughtful and difficult journey home.

CHAPTER 9

The 'Rucksack' Revisited

In the unfortunate circumstances that you have been abused in some way, does it always leave you feeling like you're constantly battling or damaged, and do these feelings ever go away? Well, I don't think they do, you simply cannot erase events from your mind but what is key here is how you manage them following counselling and I can see now that even after all the counselling I had sat through, my misjudgement was that I walked away totally healed and never had to think about it again, my 'rucksack' was empty. But that was typically me and relating this to OCD, I had everything finalised, folded and boxed and put away forever. However, following my two-and-a-half-year stint in counselling what I failed to understand is, you simply cannot box memories and make them disappear, they remain and although your 'rucksack' may be metaphorically empty and you may have a better understanding of your life's events, the hard work remains. The question is, how do you keep that 'rucksack' empty?

There is no doubt about it, I had relapsed. I wasn't quite back in Kane's world but I was close, very close, I had allowed the toxicity back into my life. On the positive side, I hadn't forgotten all my learning, all my hard work and I understood the need to revisit this, a thought I held on to but in the meantime, I had a few things to sort out. On my return from Ireland, I was not in a good place, I couldn't get back into my maisonette, that had to be dealt with, I had tenants from hell who by now had stopped paying me rent, I was living with Nyve who so kindly said I could stay with her for free for as long as I needed, I was jobless and I was penniless, my only asset being my maisonette. By the time I got to Nyve's Kyron had so kindly cleared out our bank account, well almost, he left £4.30 in there, too generous. Nyve commented that at least I could buy myself a sandwich, ever the joker but it made us both chuckle, something I definitely needed. But she was right and that was the reality of it so my priority was to find myself a job, I needed some money so I set about seeking employment. In the meantime, about a month after being back in England, Kyron had enquired about my welfare and asked where I was living. Nyve was happy for me to tell him as he said he had something to send to me so I gave him the necessary information and shortly after a letter arrived. It didn't really say much, just that he was sorry I felt the need to leave as I did, blah, blah, blah and then he asked for a legal separation. I was a little bit shocked and upset but didn't really understand my reaction, why would that bother me? Maybe it felt final or that it was heading that way but whatever it was, I agreed and signed the separation papers. It was a step in the right direction but I later found out Kyron was thinking of having a house built and the legal separation was his way of simply protecting his assets. I guess there had to be something behind it, he was already planning his life without me but on reflection, he was probably doing me a favour as it helped me to start the disconnect process. So, back to my priority, I had to find a job and had contacted all the employment agencies I knew, giving them all my details hoping that they would come up with something. In the meantime, I went into pubs to see what vacancies they might have, bar work, waitressing, I didn't care what it was, I would have done anything and everything but before I had to go up that road, one of the agencies contacted me about a temporary contract in Dartford, office based and loosely connected to the shipping trade. I was very happy and I would make sure I got this role, I had to, I needed to and fortunately I did and I was back on the ladder and most importantly, I was earning. The contract for this role was approximately six months so during my time there I kept an eye out for permanent work in anticipation of the contract ending and sure enough, towards the end of my time there, I found something. I was delighted, I had a permanent job and discussions began about start dates etc. But, before I started my new job, I took up Don's offer and went to Dubai with Don getting the flight with his air miles as he knew I had very little money, which was very kind of him. I booked two weeks and from the minute I arrived I bloody loved Dubai and quickly got into a routine. Don was working so my routine involved the gym, the rooftop jacuzzi and swimming pool, a bit of walking and a bit of window shopping including the gold souks which were a wonderful sight. I simply amused myself soaking up the wonderful atmosphere with the only challenge being the heat. My god, it was hot, it was July which is not the hottest month but it was certainly hot enough for me and quite challenging at times. Don and I had dinner together in the evenings sharing our different stories and it felt good to just relax with a man who I could have a grown-up time with, no issues, no pressure, just a nice time and I think the whole experience did me good and when I returned home, I felt much better for having taken the trip which helped me prepare for my new job. The job was based in Tilbury, a supervisory role for a logistics company in their import department. I felt pretty confident about my role, it wasn't anything I hadn't done in previous roles and I was looking forward to it but I had one challenge, I had to find somewhere to live closer to this job as travelling to Tilbury from Nyve's home in Kent everyday did not inspire me. I knew it would only be for a few months as by that time I was confident my tenants would be gone so I first approached my mother and Joe. However, Joe took me aside explaining that my mother was due to have a knee replacement and it would be better if she recovered without any disturbances which I understood and looked for another source which fortunately came in the form of Kaci. Kaci lived in a three-bedroomed house with her mother in Basildon so she had a spare room and was happy to rent it to me so I snapped up the offer. I was very grateful and I thanked Kaci for helping me out and quickly set about packing up my stuff, leaving Nyve's, saying our farewells and heading to Kaci's thinking how fortunate I was to have these friends. I settled into Kaci's, staying there for a few months and I settled into my new job and, after a few months, I was able to access my own property but not without more issues and it became a very stressful time. Being the tenants from hell, they eventually fled, taking some of my items with them and owing me several months' rent. They had been so difficult to deal with, particularly the man who had moved in a little later, he actually frightened me and I discovered he had quite a reputation, and not a good one, so when he contacted me to ask to retrieve some items left in the garage, I had to think about how to deal with him. It seems he was quite the argumentative type with serious anger issues, a bully with an attitude and given that he knew where I lived, it took some thinking about what to do for the best and I decided I wasn't going to react or play to his behaviour which meant no arguing, something he would have been expecting as it seems this was all he knew. So, with my plan in place and a date and time agreed, he turned up and I greeted him cheerfully with a handshake and I could see immediately this made him uncomfortable. I then took him to the garage making polite conversation noticing his body language was that of a child which told me my plan was working. He then startled me by starting apologise for the mess the dog had made but I responded with, 'oh never mind, I've taken all the carpets up and found some nice floorboards which I'm thinking of sanding. What do you think of that idea?' He was shuffling from one foot to the other, no eye contact, with no idea how to respond. He wanted an argument, a scene and he was met with something completely different, something he simply didn't know how to handle. Strangely enough, he didn't hang around long, he grabbed a few things and quickly left and I think I can safely say my little plan worked as I never saw or heard from him or her again. Safe to say, my reverse psychology plan was a hit and I decided to put this all down to experience and focus on the positive which was, I had my property back and even though it was in a terrible mess I knew I could put this right and set about getting the bedroom and bathroom liveable, the two main rooms that would allow me to move back there. Fortunately, it didn't take long and before I knew it, these two rooms were completed and I moved back and started planning the other rooms. I was truly home and it felt good but I must say, I am forever grateful to Nyve for getting me home from Ireland, letting me live with her rent free and helping me get myself back on my feet, particularly financially. I am also forever grateful to Kaci who offered me a room at another time of need, not an easy thing to do but she did it without hesitation. Thanks to you both, your selfless acts helped me on my road to recovery.

So, I was settling back into my Horndon home, I was working, I was socialising a little but I decided it might be a good idea to start a new hobby. I thought about what I might like to do, spoke to a few people, ran a few ideas around my head and settled on golf mainly because of the social side attached to the sport, I thought I may make a few new friends. I didn't join a club, I just took a few lessons and messed around on a pay and play local golf course, just having a bit of fun. I met a few people and eventually started going to other courses which was great as it brought new experiences. I also hoped it would help improve my game as at this point, I wasn't the best and found it a really tough sport. But I worked at it, playing, taking lessons, playing, taking lessons, and eventually I improved, albeit slowly, and started playing a few competitions. I felt better about my performance but I don't think I ever really grasped the game of golf, I always felt like I wanted to run around the course or tell people to carry on chatting when I was teeing off, I hated the bloody silence. And the rules, so many and so much 'golf etiquette', maybe I just felt it was too restricting but it doesn't elude from the fact that it's a very, very tough sport and takes a lot of hard work and skill to reach a good level. But, my appreciation for pro golfers increased 1,000 per cent once I started playing, something I think only happens when you do play and experience the sport, it left me wondering how these pros do it, so skilful. At around the same time all this was happening, my cousin Jolene had come back into my life, she had been widowed some years previously and was single so we started spending time together. Jolene also took up golf and we would play the occasional game but mostly we would go out socialising. It was nice to have someone around who was my age and single who wanted to go out and have fun which is not easy when you're forty years of age. I think at this point I needed to have some fun and spend time void of any relationships so that's what I did whilst trying to concentrate on keeping my 'rucksack' empty. In the meantime, at my new job, I had a small team and everything seemed OK, my only concern was it was somewhat chaotic so my organising skills kicked in and I set about making improvements. Most of the employees were very young so there was a lot of teaching and guidance required which had its difficulties, particularly as there was a distinct lack of good senior management, one could say unprofessional, but it seemed to be perfectly acceptable in the organisation, something I really struggled with but I soldiered on. And then, out of the blue, Kyron contacted me, first by text and then he called. My heart was beating and my stomach churned, why was I feeling like this? I didn't know but the discussion went in the direction of him wanting to have another go at things and before I knew it, I went to visit him taking my proverbial 'rucksack' with me. It was a very strange feeling seeing him, I didn't quite feel the same and when I asked why he wanted to try again he said it was because he missed me and loved me. I didn't know what to believe as he had said this with no eye contact but I made a couple of more trips thinking I would find out and in a strange way, I did. On the last trip, what had become apparent was that Kyron wanted to come back to the UK so after much discussion we agreed that he would come back and live with me in Horndon. What was I doing? I felt like I used to feel with Kane, frightened, pressured and with no voice but I truly recognised it this time. And then, whilst out one evening on this last trip with some of Kyron's friends and family, I happened to meet one of the ladies from the group in the toilet. It was strange, it was like we both wanted to say something but couldn't so I started by talking about Kyron's return to the UK and then I ventured further by saying, 'do you think it's the right thing to do?' I was risking it, I didn't know this lady very well, she could have just said what I wanted to hear, she could have said something to Kyron but somehow, I knew she wouldn't and something told me to speak to her and when I did, her response made the cogs in my mind turn faster. I could tell she felt uneasy, she was fussing with the hand towel and couldn't make eye contact but when she spoke her words went something like this 'don't change your life for him, just don't.' She then asked me not to say anything about our conversation, her nerves showing as she left to join her husband and the rest of the group. I also went and joined them, acting like nothing had happened but holding on to the words I had just been fed. I flew back home the following day with everything in place for Kyron's return to the UK but I was very uncomfortable, it didn't feel right before those exchange of words which now had just added to the uncertainty so I had a choice, stand up for myself or fill my 'rucksack' up again. I slept on it, woke the next morning, sat on the edge of my bed and knew what I was going to do. I left it until the afternoon before I called Kyron and when I did, I felt terribly nervous. It was clear he frightened me just as Kane had but this time, I had a telephone and a country between us so I got brave and told him this was not what I wanted. I waited, waited for his reaction, the explosion, the abuse but it was not as I expected. Kyron kept calm, even though there was a distinct annoyance in his voice, and said the following, 'well, if that's how you feel, what can I do?' And there ended my five years in total with Kyron, three of those being married, and it felt good. I was happy, I chose to do what I wanted and I chose to keep that 'rucksack' empty. I thought about all my past learning, I took control and I immediately felt stronger. And as for 'those' words from the lady I bumped into in the toilet, what a woman. She knew Kyron's only intention was to get back to the UK and that I was a simple solution and she seemed to want to protect me from that. I know it took a lot for her to say what she said and she will never know how much she helped. I think she knew a lot more than she was prepared to say but she just said enough to assist me making my decision. And, of course, in the cold light of day, yes, I was an easy target, a meal ticket back to the UK. Imagine how that would have turned out.

During the following year and feeling so much better about myself, I decided I needed to earn some extra money in order to get some additional work done in my maisonette and to also have more disposable cash so I decided to take a second job and it was by sheer fluke this happened. I just happened to go to a pub in the next village which was run by some very old friends of my family who I hadn't seen for many years so after our initial greetings and catch up on families etc. it became apparent that there were vacancies for barmaids and I was asked if I was interested. Well, yes, I was, I almost bit their arm off and then everything happened very quickly and the following day, I did my first shift. That went quite well so we worked out a shift pattern which involved evenings and weekends and I quickly settled in, also enjoying the social life it brought. But, the social life aside, being a barmaid in a very busy pub is pretty hard work, especially if you're juggling it with your day job but I needed the money so I kept at it. It was a great pub to work in, the clientele being mostly polite and overall, it was a lot of fun and I was meeting all sorts of people, mostly locals, who were easy to have lots of laughter and banter with and even though I was working, it became my social life. I loved the fact it was busy as each shift flew by, especially at weekends when the clientele increased but it was fun and over time, I got to know the regulars. There were those who always wanted to share a little joke, those who drank exactly the same drink on exactly the same days at exactly the same time, those who always sat in the same seats or stood at the same part of the bar, those who enjoyed a little flirtatious fun, those who only drank in the back bar and those who were pain in the arse but overall, they were good clientele. So, yes, if you want to be a barmaid, be prepared, it's quite a rollercoaster but in the right establishment, bloody enjoyable and a way of earning extra cash and making friends.

Now, somewhere between marrying Kyron and coming home from Ireland, the Thurrock netball girls from the team Flight reconnected, we hadn't seen each other in many years and it was so nice to get together. Our first meet up was hilarious, we were all talking over each other, trying to let each other know what we had been up to, trying not to miss anything out. There was so much catching up to do but what was apparent, it was like we had never been apart, so many years and nothing had changed. Well, almost. What had changed, much to the amusement of the others is, I had become a social smoker, a habit adopted from Kyron and I had had my first tattoo! It created a lot of laughter but not in a malicious way, our relationship was such that we could all laugh at and with each other. This little group of friends has remained a five for some time now and we all meet up once a year to exchange stories of our lives. Fortunately, the smoking ended very quickly after leaving Kyron but the tattoos have increased, currently sporting five in various locations on my body and I love them, I'm quite a fan of tattoos. As for other friends and family, my cousin Jolene was still around, we were still socialising together and I still saw my friend Astra and her husband Jason and their twins Kylie and Kensa. I sometimes saw my sisters Jet and Aline but we weren't the sort of sisters who socialised together on a regular basis, in fact we still don't, mainly seeing each other at the odd family gathering and it was on these occasions that I usually saw the rest of my family. Jet, Aline and I ended up being siblings who don't really spend a lot of time together but try and be there for each other if needed and I guess that's OK and works for us. So, friends and family aside, the time came when I felt open to the idea of meeting someone and I guess as a single woman with a second job working as a barmaid, it wasn't going to be long before this happened, and it did about six months into working at the pub. The man in question was a local, his name was Bret and he lived just a stroll from the pub and was one of those customers who often chose the same end of the bar and, if available, the same bar stool and was usually accompanied by a group of friends. Bret and I had spoken and laughed a lot during the times I was working until one evening, he asked me back to his house for a late supper, I liked him so I said yes and it turned out to be a very pleasant evening. Over the next few weeks, I got to know Bret more, this wasn't a man like any other I had known, he wasn't controlling, jealous or narcissistic, he just seemed OK and not too difficult to be with. I saw this as a positive, perhaps I was thinking about my 'rucksack', about what I had learnt, what I had unloaded and perhaps I was learning to make better choices. I really hoped so but I knew I had to work at it and that for me became a very conscious effort. I discovered that Bret had been married for twenty plus years but the marriage had dissolved and the family house sold. He had married quite young, had three grown children and had been separated from his wife for about a year. I was around the age of forty-two when I met him and he was about forty-six and it quickly became apparent that Bret's life was nothing like anything I had experienced previously. He had his own engineering business and worked hard but he also knew how to play hard and had a circle of friends who adopted the same style of living thus creating a very full social life. Social events were weekly, starting on Thursday or Friday and more often than not finishing on Sunday and Bret's house was mostly where everyone congregated prior to going out and where everyone gathered up after a night out, it was the ultimate party house. Sometimes when I was working at the pub, I would finish my shift on a Friday or Saturday night, go to Bret's and join in the fun, meeting all his friends and their wives who all seemed very friendly and accepting of me into the crowd. I loved everything about it, it was a knew situation for me and I found myself embracing it, it was so much fun, very relaxed with no real pressure, just enjoyment, something I liked and quickly adapted to. As time passed and the more familiar Bret and I became, the more I liked him. To me he was what I liked to call a man of old-fashioned values and by that, I mean, he took responsibility, he took the lead, all firsts for me and he also made me feel protected, another first. He had this way of making me feel like I could just be me, no mask, no pretence and it all seemed so simple. As it was something I hadn't previously experienced I had to make a conscious effort to enjoy it, it simply didn't come naturally to me so I dug deep into my 'rucksack' and my counselling – searching for all the positives whilst telling myself it was OK to have fun. And yes, it started to work, I started to grow and my 'rucksack' started emptying all the leftovers from Kyron. It all seemed so good and I got totally engrossed in the lifestyle failing to see what was really going on. I guess I was a little blinded when, after I had been seeing Bret for about a year, a discussion took place about me moving in with him which I was very happy to do so, in fact, I didn't hesitate, it didn't seem to need much thought, I loved Bret and I loved my new life and living with him was the ultimate for me. So, once everything was agreed, I started the move and eventually left my apartment in Horndon but chose to be sensible and keep it and rent it again and soon I was settling in with Bret in his house, it just seemed perfect. In the meantime, I had found myself another job, I left the company in Tilbury and went to work for a bigger corporate company in Hainault, Essex, it was a longer journey but a much better job so, all in all, life was looking pretty good. Socially, it was all still very exciting, we continued to enjoy ourselves, with friends, at functions and we had some great holidays but there were times the lifestyle could be quite overwhelming and quite tiring so it wasn't long before I got involved with something I had never experienced before, the ultimate pick-me-up, cocaine. It was used quite a lot amongst the group of friends and it wasn't something I had experienced previously but it wasn't long before I joined the cocaine club. It's quite shocking how easily available this drug is and how many people use it but it's not until you experience it yourself that you realise all of this. I remember my first experience, we had been out with the usual crowd and one of the girls offered me some, I had no idea what to do but with a little guidance I went for it. It was strange, it gives you a complete rush of energy both physically and mentally but it does go straight to the part of your brain called 'bullshit'. You get wide eyed, very gobby, often talking complete bollocks, finding conversation easy and talking about things you would otherwise avoid. Then there's the constant sniffing, which would depend on the quality of the drug (you never knew what you were putting up your snout), the immense thirst and its ability to keep you awake which married nicely with the lifestyle as all-nighters were common and with cocaine, that's very easy to do. The downside is the comedown, it's very difficult to sleep if you've been on cocaine so getting back to some kind of normal feeling can be quite difficult, it's actually pretty dreadful and your nose feels like you have a bad attack of sinusitis. But it was rife amongst the crowd as it was with extended friends so weekends were pretty crazy and full on but something I did observe is how the dynamics of a crowd changed pre and post cocaine. You could be having a quiet, sensible night and then, boom, cocaine is introduced and it's like you're with a different group of people and its effects are immediate, a few sniffs and personalities quickly change. So, I joined in, it just seemed fun and maybe I felt a bit of peer pressure but I'm not blaming anyone, it was my choice and it just seemed easier to use it when amongst a crowd of users. You see, being surrounded by cocaine users and choosing not to do it yourself is a very difficult situation to be in, you're just not on their level because their level isn't real anymore and all the intense bullshit discussions and laughter that takes place, most of which will be forgotten in the cold light of day, seems so ridiculous to an observer not using. I guess for some it's a drug that takes you to a level you're unable to reach without it, freedom of the mind, fluidity of speech and maybe that's why some people become addicted, who knows, I'm no expert, this was just my observation. That aside, my life with Bret continued which became a pattern of work during the day, which started to involve more client visits thus more travel, my second job at the pub and socialising in between so it was pretty full on. Something I did notice was, although Bret and his wife were separated, it seemed there was still some strong ties which became apparent if she had any issues with her home, job, money etc. In such circumstances, Bret seemed to get involved with the resolutions which I found strange and failed to understand, after all, if you're separated, you're separated, don't you both then get on with your own lives, isn't that how it works? Apparently not, well, not in Bret's case and he never really had an answer if I tried to address this, he used to just shrug his shoulders. I never felt comfortable with this and I never accepted it which seemed to bring out an insecure emotion in me, resulting in me fighting for his attention. I didn't like this feeling but I didn't want to feel like second best even though, in reality, that's what I was and I was at a loss how to deal with it. On reflection I should have known what to do but that could only have happened if I felt more secure in myself and had an understanding of my own self-worth. But I'd gone a little backward in that department since my relationship with Kyron and was working hard, pulling on my counselling, searching in my 'rucksack', to get that back, but I wasn't quite there yet. I guess the positives were, I wasn't throwing my current situation into my 'rucksack', I was trying to deal with it but it wasn't necessarily in the best way. There were times I was very angry and unsettled and I needed some reassurance from Bret and in my hours of need, I desperately wanted some sort of commitment from Bret, we'd been together for a couple of years and I saw myself being with him but I wasn't getting the same feeling back. We talked about this until one day during one of these conversations he offered to buy me a commitment ring and all I could think was, what's a fucking commitment ring, something you buy someone when you can't commit to an engagement ring? I had never heard of such a thing and I felt somewhat insulted. But he had clearly thought about it, thinking this was the solution but I really wasn't interested and at this point I really started to wonder what was going on and thoughts ran through my head that he would end up back with his wife at some point, after all, he had never really let go and divorce did not seem to be on the cards. Then one day, rather out of the blue, we were dining with friends when Bret returned to the table from the toilet, got on one knee and proposed. The couple we were sitting with had just got engaged so I think, feeling a little under pressure and being fuelled with cocaine may have helped this happen. I can see this now but at the time I was delighted and accepted his proposal and the next day Bret took me to Lakeside to select an engagement ring. I was still a little shocked but very happy and after trying a few different designs I selected a beautiful square cut diamond ring. I remember walking away from the shop feeling happy but the words I used really said a lot about me and those words were 'I feel like I belong'. Now it's nice to feel like you belong but what I now believe to be very important is to know whether that belonging is a need or a want and for me it was definitely a need which looking back was not very healthy as you're relying on someone else to make you feel whole. So, me thinking this would make me feel whole, give me the security I desired, make me feel settled turned out not to be the case which led to more frustration enhanced by the fact that Bret seemed to want to keep our engagement quiet and not over-publicise it, particularly to his family. The alarm bells should have rung, why keep it so quiet? His children weren't told and his wife definitely wasn't even though they found out eventually but it was like our dirty little secret, it just didn't feel like the happiest engagement story and I guess I just wanted to feel special, but I didn't. This lack of feeling special opened up so many insecurities and my feelings and thoughts about Bret ending up back with his wife increased. I found myself getting very angry and upset and way too emotional at the slightest thing, screaming and shouting in order to get my point across which really showed only weakness. Bret was very single minded but I didn't want him to be, I wanted it to be 'us' but it really wasn't and I started to wonder if I was just a time filler for him. Had I caught Bret in his very own mid-life crisis, married young, three grown children, middle aged, decided to go have a life of his own until he decided to go back to his wife, not intending to meet anyone. I think it's so easy to know the answer to that now, I just wasn't quite sure at the time and I also refused to accept it creating confusion about our relationship because Bret wasn't a horrible man, not abusive in any way, physically or emotionally and in many ways, he looked after me which were all positives but still, I didn't feel I totally belonged. However, I did feel all the positives were good for me whilst I was getting back on track and revisiting my 'rucksack' following my marriage to Kyron, they were nice experiences and I felt they told me I was making wiser choices in relationships but on reflection I think my focus was probably on the fact that he was nothing like past relationships. I can see now I was focusing on comparisons rather than the relationship itself and because it felt better with Bret, that's where my focus was, only on the good stuff, but by not dealing with the unhealthy side, an emotional anger emerged. There were times during arguments where I would completely lose the plot and scream and shout, a behaviour I didn't like and one I look back on with great embarrassment and horror, but I simply didn't have the appropriate tools to deal with this, how could I feel like I belonged, how could I stop feeling like second best? I didn't have the answers but I definitely wasn't looking in the right place. It's easy for me to see this now and if I compared it to how I would deal with this today, well, I wouldn't have even made it to this point, I would have walked long before but it wasn't where I was and to get to that point, I needed to put some work in and that's what I set about doing. In the meantime, my current behaviour was doing no more than feeding Bret good enough reason to justify not completely settling down and I would most certainly have agreed except for the fact that I felt there was another reason, the hidden agenda, the return to his wife. Strangely enough, Bret did apply for a divorce, much to my surprise, to which his wife agreed and within a few months it was all settled but it didn't make me feel any different and I didn't understand why. It felt like an action to simply prove a point rather than one he really wanted to do, his behaviour spoke a thousand words, yes, he was divorced but no, nothing changed and the more I observed our situation the more insecure I felt. Strangely enough, things really started to fall apart after this and once again, I am not proud of the way I handled the arguments. We were still socialising and cocaine was still a big part of the group. We were not in a good place and we separated a couple of times for a short while only to end up back together with me thinking it would be so much better following a break. And, as with all breaks and returns, things are good for a while but unless you deal with the reasons you split and tackle the difficulties, the old demons will come creeping back, and they did. In the meantime, I started to get concerned about the amount of cocaine that was around which was heightened by the fact that, one evening, all the guys decided that they were going to have a break, news I welcomed even though I was a user myself, albeit on a much lesser level. However, once they'd all met up at Bret's and had a couple of drinks, I noticed the atmosphere was very different, things were much quieter, conversation didn't flow and as a spectator to this, I started to wonder if they could actually survive without it. Well, they couldn't and soon a phone call was made with the motorbike carrying the goodies arriving shortly after and it was like watching a group of children in a candy store. Within no time at all everything had changed, the laughter, the conversation and the bullshit ensued confirming my concerns about the necessity for the drug. Quite sad really, well that was my thought and as the evening progressed, I did notice that I started to resent the cocaine, the lifestyle and what I thought was real was suddenly very unreal which came to a head whilst on a skiing holiday, a holiday that would prove to be our last. We travelled to the ski resort by car, there were the usual crowd all spread over three vehicles, Bret being one of the drivers. It was a very long journey and we were all happy to finally get at our destination and set about unpacking and settling in. We skied for a couple of days which was OK but once the skiing was over, I noticed a pattern emerging which was, get ready for the evening, snort cocaine, go down to the bar for drinks and, if you were able, have dinner. You see, cocaine is a massive appetite suppressant so dinner was not always on the agenda. I have been out on many occasions for dinner when cocaine was being used and all you see is people pushing food around their plate, unable to consume anything and making frequent visits to the toilet more times than necessary, I know, I did it. Anyway, back to the holiday, I didn't like the pattern that was developing and with my increasing resentment to cocaine, needless to say, I expressed my feelings but not necessarily in an appropriate fashion which led to arguments. And Bret's response, he got a flight home leaving me with the rest of the party and given that Bret had driven to the resort, which was in France, it left me to do the drive back home which thankfully I was confident enough to do. So, I spent the rest of the week on my own making the most of the situation until eventually it was time to return and needless to say it was a long hard journey home helped by the fact that rest of the party travelled with me. When I got back, for me things were never the same, I realise my handling of situations wasn't the best but I don't think I can take the blame for everything even though I was always made to feel that way. Bret had his faults, he wasn't perfect, like most of us, but one of the things I found very difficult was his incredible stubbornness, it was nothing like I had ever experienced and nothing could break it. If Bret decided on something, nothing was going to change it hence not trying to encourage him to stay on the skiing holiday, his mind was made up and once that happened, I took a step back as any efforts to try and convince him of anything different would be pointless.

And so, we muddled along until, one day, I was faced with an unexpected opportunity at work. I was asked by my company if I would be interested in working as an implant for one of our customers who were based in Leicester which would mean staying in Leicester all week and coming home at weekends. I thought about this and rather fancied the idea so when I arrived home from work that day, I told Bret about this opportunity and what it entailed. Following a brief discussion there didn't seem to be any issues from Bret's side so the following day I confirmed to my company that I would take the post and started making preparations. If I'm honest, it probably came at a good time as I thought some time apart from Bret was probably what I needed and I think the same applied to him, we both needed some space and this opportunity provided that. I had a couple of interviews at the customer's premises to finalise everything and agreed to a term of approximately six months. It was also agreed that I could live in a short-term let rather than an hotel which I was very happy to do as hotel living for six months really wasn't something I favoured plus, a short-term let would be financially favourable to the company. So I set about finding somewhere to live and finally decided on a little studio apartment in Ashby-de-la-Zouch which was about twenty minutes from my new work location. It was owned by a family who had a large house with a garage to the side and the studio flat had been created utilising the space above the garage, it truly was like a grown-up Wendy house and I loved it. The family occupied the large house with the studio flat having a separate entrance which was ideal as it created some privacy so all I needed now was for my company to agree all the finances and write up the contracts and I would be good to go. Thankfully, this all happened very quickly so I didn't have to wait long before I could start planning my time away and set about making my new dwelling a home. I made a couple of trips to Leicester prior to my final move and then, about a week before my start date, I took one last trip, taking my clothes and some personal stuff. I now had everything I needed in Leicester and took my last trip the following Sunday meaning I could prepare myself for my first day on Monday. This all went well it was a good first day and it wasn't long before I started to settle and a routine quickly developed. I would rise very early Monday morning, leave home, travel to Leicester for a 9 am start, work all week in Leicester, travel back home Friday evening, have the weekend at home and start the whole process again every Monday morning. It wasn't easy but part of me enjoyed it, I was enjoying the experience, the new surroundings, the new people, the new challenge which included trying to create a social life whilst I was there. I started taking golf lessons, I took the odd trip to a local wine bar and I sometimes socialised with the family where I was staying but as time went on this whole arrangement started to become extremely tiring. Travelling up Monday morning and back Friday night was proving to be a nightmare, particularly with regards to traffic. I felt that during these early months, I spent more time on the M25 than I had ever experienced in my whole life and I started to hate it, so in order to relieve the nightmare of the traffic, on some occasions I would travel up Sunday evening and come back Saturday morning. It wasn't ideal and although I didn't do this all the time, when I did, it was a lot less stressful even though it meant spending less time back home. On a couple of occasions Bret came to stay with me, relieving me of the journey which was extremely welcomed, it felt like a nice break and we would spend time exploring the area and going out for a nice dinner, we somehow worked it out but it really wasn't without its difficulties. There were times, when I had decided to come home Saturday morning, that I would arrive home knowing there had been a gathering at Bret's on Friday evening which would really agitate me as I knew the previous night's antics would have included alcohol and cocaine, the latter being something I so wanted to move away from and I now so hated. My obvious agitation often caused an atmosphere which wasn't pleasant and not ideal if you're only home for a day or two but as Bret wasn't the type to argue I would calm myself down with a glass of wine and maybe a line of cocaine, not ideal I know and so hypocritical. So, although my use of cocaine had lessened enormously, at times I felt the need to take part in an effort to be on Bret's level which simply created an unreal situation enabling us to avoid reality and the inevitable. The distance between Bret and I was growing, I knew it but tried to carry on, feeling like I didn't want to give in, that I could make this work, it just needed a little adjustment, but you can't do the adjusting alone, it takes two to make a relationship work and more importantly, both people have to want it to work. I know I didn't always handle things in the best way and I am not proud of some of my reactions but Bret, with his stubborn nature, often showed no give in many situations so fitting into his world seemed necessary. With my frustration growing, this wonderful life I thought I had found was quickly being replaced with harsh reality. But then, during my stay in Leicester, the company asked me to travel to Bangkok for a business trip which I was delighted to accept, firstly for the great experience and secondly for some space from Bret. It was a wonderful opportunity, I had never travelled to the Far East before and as the company sent us business class, it made the whole experience even better. Personally, I think Bangkok is a wonderful place, it's a fascinating city, full of vibrancy and warmth and it has the most beautiful temples. I really enjoyed it there but more from a personal level than a business one and although I was only there for about nine or ten days, I felt very relaxed and had no issues with jet lag, I just seemed to melt into the place. This trip was quickly followed by another but this time the destination was Hong Kong which was quite a contrast to Bangkok. I found Hong Kong a little crazy, very busy but in a different way, I didn't feel relaxed and had terrible trouble with jet lag so trying to keep tiredness at bay was somewhat difficult. Both these trips were great experiences but for me, business travel is not as glamorous as it may seem as in between the travel, the jet lag, the business dinners and the overall adjustment, you still have to go to the local office and work and that can be quite challenging, particularly with short trips. However, these trips did give me the opportunity to reflect further on my situation back home.

Soon, my time in Leicester came to an end and I was back home but things hadn't improved a great deal. The arguments intensified and soon we drifted to the point where we were just living separate lives and it was hell. I talked to a friend about our situation, a friend who happened to have a house in Spain and during our conversation she took sympathy and asked if I wanted to take a holiday and if I did, I could use her Spanish home. This seemed like a good idea so I took her up on the offer, booked time off from work and booked the flights and it wasn't long before the time came for me to go. I hadn't spoken to Bret about this, I didn't think it mattered given our separate living so while he was at work, I packed, waited for the taxi and left a note letting him know where I was going. I explained in the note that I needed some space to think about my future which I thought he would understand but he didn't take too kindly to this and sent me a torrent of messages resulting in him saying my clothes would be in black bags in the garden when I returned, effectively kicking me out. I panicked and started thinking about what I was going to do, I needed to stay somewhere for a short period until I could return to my own maisonette but where? There were a few further unpleasant exchange of messages but all I could do was think about putting a plan together, secretly hoping Bret would not follow through on his threats. The days waiting for my return home were hell and I got very angry about the whole situation asking myself how I ever ended up in yet another bad situation and what I was going to do. Well, the answer came when I eventually arrived home. It was a very tense situation. I was angry. I felt emotional. I felt sad. I felt relieved at the fact that my clothes were not in black bags and what followed was all these pent-up emotions exploding like a bomb. I ranted uncontrollably, screaming, using language that was quite unnecessary which it seems the whole street heard and I went on and on trying to make my point. Bret just sat there, leaving the back door open which I think was his way of letting those that could hear know what a crazy lady I was and what he had to put up with, smart move on his part, obviously I was the problem and he was the good guy. I eventually calmed down and took myself for a drive returning a few hours later and allowing myself some much-needed sleep. The following day I was subjected to a few comments from neighbours and this plus my own thoughts and feelings cemented the fact that serious action was needed. This was not who I wanted to be, this was not what I was aiming for, I had to face facts, this was not working, I was not working and I couldn't live with being second best. I decided to write a letter to Bret saying my goodbyes and explaining that I had made arrangements to move back to my maisonette but just needed a few weeks in order to organise everything to which he agreed. Those few weeks were strange, we exchanged pleasantries and tolerated each other in a way we probably never had. But isn't that always the irony of such situations, I think at such times it's easy to be tolerant as you know it's not forever so you play act until the time to part comes. And that time came, and that was the end of that.

But not quite. We did meet up a couple of times but nothing had really changed and eventually I stated that we should stop this for good to which he agreed wholeheartedly. But let me just finish on this final note. Not long after that final farewell, guess who moved in with him? Oh yes, his ex-wife. It came as no surprise, deep down I always knew it would happen and even though it hurt a little I was happy for them. They clearly wanted to be together, so much so that they remarried, bought a form of camper van and went travelling around France, finally fulfilling their dream, something Bret had mentioned they had talked about many years previously. On reflection, I honestly believe that I did meet Bret during his mid-life crisis, I came along at a time he wanted to be free and single and I really shouldn't have been around. I can see a lot of things now which I take as positive because, although this didn't work, my learning was immense and even though I may have handled things badly, at least I didn't throw anything back in my 'rucksack'. I had revisited my 'rucksack' but not filled it up again but what was I taking with me? Well, the biggest lesson was, trust your gut, what you feel is normally right, it's rarely wrong and the other lesson, never force a relationship of any kind with anyone, be it of the romantic kind or a friendship, it'll tear you apart. If somebody wants you in their life, you will know, you will feel it, you will see it in their actions, you shouldn't have to fight for anyone, just let it go.

I feel like at this point in my story, and before I move on, I need to recap, take a look back, look at where I am now, what I have learnt and what kind of person I've become. So much has happened but has it all been worth it? It's hard to decipher why I was so shy, so introvert, so worried and so underconfident as a child, always feeling insecure and afraid to speak up. I'm not totally certain how this came about, I have a few ideas but one can't be certain but what I do know is, it set me up for a very difficult time. Sport without a doubt helped but that in itself created different problems, the need to win was necessary in order to eliminate the disgrace I felt if I didn't as failure was the worse feeling for me as failing meant I wouldn't be liked, all traits of insecurity. What I now know is failing is part of life, it's how we learn, in fact, I call it learning, if something doesn't work out as planned you take another look and have another go, it's how we progress. And the most important part, it doesn't matter what anyone else thinks, period. Now let's move on to the Kane years. My god, how do I expect anyone to understand those years? Well, the answer is, I don't, I'm not asking for anyone's understanding or sympathy and perhaps only those who have been there will get it but what I do hope is, for those who can relate, understand there can be a way out, a way to find yourself, relieve yourself of these narcissistic, gaslighting, abusive bullies who, by the way, you cannot help, please don't believe you can, you will only damage yourself trying. These types of people are wired differently, they're extremely nasty and evil and are experts at manipulation, they care about nobody, only seeing people as some form of supply and always having an ulterior motive. This master manipulator will do anything to get their needs met even if it hurts or scares their loved ones and will not be accountable for anything. They will blame shift, make you question yourself and lose yourself and will not feel any form of guilt or remorse as, getting you to your lowest point is their goal. And once you're there, the love-bombing starts and so the cycle begins once again. They are such sad, broken people with no understanding of why they behave this way but, know this, and as mentioned previously, you cannot fix them, you will just end up in a cycle of permanent abuse, be it physically or mentally, or both, carrying your own 'rucksack' around, dragging you down with its heavy load. I am a true believer that anyone finding themselves in this situation, whatever your gender, deserves better but the key is believing it, believing you're worth it, finding your self-esteem, learning to love yourself, unloading your 'rucksack'. As you now know, I did all this through counselling and beyond, taking many years of my life to recover, working hard to understand and grow but every second, minute, hour, day, week, month and year has been worth it and I say this with utter honesty, in fact, I don't think the growth ever stops and continuing to flourish becomes addictive, in the nicest way. I do however think that, once you've experienced such abuse, it does change you and we must be careful not to get bitter and allow this pain to rule us. My advice on this would be, forgive yourself, it wasn't your fault and talking of forgiveness, some say you should forgive your abuser in order to move on, I say bullshit, it's more important to forgive yourself as we can only make decisions in life based on the knowledge we have at that time, we didn't know any different but once we heal, we sure do know the difference and we can make much wiser choices. So, heal and move on and once you have, you will never look back. And one final note from me, I do sometimes wonder if my decision not to have children post Kane came not just from believing I wasn't mentally stable enough to bring a child into this world but also from a feeling that somewhere deep down I didn't deserve them, maybe that's something that sits in my 'rucksack' and will remain. But, I'm not unhappy that I don't have children, I have lots of nieces, nephews and great nieces and nephews that I get joy from seeing grow, I hope they know this, they often bring a little bit of pleasure for me even if it is mostly through social media.

So, let's briefly recap on Heath. Heath was not a difficult man nor was he a bully or nasty in fact, he was quite a gentleman and treated me very well. The problem here was, I ran to him thinking I could leave the past behind but as mentioned previously, it doesn't work like that (if only), your mind goes with you as do all your memories and if those are not good, the chances of you recovering are probably pretty slim. It's quite sad looking back as Heath and I had a good life and I loved where we lived, I just failed to understand the impact my previous life would have on me and us as a couple with me realising eventually that I had to heal myself. I would never wish anything bad in Heath, I think it was just wrong place, wrong time.

And then there was Kyron, the testing years as I like to call them. Counselling ends, I'm on my own and believe I'm fixed so I'm now going to put it all into practice. Well, that didn't happen, it's simply not how it works, the learning continues and it's a struggle but however tough it got, I continued to learn, I never allowed my mind to stop, I pulled on all my resources and eventually came through and I dealt with Kyron quicker than I did with Kane which I saw as a bonus. I felt I was moving forward, albeit slowly, but it was definitely forward and I recognised the need to continue to work on myself if I wanted results, a bit like anything in life, I guess. Yes, I slipped but no, I didn't give up, I never wanted to.

And now, on to Bret. By now I was in a better place, I had moved through my years with Kyron and come out the other side stronger than ever and found a man who wasn't controlling but what I lacked was the ability to know how to voice my opinion. Yes, I felt able to speak up but the downside, I had no idea how to do this and I made a bit of a mess of it. I also refused to see what was right in front of me but when I did, I actually felt relieved and stopped trying to force it to work. So, what did I take from this relationship? Well, as mentioned previously, always trust your gut, it's like your guardian angel, it looks after you if you listen to it. The other thing is, never make a decision based on emotion, in fact, hold fire on anything when you're emotional, always sleep on it, it will seem very different the following morning and your reaction will reflect this, you won't regret it.

As for friends and family, my relationship with my family remains the same, my father by now had been moved to a pensioners' flat following the death of his mother, her house was too big for him to live in alone so the council moved him but he has a lovely little flat and he seems happy. My mother was still with Joe and had been for some years, I wouldn't say it was the easiest of relationships but somehow, they muddled through. I saw Aline and Jet from time to time, usually if I was doing the rounds, our relationship remains the same, don't see each other much but there if needed. I did have a lovely relationship with one of my great nieces, she used to come stay with me some weekends where we'd have fun at home or go to dinner to an Indian restaurant or go shopping (which was our favourite thing), or go to a fun park, they were good times but, of course, they grow up and move on. I often wonder if that's what having children is like, they're there, they grow, they move on to their own lives, I don't know but I guess this is the closest I came to it. And then there's Astra and her family. Well, at this point Astra and I had had a fall out, it was all about something and nothing and happened when I was with Bret but more of that later. I wasn't seeing much of my cousin Jolene, we had gone our separate ways, our lives had moved on but we still spoke from time to time. And as for my netball friends from Flight back in Thurrock, once we reconnected, we continued to meet up once a year which has been a lovely experience and has created some fun memories. I still have a couple of friends from Kent netball who I keep in touch with, mainly Nyve who I am still very good friends with. And then there's Helsey who is settled with her family on the Kent coast but who I do my best to keep in touch with.

And it wouldn't be a complete recap without mentioning our dear friend Snoopy. Oh yes, still around, still driving slowly past my maisonette in Horndon, glaring through the lounge window, which happened to face the through road, going around the block and returning minutes later and sometimes making this trip three or four times. What a moron, what an idiot, what a persistent asshole, and that's being kind but by now I had contacted the police and explained everything including the time he got caught hiding and my outburst in the street. The police suggested I keep a log of every time I saw him, day, date, time, car reg, which I did, even noticing when he had a new car which wasn't difficult as I could see his face glaring in, he gave himself away so I logged the new car details and kept this log running for many months. The problem was, during the times he stalked me, stalking wasn't a crime as such, the stalker had to do something to you before they could be arrested but I do believe this has since changed and rightly so in my opinion as it's a very unsettling experience and harassment with a restraining order should be the very least charge. But, on the bright side, I had no remorse whatsoever contacting the police and no remorse naming and shaming him and in doing so I knew I had come a long way. I would never have done this ten years previously but now I was looking out for me, understanding when to stand up for myself and my god it felt good.

In finishing this chapter, I can say with great confidence that my years with Kane had to be the worse of my entire life but with a lot of courage, hard work, self-love and the incredible want to understand and find myself,

I am at a point where I feel more comfortable with myself than I ever have. Yes, I have to revisit my 'rucksack' occasionally and yes, it has been quite a journey, a tough journey but hand on heart, a worthwhile one, and one I don't believe will ever end as I still have remnants of my past that I work on, one being my eating disorder. My association with food is far better than it's ever been, I eat much healthier than I ever have but on the odd occasion I slip and if this happens, I try to associate it with what's going on in my life which helps me understand and hopefully eliminate a repeat performance. I use this method with a lot of things, it's something I have learnt and it helps tremendously, I'm not afraid to ask myself awkward questions which I now see as very healthy. My tidiness has remained but this really doesn't bother me, I'm more relaxed than I used to be about it and I really enjoy being tidy so for me this is not an issue. Yes, I'm a bit of a tidy freak but nowadays it's for different reasons, it helps me remember where I've put things!

So, this is where I am at this point in my life. I had no idea what lay ahead, in fact none of us do, but I felt better equipped mentally than I ever had. It took a long time to get to this point but it was worth the journey, a journey I continue to this day as self-improvement has become a way of life. A life I thoroughly enjoy.

CHAPTER 10

Loving and Losing

I had come to the conclusion that, maybe I should stay on my own for a while, relax a little, no interferences, except those that are unavoidable, like work. I was still playing golf here and there but one decision I made at this time was to join a local club so I could hopefully meet some lady golfers and even play the odd competition. I looked around and concluded that a club in Stanford-le-Hope which was only a few minutes away from me would be ideal so I went along and made some enquiries. The people I met were pleasant enough, they explained everything like, when the ladies played, when the competitions were, what the clubhouse had to offer, when they had their presentation dinners and so on. I met a couple of the lady golfers, had a chat with them, they seemed OK so I made the decision to join. Running alongside this I was also a member of a local gym which I tried to attend as often as possible. It wasn't just the gym I enjoyed but the classes, I loved aerobics and step classes which were the big thing around this time, in fact, I had been doing both for many years, particularly after retiring from netball as I had always attempted to keep myself fit and healthy. So, I had a few things in place to keep me occupied after work and at weekends and hopefully, golf would help enhance my social life.

I was doing OK at work, still located in Hainault, climbing the ladder, slowly, but heading in the right direction. It's strange but I was often described as a career girl, a term I actually hate because I wasn't, but I can't help thinking that not having children probably encouraged this term, believing I chose work over family. Well, now you know, that wasn't how it was, I worked hard because I had to, I needed to earn a fair wage in order to survive and enjoy better things. And, at work, I had to apply myself as best I could so I gave myself promotion chances or the chance to earn good bonuses for my achievements. It wasn't easy, I wasn't well educated and I often struggled but the one thing that helped was counselling, the more I understood myself, the more I believed in myself and the more I forgave myself, the more I loved myself which led to me having more confidence. This confidence and self-love gave me the ability to not be afraid, to feel comfortable asking questions about things I never understood and it also made me a very good people manager. I became good at reading people, finding their passion, using individual skills and not treating them like robots which unfortunately is common in big corporate companies which, in my opinion, creates a lack of commitment. My belief is, you're only as good as the people that work for you, so treat them accordingly. I listened to all my staff, I had empathy and I knew how to make them feel part of a team, part of something we had all created but it was hard battling against what I believed and what was expected and even harder dealing with intercompany politics. I was too honest for that shit but had to bow down at times and keep quiet as too much voicing of opinions could lead to trouble, after all, you really are just a number and replaceable at any time. However, love it or loathe it, I did my best, embracing the fact that I had come a long way and was happy with my personal growth and my growth as a manager, and I hung on to that.

I found work quite stressful at times but what I did know is, exercise is a great stress reliever, believe it folks, it's true. When you've had a tough day, particularly mentally, and you go do some exercise, it releases all those 'feel good' hormones which automatically make you feel better. You also get a sense of achievement and self-discipline and that you're doing something good for yourself, which can't be bad. I know this helped me get through a lot of bad times in the past, even if I didn't always realise it. These days I exercise out of choice, my choice, and for my own love of health and fitness and now I had added golf to my exercise plan, it was time to go along and make my first appearance at the golf club. I was a little nervous but I had to start somewhere and get all the 'firsts' out of the way, first arrival, first hello, first explanation of rules, first registering for a game, first analysing of my fellow golfers and the dreaded first tee! But I got through that and started playing the odd game and competition and soon got to know a few people and would often go into the bar afterwards for a drink where the male golfers also congregated. I did meet and chat with some of the male golfers and there were a couple who paid me attention but I really wasn't that interested. There was also one who enjoyed helping other golfers so I often took tips from him which I found useful but this led to me realising I needed some help so I decided to take lessons which overall, was a wise move. Sometimes I would play with both ladies and men and I must say, the men were more relaxed which made it more enjoyable. I didn't want things to be too stiff or too strict and whilst I appreciated the rules and regulations during competitions, when I played for fun, I liked to just enjoy myself which I found easier with the male players. Then one day, whilst having a late afternoon game with a golf friend from another club, just across from us on another tee was the male golfer who enjoyed helping others with their game. He was alone and was waving and gesturing to come and join us which we were more than happy with so he wandered over and the three of us continued our game. I had got to know this man during my times on the course and in the clubhouse, he was a nice man, very helpful, very polite, well-mannered, particularly with the women, but also knew how to handle himself with the men so all in all, he was very likeable. Our game finished and given that it was now early evening the discussion quickly turned to food as we began to check who did or didn't need to eat. My friend being diabetic had to decline and go home but suggested the two of us go and have something and after agreeing we were both ready for a bit of supper, we decided to go to one of my village pubs called The Bell. We had a drink first and started sharing things about our lives, what we did for work, age, where we were from, where we lived, all the standard stuff but the conversation rolled so easily that we forgot all about the food, we just enjoyed the moment. And when the time came for us to leave, we walked to the car park where he sheepishly and politely asked if he could kiss me and I felt utterly sure of my next move. I let him, and what a kisser he was. We decided to sit in his car for a while where we exchanged telephone numbers and went in for another kiss which felt like melted chocolate. I eventually went home thinking, that was unexpected but a rather nice unexpected, not something I was looking for but not something I wanted to deny myself either, it felt good, it felt different and I looked forward to our next liaison. We saw each other a lot at the golf club, we spent time together in the clubhouse and we played a lot together and quickly became the subject of discussion amongst other golfers. But he had manners and never spoke about 'us' to anyone, politely avoiding questions and jibes from fellow male golfers. And I did the same which wasn't any type of agreement between us, it's just how it happened. And when we didn't see each other at the golf club, we spoke on the telephone, long into the night hours, we also went on dates, a drink or a meal and I quickly realised that this was turning out to be a little bit special. So, more about my mystery man. He was forty-five years of age, two years my junior, he originated from Aberdeen, Scotland so had a wonderful Scottish accent even though he had lived in the South of England for approximately eighteen years, he had been married many years ago, was divorced, had a daughter resulting from that marriage who resided in Aberdeen and was around twenty years of age and he had been living alone for around seven years. He worked, he had been with his current company for about nine years, they were contractors for the Bank of England and dealt with the printing of money and he worked in the quality control department so all in all, he seemed a steady man. And his name … his name was Fraser.

Fraser and I became very close, very quickly, he seemed to be certain of what he wanted, giving me lots of attention and a warm feeling not previously experienced. I was completely myself with him, no pretence, no game playing, it was what you might call a very grown-up relationship. And there was a very important aspect to Fraser, one I never realised the importance of until I experienced it, I trusted him. It's such a wonderful feeling trusting your partner, and to share trust, it creates a very relaxed foundation, something I would urge anyone to search for in a relationship. Trust changes everything and, in my opinion, makes everything so much more relaxed, and happy. So, for us, there was no guessing games, in fact, there was no game playing at all, we were just two people who knew what we wanted, and it clearly showed. Fraser was very kind he would bring me little gifts and flowers and he quickly learnt that lilies were my favourite flower so my maisonette would often have a wonderful aroma thanks to Fraser. He also had a fun side and I remember him knocking at my door once, unexpectedly, standing there in full kilt ensemble, he looked great and I've always loved kilts but after this, I loved them even more. He also shared stories of his holidays, playing golf in Portugal and going twice a year to a small resort in Kos called Kefalos. He wanted to take me to Kefalos so we talked about planning a trip but we couldn't do it until he had returned from a holiday he already had booked there, so we would have to wait a while. He talked about his home town of Aberdeen and we talked about visiting there also and I felt we had so much to look forward to, he was a breath of fresh air. So, the time came for him to go off on his already booked holiday to Kefalos, he said he didn't want to leave me for two weeks so I encouraged him to just think about having a nice relaxed time and very soon the two weeks would come to an end. I took him to the airport where we said our goodbyes and, off he went not really looking like he was going on holiday but looking a little sombre. Once he was there, he called me every day mostly to tell me how much he missed me and that he wanted to come home. He was so serious that he said he was looking at flights and guess what, he found one and came back after about six days! I went to collect him from the airport and when he came through, I was very pleased to see him and he looked divine, white linen trousers, white linen shirt and a fedora style hat. Two things here, he always wore linen very well, it looked good on him whereas on me it just looked scruffy. And he always wore a hat extremely well, particularly the fedora style, in fact, it was Fraser who got me started on hats which I do enjoy wearing these days. So, he was back and it was great and our lives continued to grow together and by now we had been dating for three to four months. Sometimes we frequented The Bell, the pub where we had had our first date, which was always nice as it held fond memories. It was a nice relaxed pub most of the time and the food was good in the restaurant, albeit very nouvelle cuisine which I'm not a complete fan of, all overpriced and pretty and not enough. However, we booked to dine there one Saturday evening so we put on our glad rags and proceeded to walk there, this way Fraser could stay at mine (which he often did anyway) and we could both have a drink. It was a very pleasant evening, it was busy but had a nice mellow atmosphere but little did I know, very soon, that was about to change. We finished our main course and were chatting about all sorts of things when suddenly Fraser produced a small box and placed it on the table. I looked at him, he was smiling but, dare I say, nervously as he proceeded to say 'it's for you, open it.' I took the box, opened it and was greeted with a beautiful diamond ring of oval shape, quite unusual, which showed how well Fraser knew me, I was never the conventional type. I looked at him thinking, tell me it's what I'm imagining and he must have understood my need for reassurance as he confirmed very happily that it was an engagement ring and then he asked me to marry him. He looked so pleased with himself, as pleased as I was, and my eyes filled with tears as I put it on and said yes. I had to take myself to the ladies to freshen up and was confronted by some females who thought something was wrong and asked if I was OK. I told them everything was fine and they were happy tears and showed them the ring whilst relaying my story. They were very happy for me, congratulating me before leaving me alone to compose myself. Eventually I ventured back to my table and as I entered the restaurant several people began to applaud and for those that didn't, they quickly joined in when they realised what the celebration was. I have no idea who those ladies were, I had never met them before but they sure helped make it a special evening for which I am very grateful. And the look on Fraser's face, well that was something I'll never forget, he looked like he'd just conquered Ben Nevis. He loved me dearly, he knew what he wanted and was not afraid to show it, he made me feel comfortable, safe and he introduced me to trust and for that, I loved him.

So, there we were, engaged and planning our wedding. I telephoned my mother and told her the news, she said she was happy and I guess she was, I think maybe because I was no longer alone, I was safe and I was settled. News spread quickly but not necessarily from me, just word of mouth, I wasn't the type to go advertising my life, never have been, but it was often not necessary as once one person knew, everyone knew, that's just how it was. Fraser and I talked about what type of wedding we would want which was narrowed down to Kefalos in Kos or a traditional Scottish wedding somewhere like Gretna Green with bagpipes, kilts and probably haggis. In order for me to decide we booked a trip to Kefalos to see if I liked it, we went for two weeks and I fell in love with the place and it was during this trip I decided this was where I wanted to get married. We told both families of our plans and it turned out we were to be blessed with eleven guests, my mother and her partner Joe, my sister Jet and her husband, Fraser's sister and her husband and their two children, Fraser's brother and two of my very good friends from Kent netball days, one of them being Nyve. We had already visited one of our favourite restaurants whilst in Kefalos and planned the food based loosely on twelve guests so we weren't far out and we had also planned what church we wanted to get married in. Well, I say married 'in', in fact you are married outside the doors of the church, we were not allowed to marry inside the church due to Greek Orthodox religious beliefs, if you're not Greek Orthodox, you're outside. But that wasn't a problem and we had to respect their rules so just to make sure we covered everything and understood all the rules, we hired a wedding planner in Kefalos, someone with local knowledge, to guide us through the process. We also hired a translator as all documents required to get married had to be translated to the Greek language. So, all in all, we got everything organised during that trip and decided we would marry on 14 June 2010 when I was forty-nine years of age and Fraser forty-seven. I personally had to make one more trip to Kefalos before the wedding, I went in May 2010 to take all the translated documents and ensure we were all ready and that everything was in place.

So, the time came, we were to be married, we had travelled to Kefalos the week before as had our guests, all staying in two different hotels and on the day of the wedding, in order for me to be alone and get ready, Fraser took his wedding outfit and went to get ready at his brother's apartment. We had a minibus organised to take everyone to the church and I was being taken separately by the wedding planner. It was a beautiful little church, tucked away along a track, overlooking the sea, the guests went along before me with me following shortly after. We were married at 6 pm just as the sun began to set and it was still extremely hot, thirty-six degrees in fact, and as Fraser and his brother had worn full kilt outfit, they were very, very hot. Whereas I wore a long green satin halter neck dress, much lighter and more fitting for the weather but my love of kilts made me very happy that kilts had been chosen. Once we were married, which was conducted by the local mayor who looked like an older George Michael with no style, we all made our way to the restaurant and enjoyed great food, plenty of drinks and some live music. It was a really great day and night, everyone enjoyed themselves, Fraser in particular who at one point was dancing on the bar and if you understand what is worn under a kilt, you will know the dangers of a kilt flapping anywhere above eye level! It was fun and I was now a wife to a man who loved me dearly. We enjoyed the rest of our stay in Kefalos and arrived home as Mr and Mrs.

Married life was good, we enjoyed sharing our wedding memories with family and friends and we quickly settled into our new life. When not working, we both enjoyed shopping and eating out and sometimes strolled down to the local pub and, of course, Fraser enjoyed his golf and I the gym. I was still playing golf and sometimes we would go away to a golf and spa hotel for the weekend, these were fun times and something we both really enjoyed. We also enjoyed the odd dinner party with friends which was a new thing since becoming a couple, we both enjoyed them and, of course, we enjoyed our holidays, mostly frequenting Kefalos where we married. I had found a man who wasn't difficult to be with in most situations which is always a bonus. Fraser had manners, he could talk to people, he was comfortable holding court and he was very good at talking to a crowd as he sometimes did at the golf club presentation functions, it just seemed to come naturally to him and I loved it. Something I learnt to appreciate with Fraser was how he always made sure I was OK, he looked after me, checked on me but not in an oppressive controlling way, in a way that comes from love. But his whole behaviour was new to me and although I tried to just enjoy it, I had looked after myself for so many years I struggled to understand that I could rely on him, to let go a bit. I also discovered that I struggled with having someone who truly loved me, I had never experienced it and, if I'm honest, there were times when I fought it and was probably quite a challenge for Fraser. This whole relationship was the type I had always wanted but once I had it, I struggled to know what to do with it, it was quite frustrating and something I had to work on. And work on it I did as this was where I wanted to be and who I wanted to be with, I knew it was right and fortunately Fraser had the patience to deal with me and help me. Sometimes I had to dig deep to try and understand why I just couldn't relax into this relationship and enjoy it, which often entailed visiting my 'rucksack' in order to get to the root of my thoughts. This often helped, plus my years of counselling had taught me how to manage situations and taught me how to use coping mechanisms, I understood my dilemma, I just needed to work on solutions and I had the tools to do so. I did often wonder why I still carried certain issues and it always led me back to Kane, I think there were probably other factors prior to Kane but ultimately, the majority sat with him, well, that's how it felt. This made me wonder if there would ever be an end to my chaotic mind and whilst memories cannot be erased and I had dealt with the majority of my stuff, there always seemed to be something that would crop up and take me back which I then had to work on. Maybe that's just the result of being abused but whatever I had thrown at me, I worked on it, I knew how to, most of the time, and I didn't want my past standing in the way of my future. But anything I had to revisit, I took as learning, I tried not to see it as negative, only positive, this is the stage I had reached and one I felt comfortable with as I had come to believe that all life's experiences are sent to teach us something, and if we look, we will find the learning from it.

Before I move on, let's just catch up on a couple of things. My old nemesis, Snoopy, was still around, still driving past my home even after Fraser had moved in. Once, he drove past the Horndon maisonette when both Fraser and I were home and having noticed him, I told Fraser. Fraser suddenly dashed to his car to drive out and find him but was unsuccessful, maybe not a bad thing although, perhaps it would have stopped Snoopy, I don't know. And as for friends, the five netball girls from Flight remained very dear friends and, if possible, we would meet up and exchange and update stories of our lives, it was and still is very precious. And then there's Astra. As mentioned previously, Astra and I fell out and didn't exchange any communication for five years, I still spoke to her children Kylie and Kensa but the situation did, at times, make things awkward. Then one day, one of the children told me that neither her or her sister liked the fact that we didn't speak and so a plan was put in place for us to reunite. That plan didn't happen however, shortly after, when I was fifty, I celebrated at the local pub and right at the end of the evening Astra and Jason walked in. The ice was broken, I was so pleased to see them and they quickly joined in the celebrations and I'm pleased to say, our friendship was rekindled and we have remained friends ever since. I didn't see much of my cousin Jolene anymore, the odd phone call to see how we both were but I did see more of her elder sisters, Fraser and I used to share the odd function or dinner party with them. Anyway, let's carry on.

About three years into our marriage, Fraser and I were to be met with some challenges. The first was, my mother contracted cancer and whilst initially there was talk of an operation, it was later confirmed that the cancer had spread and it was terminal. We were also told that her life expectancy was approximately eighteen months which came as quite a shock to us all and created a bit of chaos. Tensions were high and as Jet and Aline had no contact with Joe, the pressure of helping Joe deal with this landed with me. I have to say this was very tough, I don't think Joe believed the diagnosis in fact, I know he didn't, but somehow, we all had to come to terms with it, there was no other answer, we couldn't change the inevitable. I think it's fair to say that people deal with such news in different ways, it's very personal and can depend on many things making it harder for some than others. The other challenge was, during this time, Fraser's father passed away, he had been unwell for some time with dementia, in fact, he barely knew me as he had the illness at the time Fraser and I met, which is rather sad. Fraser managed a trip back to Aberdeen to see his father before he passed away and then made the final trip to his funeral. I didn't join Fraser as there was too much going on back home and then, amongst all the sadness, Fraser and I were faced with a situation or one could say, an opportunity. The company I worked for in Hainault had some years previously been purchased by a larger shipping company, a very well-known one, and they had decided it was time to close the Hainault office and relocate to Felixstowe. I think the decision was prompted by the fact that the lease on Hainault was due to expire and as they already had an office in Felixstowe amalgamating everything rather than renewing the lease made sense. However, Hainault and Felixstowe are quite different locations so we were all given an option, take redundancy or relocate. There were many who would not relocate, they either simply didn't want to or they had too many commitments, family etc., which they didn't want to disrupt. Fraser and I had none of these so discussions began about whether I should take the redundancy and search for another job or whether we should relocate. I must say my boss at the time was encouraging me to relocate, assisting me with areas to possibly live which had to be between Felixstowe and Epping as Epping was the area Fraser's company resided. There were lots of discussion both at work and at home and eventually, after a lot of searching, I found a location we both liked and felt we could live if we were to take this opportunity. At this point we decided that the next stage would be to stay in our preferred area one evening and both do a test run to work the following morning which we arranged, staying at a little hotel in the high street of the village. That all went very well which shifted Fraser into favouring relocating but I still had reservations, although I wasn't sure what they were, and at this point I was still sitting on the proverbial fence. However, when I got back home later that day, I had an email detailing my relocation terms if this is what I chose to do and quite frankly, it was hard to refuse. It wasn't just the salary increase but the financial help with moving plus additional funds for white goods, curtains, blinds, carpets etc. and I had to admit, I probably wouldn't get another offer like this either professionally or personally so I joined Fraser on team relocate and everything went a little crazy after that. Once the decision was made, the first people I spoke to was my mother and Joe explaining what the opportunity was and that Fraser and I had decided to take it which meant we were relocating. That was a little tough considering the situation with my mother but I explained I would only be an hour away so would be around when needed. The truth is, having already been given some idea how long my mother would live, and even though one can never be certain, what we were certain of is, she was dying and none of us could do anything about it. I had to think long and hard about this and it was probably part of my initial hesitation but I couldn't miss this opportunity and wherever I was, I couldn't change the inevitable. I think Joe panicked a little, with me being his 'go to' person, I could see it in his face but I explained I would be at the end of a phone or around in person if really needed and, of course, I would visit as much as possible. With that step done, the next step was to sell the maisonette in Horndon and find a property in our new location which was Earls Colne in Colchester. We were fortunate enough to sell and buy very quickly and what was really nice was that our new home in Earls Colne would be ours in every sense, we would both own it, it was like a new start, a joint venture. During the whole buying and selling process I was travelling between Horndon, Hainault and Felixstowe, often staying in an hotel in Felixstowe in order to spend time at the new office for the set-up process. Hardly any of the Hainault staff came to Felixstowe, there were a few senior managers and two customer service managers, one of them being me, so we had a whole department of new employees, every one of them having to be trained, something I think was hugely underestimated by the powers that be. At this point I started to feel the pressure and it was bloody tough. There was pressure from all directions, buying and selling properties, moving, travelling, staying in hotels, training staff and establishing new teams, management pressure, trying to see my mother and trying to support Joe and yes, I started to feel myself crumble. I hadn't felt 100 per cent for some time but I ignored it, I had tingling in the ends of my fingers, dreadful pain in my right shoulder and terrible waves of utter fatigue which I put down to the fact that life was a little crazy right now. But eventually, I had to go to the doctor who referred me to BUPA in Brentwood as I had private health care with my company. The doctor at BUPA couldn't identify what the problem was so he referred me to a consultant in London and it was here that I discovered I had Systemic Lupus. Now I had no idea what that meant, I had heard the name Lupus but didn't know what it was, so as you can imagine, I overloaded on Google. It turns out it wasn't great news, it's a serious autoimmune disease, not curable but manageable with the right medication. I had to see my consultant a few times and undergo various tests and one operation before they decided what to do with me and there began the rollercoaster of finding the right medication, and it was hell. Fraser was very supportive but there was very little anyone could do, I just had to get on with everything that was going on, which I tried to do but was very unaware of what I was doing to myself. We eventually moved and settled into our new lives but I was getting more and more tired which no amount of sleep would alleviate. I carried on working, which I now know was a big mistake but being conscientious and having so much to do I felt I had to be there and by now the pressure was immense. A few months went by, life was great with Fraser in Earls Colne, we liked our new home and our new village but life at work was the toughest I had ever known and I still wasn't in the best of health despite starting some medication. The other issue was, my mother was deteriorating so I spoke to Joe more than I normally would as he was not holding up well. I remember the last time I visited my mother at her home, Joe and I had very severe words, we argued about my mother but she just sat on the sofa smiling, she had no idea what was going on, this was the stage she was at and I knew at this point she was nearing the end of her life. Joe called me on my way home after that visit, there were many tears and apologies from us both which I said was simply down to stress, we had to be strong and move on, and we did. Not long after this I felt like I was falling apart both physically and mentally, I did not know which way to turn and if I'm honest, I think I was on the verge of a breakdown. I had to do something, I was a mess so I decided to call my eldest sister Jet. I was crying whilst Jet was asking me what was wrong, I could hear the concern in her voice. I tried to explain through my tears everything about my diagnosis and everything else that was going on and asked for her help where Joe was concerned, I said I was falling apart. Jet hadn't spoken to Joe for many, many months, it may even have been years but I needed someone, I needed a little bit of pressure taken off of me so Jet said she would help. It was Mother's Day that Jet broke the ice and took a gift to my mother and from what I understand, Joe welcomed her but I don't honestly know how it went as I wasn't there but what I do know is, it didn't change much for me. Joe still liked to talk to me, I had always got on with him, my relationship with him compared to my sisters was very different so he probably felt more comfortable telling me what was going on and I tried to help as much as I could. My mother eventually had to go into a home which I thought was the best place for her, Joe simply couldn't take care of her as she deteriorated further. I felt relieved that this was happening and that she would be cared for by professionals, it was what she needed at this stage of her illness and if I'm honest, I knew it would be easier for me. My mother stayed at the home for approximately five months before passing away, it was June 2014, I was fifty-three years of age. I felt very mixed emotions after she passed but the biggest one was relief. Relief that she was no longer suffering, it's awful waiting for someone to die, just watching them lying there knowing what's coming but also, relief that we could lay her to rest and I could eliminate this pressure from my life. Looking back, that was a strange thought and I think confirms my mindset at that time, I wasn't great. I took a short period off work after my mother passed away but when I went back the Lupus had worsened. I felt absolutely dreadful, I was all over the place both physically and mentally with medications changing regularly in an effort to find the right ones. It was hell, but still I tried to carry on which was utterly foolish, I was so conscientious, but all at the expense of my health. I really couldn't provide the level of commitment and the ability required to carry out the role, the fatigue was extremely difficult to manage and the medication impossible but Fraser and I had a holiday booked, we were off to Kefalos, so I had high hopes that a break would help. But it didn't, I slept constantly and my skin came up in lumps which I now know is a lupus reaction to the sun. I was gutted, I came back, went back to work and carried on but I think everyone could see I was struggling and I eventually spoke to my boss asking if there were any other roles available as this particular role, I was finding difficult due to my health. I personally don't think I can take all the blame for this as the demands were impossible most of the time and there was sympathy zero. I worked for a huge organisation but I felt very much alone just waiting for them to decide what to do with me and eventually they offered me a place in the finance department in a role I never really understood, I think it was just somewhere to put me, I felt like I had become a problem, a spare part, which was sad as I had produced some very good work in the past but, of course, that all got forgotten as it always does. I lasted two years in Felixstowe and I didn't enjoy any of it, in fact, I hated it. I was unwell and very stressed and, on most days, didn't want to go in. Fraser was aware of the situation and tried to support me as best he could but I wasn't going to be happy until I was out of there, and that was my mission. But Fraser had another concern as, during my time in Felixstowe, his mother was taken into hospital for an operation relating to her heart. The operation, I believe, was successful but during her stay she had a fall, causing an open wound on her leg. It then seems her care at the hospital was inadequate so she was moved to another hospital but unfortunately, she had contracted sepsis which would prove to be fatal. Fraser's mother had passed away which should never have happened, it was very sad, she was a nice lady who called regularly to see how we were and was lovely to chat to. Fraser went back home to Aberdeen for her funeral but unfortunately, I couldn't attend, I stayed home. Time off work for me would have been OK but I simply wasn't well enough, physically or mentally, which is sad as I would like to have paid my respects. However, this whole time for us was very difficult, we had quite a lot going on during our first couple of years in Earls Colne but this aside, on a personal basis, I think the move to Earls Colne was successful as we had really settled and enjoyed living there. But, on a professional basis, my move to Felixstowe was a disaster so when there were whispers of redundancies, I jumped at the idea. Of course I was successful, I was a problem that could quickly be eliminated by accepting my redundancy request and once this was all confirmed, I couldn't wait to get out. When the time came, I said goodbye to a few people, left, got in my car never to return and all I could think was, what a relief. I spent fourteen years at this company and was destroyed in the last two which left an unfortunate bitter taste in my mouth, but I was gone now and a new life awaited and I had to let the bitterness go. And, on the bright side, something good had happened, Snoopy had disappeared, we seemed to have lost him when we moved to Earls Colne. Neither Fraser or I had seen him once since we had moved although we were a bit of a distance from where we previously lived which was probably the reason, not that that had held him back in the past. I think he was finally gone and, once again, all I could think was, what a relief.

The time came when I finally got my medication correct which made me feel better but some parts of this illness were to permanently change a few things. It took me two years to accept this illness but when I did, and worked with the illness rather than against it, I felt better and it was all down to mindset. Once I accepted that I had this for life and that the only way was to get on with it, things seemed to improve and even though I had ups and downs, sometimes experiencing 'flares', which can be difficult, mostly I was OK. I guess the things that lay in the back of my mind were the side-effects that come with the medication. My consultant explained everything to me right at the beginning of my diagnosis but, all I said was, 'just give me what I need to live a normal life.' So, that's how we looked at this and, quite frankly, there was very little choice. I know what the side-effects of my medication are, both steroids and immunosuppressants, I know they can shorten your life and I know my cancer risk has increased by 50 per cent. In fact, people with systemic lupus tend not to live as long as the average person but it's not lupus that shortens your life, it's often the drugs. But, hey, choice is not something I had so the best thing for me to do was to get on with it and you never know, there just might be a cure around the corner and this thought gave me hope. So now, having got my redundancy and with all my medication in order, I had to find myself a job. Remaining local was important and I quickly found work in Earls Colne and it was heaven, no long drives, no sitting in traffic and no real pressure as I had decided to take administration roles at a much lesser level. I was happy with this decision and with less pressure, it was better for my health and Fraser was completely on board. Fraser and I continued to enjoy our lives, his love for me never failing and my ability to show love for him still a work in progress. And by saying that, I don't mean I didn't love him, I was just figuring out how this all worked, but I was getting there. We had a good life, we continued with our holidays and our socialising, sometimes just us two, sometimes with friends or family. We often met Jet, her husband and their friends in Kefalos, sharing holidays with them which was fun. I do remember one year Fraser and I had gone to Kefalos alone and about three days into the holiday, we came back to our hotel and was met with a huge surprise. Jet, her husband and two friends were hiding behind the sunbeds and jumped out as we walked past, I have never been so shocked in all my living days. Fraser and I looked at each other in disbelief, but it didn't end there. Two days later, whilst sitting in the foyer of the hotel, someone came up behind me and put their hands over my eyes, I turned around and found Astra and Jason standing there, another surprise. Needless to say, that was one of the best holidays in Kefalos, apart from our wedding of course, great surprises, great company and great fun. Life was really good and then, it was requested by my consultant that I start reducing my steroids as it's not preferable to be on them long term which was something I was fully aware of so I happily went along with it. However, as time passed and the steroids gradually decreased, I found myself feeling quite unwell and extremely depressed, so depressed I just didn't want to be here, I didn't want to deal with any further issues. It was the strangest feeling so I contacted my doctor and once I said I wanted out, he quickly referred me to the mental health team. I explained to them that I wasn't going to go and jump off Beachy Head, but I knew I shouldn't feel like this so they suggested I see a counsellor. There was a bit of toing and froing, a few discussions and in the end, I said I would go private as unfortunately, there is always a long wait with the NHS, it's just how it is. Being fortunate enough to be able to pay for sessions privately, and following discussions with Fraser, we both agreed that this was the best route so the hunt for a counsellor began. During my hunt, I came across a counsellor who was a lady who happened to live in Earls Colne whose name was Rica. In the meantime, I had contacted my consultant in London explaining how I felt, and he decided to send me to a specialist in Chelmsford, I think he had some idea what was wrong but needed it confirming. So, I went through the testing process at Chelmsford and it was confirmed that my system wasn't responding to the reduction in steroids with one of the side-effects being depression, and so began the process of trying to correct it. I was gutted, I had been doing so well and I didn't want to deal with anything else, I'd had enough, but the depression made this seem so much worse and I had to remind myself of that. Eventually I started a new medication, I didn't like it but I had to try it if I had any chance of removing the steroids. I felt better on the steroids but with the aim to get you off them due to the side-effects, I had to persevere with the new drugs. This whole process made me feel dreadful which I think was both a medical issue and a mental health issue and I couldn't wait to see Rica. I had made my first appointment and was eager to see her.

I liked Rica immediately, there was something very welcoming and approachable about her which I know should be the case with counsellors but this doesn't always follow. In time I came to the conclusion that Rica was a good counsellor, I liked her approach and her honesty, in fact, she was one of the best I had seen and she was so nearby I could literally walk to see her which was a real bonus. My first visit was a bit of a rundown of my life, I explained my previous counselling with Kane being prominent in our discussions. I shared everything with Rica as I believe being completely honest with your counsellor is vital and assists in their effectiveness, helping them understand your path and growth. So, amongst all the confusion and my need to see Rica, there was one thing I really wanted to discuss, something I was having difficulty with and it was my life Fraser. I didn't feel the same in our relationship and I didn't understand why, Fraser had not changed, his love for me was the same as when we met, but I was struggling, struggling with my feelings and although Fraser and I spoke about it, Fraser did not do deep conversations well hence my need for Rica. I needed to understand what had happened, was it me, was it the medication changes? I didn't know but I needed help finding out. My sessions with Rica were very interesting, they were different from any previous counselling, mainly I guess because I was different, I wasn't starting from the beginning, I had grown but at this point in my life, I needed a little help. It was very strange but Kane came up quite prominently in my early sessions with Rica, well maybe it wasn't strange, after all, he had been a big influence on my life albeit not in a good way. What transpired was very interesting. Following a few sessions it became obvious that somewhere in the depths of my subconscious mind, sitting deep in my 'rucksack', I unknowingly blamed Kane for anything bad that happened in my life, it was one of those, what I call, light bulb moments where it all made sense and I understood it totally but hated that I was doing this as it meant he was still influencing me, so I had to work through this with Rica's help. The room where I met Rica had a little chair opposite me with a cushion sporting the print of a stag neatly placed on it and whilst we were working through my remnants of Kane, she asked me how I would feel if Kane was sitting in that chair. My reaction even shocked me, it was immediate, I jumped out of my skin accompanied by a huge intake of breath and felt fear, just like I had previously known. Rica watched and then commented, 'that was quite a reaction,' and it was, so I worked through why I still felt like this, I didn't even know I did, it was very subconscious, stuck in my 'rucksack' but now it was out I could learn to understand it and I worked hard to process this and learn to let it go. This somehow led to me talking about my parents and my relationship with them but particularly my mother. I discovered I felt blame here also as I felt I had never been protected, which was hard to discuss, so Rica suggested I write a 'no send' letter expressing my feelings. I went away and thought about this and before my next session I had put pen to paper, taking it along to read to Rica. I read it, looked at Rica and before she even commented, I knew it sounded safe. It's strange how things sound when read aloud, it can take on a whole new meaning but this is all part of the process so I was prompted to go and try again. The second letter was quite different, I would say harsh, but I had to write how I felt in order to release myself from my feelings. I did, however, explain in my second letter that part of me understood, and that's all I had to say. This process really helped me, I was letting go of blame and anger, neither of which are healthy to anyone as it only prohibits your life but following this, I had another breakthrough. I had always had trouble saying Kane's name, I hated saying Kane, in fact, I had a pet name for him, it was cunt. However, following the chair incident and working through my leftover fear and blame, I started referring to 'cunt' as Kane, much to the delight of Rica, I'm sure. And eventually, during our sessions, I would casually mention Kane, as Kane, without even thinking about it and it felt really good. I would say Kane, carry on talking, then backtrack and delight in the fact that I had said Kane which made me really feel like I had finally rid him from my life. And I had, Kane was a remnant in my 'rucksack', a thirty-five-year-plus remnant sitting there, tapping on my shoulder. But not anymore, he simply didn't deserve any more of my precious time and getting to a point where saying his name was no longer painful was a real breakthrough. Of course, I would never rid myself of the horrific memories, the scars Kane left, the losses, but I had finally got to a place where I felt he didn't affect or influence me anymore, knowingly or unknowingly, I had woken up, had an eureka moment, call it what you like, but it had happened and not for the first time in my life, I knew this was great progress. My sessions with Rica were incredibly helpful and as for Fraser and I, she recommended some methods of communication that would prove to be very successful. We were back on track, or should I say, I was back on track as Fraser never went off track. We were communicating, we were laughing again and it felt great. I also opened up more and allowed Fraser's love into my life, letting down my barriers, which helped me show my love back which I discovered to be very enjoyable and beneficial to us both. The other thing I did was embrace his help, mostly with regards to my illness. I had always been so fiercely independent, probably originating from feeling I had to look after myself for years but this wasn't out of choice, it was just what I did to survive. Here I had a man who wanted to help and I learnt that that was OK. It was OK to accept his support, OK to lean on him from time to time and even OK to ask for help and I started to enjoy what we had again, in fact, it was better.

Around this time Fraser and I started discussions about how we could free up our lives more which led to discussions about being mortgage free and asking the question, was it possible? We had already tried to pay any extra money we had off of our mortgage but in order to free ourselves completely, we would have to downsize. When we moved to Earls Colne, we bought a three-bedroomed detached house so downsizing wouldn't be too much of a problem as in reality, we didn't need three bedrooms, two would be adequate. Also, if we achieved the downsize and became mortgage free, in the not-too-distant future we wanted to travel a bit more so ideally, we wanted something we could lock up and leave. So, we kept all this in mind and started to think about how we could achieve our goal. The same year this was under discussion, we had a very nice holiday in a place called Benahavís, on the Costa del Sol, Spain and we loved it there so much that we wondered if living in Benahavís could be an option, so much so, we actually viewed a couple of properties and started talking about the possibilities of living there. Neither of us really objected to living abroad, mostly because the warm weather was good for both of us, as it is for most people, so on our return we started investigating the possibility. We were both very keen, even excited, about the possibility but I had one very important hesitation, health cover. Lupus is lifelong, I had my consultant in London who I saw twice a year, I also had one in Colchester hospital and I was also under Chelmsford hospital for an associated illness, so leaving this all behind for a health service I didn't know was quite daunting. We investigated this quite a bit and discussed it at length and had to conclude that having a UK base would be the best option and as much as it proved to be a real challenge, we had to accept that staying in the UK was the way to go, so we were back to looking for a lock up and leave back home. And so, the hunt began. We decided we wanted to stay in Earls Colne but properties in our category were limited so we looked slightly further afield in neighbouring villages but always keeping our search in North Essex. The search went on for a little while until a little two-bed bungalow appeared on Rightmove in Earls Colne but neither Fraser nor I knew the address so we set about finding it. We were delighted to find that it was a very secluded location off the High Street behind a home for the elderly and we discovered they were associated with the home meaning they were for the over fifty-fives. This didn't deter us, we loved the quiet location and we were both by now over fifty-five, I was fifty-eight and Fraser fifty-six, and its location made it the perfect lock up and leave. There were only ten of these bungalows, two rows of five and the one available was a mid-terraced so we quickly arranged a viewing which highlighted the fact that it needed a lot of interior work so we organised a quote to refurbish so we could establish what price we wanted to pay. At the same time, I noticed another one of these bungalows empty which I preferred as it was an end of terrace but there didn't seem to be any information on it and at this point in time it wasn't for sale so, we pursued the first one. We had to immediately put our house up for sale which was organised with a local estate agent and then we simply had to play the waiting game, hoping to marry both sale and purchase together. However, this didn't quite go to plan as there was another party interested in the bungalow who were in a better position than us and were able to move quicker, and so the inevitable happened, we lost the purchase which made us a little upset but we couldn't do anything about it so we went back to our search hoping for something similar. And then, to my amazement, whilst looking through Rightmove a few weeks later, the other bungalow, the end of terrace, was up for sale. We were excited beyond words and quickly enquired and arranged a viewing finding it was similar to the other one, needing full refurbishment, in fact, it was slightly worse but this didn't deter us and we quickly entered into negotiations, in fact, we didn't negotiate, we offered full price if taken off the market and it was agreed. And so, we found our next home and it wasn't long after this we sold our house and everything started falling into place.

Once everything was finalised, Fraser and I found somewhere to rent for a month so all the work could be carried out on the bungalow, our new home. We found a cottage in a nearby village, the owners of which were happy to accommodate a short-term rent agreement and when the day came to move out of our house, Astra and Jason came to help us move to the cottage, with Jason driving a hired van. It was bloody hard work that day, but not for me as I took on the role of supervisor! But seriously, lupus had caused my hands to lose feeling, affecting day-to-day activities but it was strange, as although I'd lost feeling, the pain could be intense if I happened to knock them or catch them in some way, it was all to do with the type of nerve damage lupus had caused, so lifting, holding etc. was a problem as I could either not feel or hurt myself so supervisor was the obvious job for me. But, that aside, the move was completed and it was very hard work for everyone, something Fraser, Astra, Jason and I reminisced and laughed about for many weeks to come, in fact, we still laugh about it to this day, it was hard work, but eventually, we got there. So, we settled into the cottage, waiting for the work to be completed on our new bungalow and then, it all got a bit stressful as the work was not completed in the time frame promised and the month's rental turned into two months due to delays with the builder and in the end, I couldn't even speak to the builder and I left Fraser to handle that side of things as I was getting more and more angry about the delays and, of course, the additional money it was costing in rent. However, leaving this side to Fraser meant that I, in fact, got the fun side, shopping for all the cosmetic stuff, colour themes, furniture etc., with Fraser helping if I there was something I couldn't decide on. We needed most things new as it was a much smaller property and our previous furniture was either too big or there was no place for it. This downsize also meant we had to be ruthless with regards to clothes, shoes and all that 'stuff' you hang on to that you never really use which I'm quite good at but Fraser found this quite difficult. I learnt that departing with 'stuff' was something Fraser wasn't very comfortable with but having no choice, he soon got into the swing of things but he did end up with a few boxes eventually making their way to our new loft, things Fraser simply didn't want to part with, and I just had to give in as he was very adamant about keeping them even though most of it made no sense to me but it clearly did to Fraser, so we called a truce. And very soon, the day came to move to our new bungalow and, needless to say, we didn't ask poor Astra and Jason to help, we got professional movers to do the job to save everyone's backs and various other joints. We planned everything precisely, the carpets fitted, the new furniture being delivered, it was a hive of activity and eventually we settled into our first night in our new home, mortgage free with many plans. The future definitely looked bright.

We loved our little bungalow, finally settling there in October 2019 with only a few small things to finalise but overall, everything was done with one exception, the garden. We had discussed what we might do with it as there were a lot of overgrown trees and bushes which crept into the garden space making it seem much smaller than it was. We cut some of them back and made space for a new shed which would mostly house Fraser's golf equipment, of which he had a fair amount. Fraser loved his golf and was actually a very good player and played as often as he could, so once we settled in he decided to join the golf club in Earls Colne where he quickly made new acquaintances and joined weekend groups playing little competitions known as swindles. In the meantime, we made loose plans for the rest of the garden but weren't in a hurry, we just lived there for a while, getting used to our new environment before deciding what to do. We did decide to organise a little gathering for all the neighbours, asking them to join us for drinks and nibbles one evening to give us a chance to get to know everyone and them us and, all in all, they seemed like a nice bunch of people and good neighbours. This was somewhere we felt really happy and safe enough to go away on holidays knowing everyone would keep an eye on things, something we quickly learned to do for others. And then, in early 2020, we would all find ourselves in a very different situation, as did most of the world. The virus Covid was upon us, we were in a pandemic, something none of us had lived through before and something nobody seemed to know what to do in order to slow it down. It gathered momentum and started to affect many people, particularly those with vulnerabilities, and the government had to take action, providing us with regular updates on what action to take and the position we were in. It was pretty scary, made more worrying when one day I went to work only to be told to go home until further notice with the explanation that, as I was vulnerable due to my illness and medication, mostly immunosuppressants, I should go home, stay home and stay safe. It was explained to me that I would be on full pay as I was being furloughed which meant the government would pay part of my salary with the company making up the difference which was very lucky as it turned out not all companies were doing this. However, it wasn't long after this that the rest of my colleagues were furloughed, as was much of the country so we knew it was serious and we had to adjust. And then came lockdown, the government decided that in their quest to get things under control, they would lock everything down apart from key businesses, key workers and supermarkets which led to businesses having to adjust, with many people unable to travel and working from home. We had restrictions everywhere and rules we had to follow, one of which was, if we were able to venture out, we had to wear a mask and we were not allowed to remove it whilst in public. We also had what we called 'social distancing' where we had to keep a suggested distance from people so supermarkets marked out the distance for the queues outside and whilst walking around the shop in order for us to adhere to this rule. It was pretty bizarre, with some people in supermarkets jumping out of the way if it seemed you were slightly inside the distancing rule but, as only a certain amount of people were allowed in at any one time, on the whole we seemed to manage to avoid each other. I think it's safe to say, there was nobody living who had experienced such a situation, it was new to all of us including our government, so we all did our best to listen, understand and follow the rules. It's also safe to say that it was the worse time ever for our NHS, they were under immense pressure which seemed to have no let up and some of the stories emerging were heartbreaking, I have no idea how the NHS workers saw this through. But the NHS were key workers, as were supermarket staff, doctors, carers and many others so they had to continue working but with caution. And talking of key workers, Fraser fell into this bracket, working for the Bank of England contractors responsible for printing money, he continued as he always had along with all the other key workers. And then in April 2020 I received a letter from my London hospital saying they recommend I shield for three months due to my medication as it weakened my immune system and made me particularly vulnerable. This meant I couldn't go anywhere, not even to the shops but I was scared and decided I should do as I was told and as Fraser was working, I started getting my groceries delivered which proved to be troublesome as the world and his wife were trying to do the same. The only saving grace was, those with vulnerabilities which included people of a later age and those with illnesses that would prove troublesome, if affected, were given priority so at least I had a better chance should I catch this virus. It was crazy but what could we do, we just listened to our government's updates and waited with me shielding and Fraser working but we managed, just like everyone else, it was simply what we had to do. It was a very strange time, the world felt different, and it was, different in ways we could never have imagined with people having to find ways to amuse themselves and their families at home by playing games or doing puzzles. But the biggest saving grace was FaceTime, everybody took to face-time to communicate with friends and family, it was the only way for people to keep in touch with each other and thank goodness for that, it was a lifesaver for many, particularly the lonely.

With Covid ruling our lives, Fraser and I couldn't plan any holidays but there was good news for Fraser just around the corner. His company were making redundancies and Fraser was keen to put himself forward. We discussed this and came to the conclusion it would be a good idea, Fraser would take his redundancy money and find a local job, just as I had done a few years earlier. And with us having the luxury of being mortgage free, it made this decision a lot easier. Fraser was delighted and once his company confirmed acceptance of his application, plans were put in place for his exit date which would be September 2020. I could see Fraser was happy, he even talked about a golf trip with the boys to Spain at one point which I knew he would love even though he hated going away without me. I remember him mentioning a weekend golf trip to Wales a couple of years earlier that was being organised by the club and when I asked why he wasn't going, he said he didn't like going away without me. I told him not to be silly and that he should go and enjoy himself as they play at some beautiful courses that I knew he would enjoy. And so, he went and needless to say, he had a great time. The following year he took advantage of his new-found outlook and went on three trips with the golf club, each time, sheepishly mentioning it to me thinking, for some reason, I would mind. So, I had a bit of fun with him and told him he was taking advantage, the previous year, one trip, this year, three trips! He knew I was joking and we had a good laugh about it, with me saying, one day, you won't be able to play so play as much as you like, after all, it's something you're good at and something you enjoy. So, now he was talking about Spain but, of course, with Covid ruling our lives, plans were put on hold awaiting our freedom. In the meantime, Fraser was very upbeat which seemed to be down to the fact that he had had his redundancy accepted and I totally understood that feeling as I had been through the same. The only thing was, he started to feel unwell on the odd occasion, complaining of tiredness and pains in his chest and arm. Then, one night, when Fraser had already gone to bed because he was on earlies, I went to bed around midnight only to find him still awake drinking sparkling water. He said he had the pains again and the only thing that seemed to help was sparkling water. I then had to have very strong words with Fraser about going to the doctors as it was a place he never ventured to, I also said he would go the next day and not go to work as he had to get up at 4 am being on earlies and it was now well past midnight. For once, he agreed and later that morning he made the necessary arrangements with both work and doctors. His appointment with the doctors was the following day and when he returned, he was all smiles, he had been signed off with anxiety for a week with a further review the following week. The doctor had performed an ECG and all was fine and it was believed he was worrying about his redundancy, the anxiety symptoms being just as he had described. Happy days, he could wind down, relax and see how he felt the following week. A couple of days later I was trimming some hedges at the side of the bungalow when he came to join me. He was having a great laugh with some of the neighbours, swinging in a hammock he had erected between the trees, laughing and joking. But eventually that stopped and he came to help me until he said he felt unwell again and went to have a lie down. I carried on cutting hedges and trees and about twenty minutes later I heard Fraser calling me. I ran inside only to find him on the floor in terrific pain and, to be honest, in a terrible mess. I tried to help with the little first aid I knew then dashed outside to get a neighbour who came inside, saw him and immediately called an ambulance. I spoke to the emergency services whilst waiting for the ambulance who relayed instructions on what to do. They said I was doing good and to continue with their instructions which basically were to keep Fraser talking and to encourage normal breathing. I sat on the floor next to Fraser relaying encouraging words, calling his name when he drifted into what seemed like a sleep and telling him to breathe with me. He said he was very hot so I grabbed some kitchen towel, ran it under the cold water, and placed it on his neck, head and chest. I stroked his head, still encouraging the breathing and all he could say was 'I'm in trouble.' He said this several times but I just kept dismissing this telling him he was going to be OK and soon help would arrive. He continued drifting into a sleep with me immediately shouting his name to bring him back with me and to continue with the breathing but he was struggling, and I knew it. Soon, the ambulance arrived which was quicker than expected considering Covid. They started by cutting off his clothes and checking his heart which seemed to be utterly erratic, so at this point I left and waited outside leaving Fraser in their capable hands. At one point one of the ambulance crew came running out, collected something from the ambulance and ran back to Fraser then, following a short period of time, Fraser was bought around the side of the bungalow on a stretcher and my heart sank as he looked worryingly grey. I'm not sure at this point if he knew where he was or what was happening but he was put in the ambulance ready to be transported to Basildon hospital heart unit. But then that changed and they said they were going straight to Colchester which I didn't understand why but I trusted their judgement. As they were about to go, one of the ambulance crew asked if I wanted to say goodbye as I wasn't allowed to go with him due to Covid restrictions. I walked to the back of the ambulance and waved, Fraser looked at me but I have no idea if he knew I was there, I just had to believe he did. The ambulance went and a paramedic asked to speak to me in private so we went inside. He told me that Fraser was quite unwell and at this point I looked at him and said, 'please don't sugar-coat it, tell me the truth.' He looked back at me, hesitated for a while and then said, 'he's very unwell, he actually died in the garden (hence the ambulance crew running back and forth) and had to be recused which is why we're taking him to Colchester hospital.' I took from that that he wouldn't have made Basildon as it was a much longer journey but, in the end, the paramedic gave me a number to call, he said to leave it for a couple of hours which meant I had to call around 7 pm. The paramedic left and I went into clean-up mode, I couldn't go to any of my neighbours as we were social distancing although one of my neighbours did say to knock on their door once I had an update. The cleaning continued, I was like a woman possessed and soon the time had passed, it was 7 pm. I continued cleaning, ignoring the time, but not ignoring it. I knew I had to call but I was putting it off and then, at about 7.20 pm, I called. I asked for the correct department, was put through, was passed to the correct doctor who had to ask some security questions and then he asked the question you do not want to hear, 'are you driving?' My heart sank, I knew this meant a shock was on its way and they like to know you're not in a dangerous or vulnerable place. No, I said, I'm home, and I waited for what seemed like a lifetime.

And then the doctor in his most sympathetic voice gave me the news. He said they had worked on Fraser for about an hour but his heart, so full of love and excitement for the future, had stopped working, he'd had a fatal heart attack and they simply couldn't do any more for him.

Fraser was no longer with us, he had passed away, he was fifty-seven years of age.

I stayed calm, thanked the hospital, ended the call and ran to my neighbours where we broke all the Covid rules.

And there I was, in this surreal situation facing the biggest challenge of my life. I don't think I actually believed it, it couldn't be true, could it?

But it was, and there I was, someone who had learnt to love, been taught by the best, only to lose it all.

And Fraser, with so much to look forward to, had had it all taken away from him, and he really didn't deserve that.

And for everything that had gone on in my life, the years of searching, the challenges, the confusion, the pain, nothing compared to the way I now felt. My heart ached in a way I had never experienced, but it wasn't something I could simply change or fix.

And it definitely wasn't something I could throw in my 'rucksack'.

RIP dear Fraser, forever loved, forever missed.

Ever Thine

Ever Mine

Ever Ours

Xxx

EPILOGUE

I raised a question at the beginning of this book about early life experiences shaping our lives. Do you believe it? I am one of those people who do, I just think you have to open your mind and see beyond what's in front of you. The hand you've been dealt doesn't have to be the life you lead, especially if you feel a deep-seated unhappiness or confusion, it's worth exploring no matter who you think you might upset. And even if the upset extends to those close to you, those we feel we should respect, don't be afraid, what's the alternative, carrying a 'rucksack'? Of course, there are many people who feel they have had a very fulfilled life and are happy with their lot, I say amen to that, enjoy and remember to be honest with yourself, always. But for those who feel they haven't, explore those demons, learn, understand and find the real you, the happy, confident you. After all, it's 'you' you have to live with 24/7 so why not love who you are, who you want to be, and find what makes you happy.

Which leads me nicely into the subject of abuse. Many people, both men and women, experience different forms of abuse. Abuse can leave both physical and mental scars but for me and my experiences, mental scars were the toughest. I was already insecure when Kane came along, that seed had already been sewn and I have my own understanding of that. But Kane then played on this, that's what people like Kane do, they hunt down their victims, knowing they can control and manipulate them. He was a bully and the ultimate narcissist, controlling me, gaslighting me, frightening me, beating me, fucking me, at every opportunity. It's quite difficult to put into words this whole episode of my life, trying to write down your feelings, your fears, your loneliness, your embarrassment, whilst trying to do it in a way that people will understand. I guess you either will understand, or you won't but whatever you conclude, remember, abuse happens every day of every year and there are many people like me who suffer, often in silence, afraid to speak out, fearing for their lives. Yes, this really happens, even today. It would be nice to think, unlike my years of abuse being the seventies and eighties when subjects relating to abuse and mental health were not understood or not spoken about, that in today's society, people might feel it's OK to speak up. We have much more exposure to these subjects, it's better understood and it's OK to talk about it, but I don't believe it's supported enough. However, having read my journey and bearing in mind the years it took to finally get to a place of self-love, how can this possibly be supported by the NHS. There are, no doubt, many people in need of help and support, my god I know some, who have nowhere to go and who's only real option is the private route. And, of course, this is not always possible but, it wasn't really possible for me, I just made choices, made sacrifices in order to afford my counselling and I did this for one reason, and one reason only, I wanted to understand and eventually heal, and that need was greater than anything I ever owned.

So, what happened to Kane? Well, he met a lady not long after we split who I understand he is still with today. I know they married, got the house, the kids and, I believe, a grandchild and maybe there's a dog thrown into the mix. All that stuff I used to dream about in my unrealistic world, my world before counselling where I learnt to decipher fantasy from reality. I don't ponder on Kane's life but, sometimes I wonder if he feels anything for the children he never had. I somehow don't think so, he managed to create and build his family and no doubt put this behind him whereas me, I have wondered if, given all that happened, deep down I felt I never deserved a child and maybe there's a fragment in my 'rucksack' that, one day, I will address. However, that aside, I don't feel any regrets about not having children as I was aware that I wasn't up to it mentally, which I hope is understood, as although being childless tends to put you in the selfish bracket, I believe the choice I made was very unselfish. I simply could not have been a good supportive mother or parent, not just with Kane but beyond those years whilst I was healing and being able to provide as I believe a parent should, is something I feel very strongly about. Kane, on the other hand, well, I would have to decline to comment. I really have no idea if he became self-aware, saw the light, whatever you want to call it, in order to become a good parent but for the sake of his family, I do hope so. And finally, my last comment regarding Kane, I often wonder what I would I do if I ever came face to face with him? Well, my response may surprise some people, so I think I'll just leave it there.

Stalking. It appears, the stalking laws of today are much improved, I can't be certain but they are definitely better than they were when I was growing up. Snoopy was most definitely a stalker and a very odd individual. These people have something seriously wrong with them but it's not something I totally understand, nor is it something I need to understand. Back when this was all going on with Snoopy, I felt the need to protect him but this came purely from my own insecurities and my need to please people and be liked. It's quite dangerous having these types of issues as many people can take advantage of it and, in my case, that was definitely what Snoopy did. I'm so glad that the day came where I found the strength to face up to Snoopy and tell him exactly how I felt and even though he still stalked me and unnerved me I still felt like that day I'd achieved something within myself and that I was becoming stronger. It was a very good milestone for me only made better by the fact that, once Fraser and I moved to Earls Colne, I never saw Snoopy again and I have no idea what happened to him, nor do I care.

As for my friends and family, my relationship with my sisters, Jet and Aline, remains the same. We don't see or speak to each other that often but, I think it's safe to say on behalf of us all, if needed we'll be there, and that's just the way it is. My contact with my cousin Jolene and her sisters remains, although I mainly see the eldest sister, the others I speak to and see from time to time. I think it's fair to say that, like a lot of families, weddings and funerals are the main gathering times and I guess that's OK, it just depends on what sort of family you are. I don't think my parents' separation and subsequent divorce affected us as a whole but I do believe individually we were all affected, just in different ways. As for my father, my respect for him continues. Once I understood him more and erased any negativity I had been subjected to, I actually came to the conclusion that he is a good man. He is a very simple man who had his years of losing his way after he separated from my mother but, overall, he has good intentions. And I will always have utter respect for the way he eliminated any scornful words about my mother following their split. He was broken after they split but on the whole he kept his thoughts on this to himself and whether he was a good husband and father or not, he did what he thought was best as did my mother, they both did their best armed with the knowledge they had at the time, and I guess that goes for a lot of people in life. I speak to my father every week, often more than once. He sits and watches a lot of sport on TV and always calls me if netball is on or my tennis icon is playing. And if a big event is on, we often give each other regular updates and opinions of which he has many, particularly with netball, being an ex-umpire. We may also, on occasions, drift into discussions about current affairs, politics or particular politicians, of which he can have strong opinions and although this can be fun, I have to remind him to be careful and not believe everything he reads in his chosen tabloid. I give my opinion but, if he's happy with what he reads, that's fine with me, as long as he's happy. My friendship with Astra and Jason continues, I see them regularly and try to see Kylie and Kensa when I can but they are both married now and have their own families. My friends are few but that's how I like it, these days I don't need a lot of people in my life as I'd rather have quality over quantity. I have, over the years, tried to eliminate negativity which includes negative people. I try to stay away from people who are draining or bring you down or use you, leaning towards circles where positivity prevails. I like to be around people who are encouraging and happy for your achievements and I try my best to give the same back as for me, this is what life is about.

And just a little update on my health. Mentally, I've got myself into a good place, it took a long time and was a lot of hard work but was totally worth it. Physically, lupus is the bane of my life. It's a very unpredictable illness with 'flares' happening whenever they feel like it, causing terrible fatigue, so much so that I can spend whole days in my dressing gown drifting in and out of sleep. And the other real issue is the vasculitis, which is all part of lupus and has damaged nerves in various parts of my body most of which I can deal with but, the worse part for me is my hands. My right hand has very little feeling which is also the same for the left except for my forefinger and thumb causing so many day-to-day issues. I'm constantly dropping things and have trouble with everyday activities, having to use my eyes constantly to ensure I'm holding things correctly, not cutting myself with knives or burning myself unknowingly. It can be pretty draining and the unfortunate part is, Fraser was a great help, always helping with things I struggled with, teaching me that it's OK to ask for help. Fraser was so patient, never complaining, always there to assist me when needed. So, how do I keep myself positive about this illness? I hit the gym several times a week, it's my solace, my happy place where I can improve myself not just physically but mentally which for me is very important. This lupus isn't going anywhere, it's something I just have to live with so I am constantly finding ways to improve how I live my daily life. And as for the bulimia, that is very much under control even though it would be fair to say, my association with food remains a little strained. However, I eat mostly healthy whilst enjoying treats as I have a wonderful sweet tooth that I do not deny myself, it's just a case of, everything in moderation. So, overall, positivity is the key and it took me a long while to get there and now, my glass is always half full.

So, whether you understand my story or not, my journey has required a considerable amount of physical and mental effort. It's been extremely challenging, demanding, lonely, sad, scary, tough, confusing and arduous but the rewards for all this are priceless. I think, whilst this is in no way a self-help book, I hope it shows that, in the face of adversity, it can be overcome, you can change your life. And whilst I understand circumstances are different for different people, if you find yourself in an abusive situation, it's worth investigating all your possible options in order to free yourself and live a fulfilled life. It's so easy to become comfortable with your surroundings, and I use the word comfortable loosely, I guess what I mean is, it's never healthy to become institutionalised in a world you know is wrong. We can feel safe in the craziest situations and escaping from that bubble and daring to see what's on the other side, that's the scary part. I sometimes ponder on how I ended up where I am now and I guess the best way to sum it up is, I listened to myself, I trusted my gut and my need to free myself was greater than my need to stay. I had no idea what lay ahead, how tough it would be, the dedication required and if I could give my old self any advice, I would say, prepare yourself for some very difficult times, be honest with yourself, don't be afraid, let go, open your mind, never give up and try to find someone you can trust to talk to. In other words, try not to use a 'rucksack' as a solution, it will only get heavier. But, that aside, the most important part, you have to want to do it, really want to, and that for me is crucial to succeeding. This journey I have been on has been a real education, an education that continues today. I will always seek to understand, to learn and I will never be afraid to ask questions, it's simply a way of life and one I thoroughly enjoy. And the funny part of all this, a 'rucksack' is often my choice of bag, I have several designs in different colours and I find them extremely comfortable to wear, perhaps because I only carry essentials and not my whole damn life!

And finally, little did I know, a whole new challenge awaited me, so unexpected and so painful and very different to anything I had experienced previously, the loss of dear Fraser. Pain is a very personal thing, as is grieving and although I had a support system around me, I had to dig very deep to find ways to cope. But there was no answer, yes, I could try and use coping mechanisms like writing or drawing but this wasn't successful, nothing was, the only thing that kept me going was, I thought Fraser was going to walk through the door and say he had had a great game of golf. For me, it was so surreal, was it really happening? But, of course, it was, Fraser wasn't going to walk through the door and somehow, I had to come to terms with it.

And this was to be the biggest challenge of my life.

Life can surprise us, nothing in this world is promised, the only sure thing about life is death so please, live the life you love, love yourself and be happy with your life's choices.

And a final note from the author. This book has been a very enjoyable hobby, I've loved writing (if you can call it that ⊠), reminiscing and seeing how life has changed and most importantly, how far I've come. And even though I know this, when you write it down it hits harder, you see it even clearer, all the ups and downs are staring you in the face but, what a cathartic exercise it has been which I do not regret nor do I regret sharing it with you, as even if it inspires one person, it'll be one person leading a better and happier life and I think that's all we ever really want. So, having enjoyed this so much, I think a sequel is on the cards with all its new challenges, and that's the thing about life, you never know what tomorrow will bring or what challenges lay ahead so make sure you live one you are happy with. Life is very precious.

POETRY

I do enjoy writing poetry and during the course of this book that's exactly
what I did. There were times during writing that something would come to
me which I felt the need to put into poetry so here they are, a few from me
which I hope resonates with my story.

CONFUSION
The sun is shining, it's a beautiful day

I get up feeling great, and then I lose my way

The birds are singing, spring flowers appear

I hop, skip and jump, but then it's all unclear

I feel I have enough, I don't need any more

I'm happy with my lot, but I suddenly feel poor

I'm surrounded with laughter, I smile with my friends

Everything's happy, then sadness descends

It's such a rollercoaster, emotions so confusing

I fail to understand why I feel I keep losing

But what am I losing? I have no idea

This confusion in my head makes it all so unclear

If only I could understand what I'm supposed to do

Someone please help me, I have no clue

I'm screaming alone in the dark corners of my mind

But you'll never see that, my expertise is to hide
It's a skill I adopted, a coping mechanism
Little did I know I had created my own prison
I had nowhere to run, I was under lock and key
And sadly, I accepted I would never be free
So, I carried on with the confusion, day in, day out
Constantly wondering, is this what life's all about?

CORNERS OF MY MIND

It's dangerous in here, dark, messy
There's confusion in here, what's right, what's wrong
There's a rollercoaster in here, flying high, speeding down
Dark thoughts, happy face, messy mind
I'm sure my mind is a box, with corners so dark
I can't open the box, nor can I see the dark corners
Can I open the box, show some light?
Does Pandora live there? This scares me
But I want to understand, how do I do that?
How do I release the darkness, the confusion?
How do I stop the fear, the insecurities?
I need to understand, but I don't know where to start
Help me

DIRTY LOVE

The day will come and it won't be long
When a decision will be made
I need to listen to myself
And try not to be afraid
My self-respect in question
My happiness compromised

These feelings have crept into my life
And should no longer be disguised
I don't like feeling worthless
Or not good enough for you
I don't match up, I'm being compared
In everything I do
It's the strangest situation
Which I don't fully understand
But I'm now all out of answers
And I'm holding up my hands
I've tried to understand you
And respect the man you are
But in doing so I've lost myself
And I feel it's gone too far
I need to keep my own beliefs
And never compromise
I need to find myself again
And from this I will rise

THE STAIRCASE

This flight of stairs represents us
They're not moving, they're not an escalator
They're still, they're steep, they need climbing
You start at the bottom, feeling the strength
To climb those stairs to your destiny, the top
It's a rocky climb but you battle on regardless
Sometimes feeling the loss of dignity
Sometimes you're halfway up, then you drop to the bottom
One word, one sentence, one action is all it takes
You keep trying with no idea why

Your vulnerability in full action
But he knows this and plays a wonderful game
He plays the staircase with ease, at his pace
You sometimes feel special, like you're at the top of the stairs
You're sometimes left wondering when quiet descends
And at these times, the staircase decline is long
Each step encompassing our insecurities, our vulnerability
And when we reach the bottom and feelings are questioned
One word, and we feel like we were wrong
We question ourselves, our thought process, were we wrong?
And then we tell ourselves we were, and start the climb again
Feeling light under foot, the climb seems easy
There's hope, we read the writing wrong ... for now
Be aware, the narcissist is everywhere
But in time, you find the strength from deep within
To tackle those stairs at your pace, alone, with dignity
After all, we are only a reflection of how we're treated
And in time, that will surface
After all, we know how we feel and we know what's right
It's simply our strength and self-love we have to find

TRUST YOUR GUT

You're faced with a situation
A decision needs to be made
There is a lot of indecision
Your mind is all ablaze

You're faced with a situation
And it's you who has to decide
Your head and your heart do battle

THE RUCKSACK

Will you conquer or will you hide?

You're faced with a situation
Do I do what's right for me
Or give in to the needs of others
And ignore my own feelings?

You're faced with a situation
And deep down you know what's right
Don't ignore that feeling
Don't start a personal fight

That feeling that is present
Is well worth listening to
It comes from deep down in your gut
Listen, and you'll know what to do

You're faced with a situation
Be brave and sing your own song
Listen to that inner voice
'Cos that gut feeling is rarely wrong